The Politics of Everyday Europe

The Politics of
Everyday Europe

Constructing Authority in
the European Union

Kathleen R. McNamara

OXFORD
UNIVERSITY PRESS

Great Clarendon Street, Oxford, OX2 6DP,
United Kingdom

Oxford University Press is a department of the University of Oxford.
It furthers the University's objective of excellence in research, scholarship,
and education by publishing worldwide. Oxford is a registered trade mark of
Oxford University Press in the UK and in certain other countries

First Edition published in 2015
Impression: 3

Published in the United States of America by Oxford University Press
198 Madison Avenue, New York, NY 10016, United States of America

British Library Cataloguing in Publication Data
Data available

Library of Congress Control Number: 2015931230

ISBN 978–0–19–871623–5

Printed and bound by
CPI Group (UK) Ltd, Croydon, CR0 4YY

For Henry Diego

Preface

Decades ago, William Fulbright, a US senator from the Ozark foothills of Arkansas, corralled his colleagues into creating the Fulbright Program, a massive, government-funded international research and teaching fellowship program closely linked to the US State Department. The goal, as the Fulbright website states today, was to "strengthen the basis for peace by strengthening mutual understanding between the people of the United States and the peoples of partner countries around the world." I was lucky enough to get a fellowship in the 1990s to write my doctoral dissertation in Brussels, at the epicenter of the European Union (EU) in the midst of the excitement over the creation of the Maastricht Treaty and the euro. But I did not apply for the Fulbright to Belgium program. Instead, among students applying to study in France, or Kenya, or Japan, I competed for a newly created Fulbright to the European Community (the former name of today's European Union). At the time, it struck me as a little odd that the US would be interested in "strengthening the basis for peace" with an entity that was not a "partner country," and therefore could not have its own "peoples." Enjoying my *moules* and *frites* while learning first-hand about the invention of the European Monetary Union, I didn't spend much time thinking about this seeming anomaly. But in many ways, the fact that the EU was put in a category alongside all the world's nation states constituted a political puzzle that informs the book you are reading. The Fulbright to the European Union continues to this day, but it remains the only Fulbright fellowship assigned to a political entity that is not a state.

I put aside my musings about this diplomatic curiosity, and set out on my professional career. For many of the years that followed, I studied the development of the euro, the single European currency that has replaced German Deutschmarks, Portuguese escudos, Slovakian koruna, and 16 other national currencies. The breaking of the link between nations and currencies puzzled me, and I decided to learn more about how money became nationalized in the first place. The story of how consolidated national currencies initially arose was fascinating and surprising to me. It turned out that before the second half of the nineteenth century, multiple types of money circulated and were used for transactions, including bank credits, IOUs, local currencies, and foreign currencies circulating outside their borders. The story of how exclusive, national monies such as the US dollar arose was a deeply political story of a broader set of dynamics often involving warfare and intense political strife. Currency, it turned out, was jealously fought over as part of highly contested projects to concentrate political power through taxing, spending, debt creation, and control over the national money supply. All this was done in the service of what scholars now call state building. Currency consolidation was just one part of a broader story of political development, with the outcome being the sovereign nation states we know today.

Learning this raised an important question for me, one that fundamentally shifted the way I think about the European Union. If currency is part and parcel of larger political projects, what did that mean for the euro, which was usually understood as a technical project, a tepid and partial consolidation of economic power? Was the euro a historical anomaly, just as the Fulbright to the European Union was an anomaly for US policy? Or were there lessons to be learned from these historical episodes about broader political processes at work in Europe?

My conclusion, and the proposition that drives this book, is that a vast array of policies and processes under way in the European Union should indeed be considered in terms of a long trajectory of profound political development now occurring at the European level. The EU's single currency is but one example of the accrual of political authority at the center of a bounded polity in Europe, in ways that look a lot like the burst of innovations in political forms of the late nineteenth century. That burst created the modern nation state. It is time we consider the EU as an emergent political entity of its own, and tell the story of the EU in terms of this broader historical process. Yet though the term political development implies a linear and forever forward process, as with any other political project, the EU's trajectory involves dramatic ups and downs. Often not very pretty, involving name calling and deplorable dysfunction in governance, the transformation of political authority to new governance forms is messy and contested. In the end, the EU might collapse of its own weight—there are no guarantees of success in political life. But thinking about the EU in terms of political development, not as a unique case we call "European integration," we can appreciate the EU as an innovative new governance form with similarities and differences to what has come before, and be less surprised by the political conflicts and seeming dysfunctionalities at work in the process.

Once I saw the EU through the lens of comparative political development, I began to notice that along with efforts in the economic and security realms, the EU was doing curious things in social and cultural arenas, using its symbolic powers in an attempt to shape citizens' views and expectations. Although not displacing the nation state and its strongly held national identities, the

EU was attempting to solidify the process of political development and the building of power and capacity by making itself seem a natural source of legitimate governance. Once again, a comparison with historical examples, namely the powerful process of nationalism, proved helpful. Although very different in certain ways, the EU has used everyday practices and an array of social representations to construct itself as a taken-for-granted actor and source of political authority, just as nations have. From the use of architecture in the key public spaces of EU governance, to the collection of data by the EU-wide statistical agency Eurostat, to the creation of a European diplomatic corps, to the iconography on the euro itself as it passes from hand to hand throughout the 19 states that use it, the EU has been working to become a "taken-for-granted" fact of life, despite its oddity as a political actor. From this perspective, the US Fulbright organizers were right to include the EU because of its status as an emergent political entity, but they were also participating in its legitimation by placing it so visibly in a category alongside sovereign states.

This new Europe is being imagined by its citizens, and those in the international realm who interact with it, in a process of meaning making that involves EU officials, national leaders, lawyers, business people, students studying abroad within the EU, and all who live day-to-day in the symbolic and practical environment shaped by the EU. The fate of this endeavor is not only of academic interest, however. Quite simply, it will help to determine the fate of the EU. A sense of commonality and belonging is critical to hold any polity together, particularly a newly created one. This book is a story about political technologies that label, map, and narrate Europe and how they form the cultural foundation for the EU's particular trajectory of political development. The punchline to this story, however, is that Europe does have a sense of commonality but it is one that is deracinated, not rooted in any passionately felt identity. The symbols and practices that the EU's legitimacy is built on are unusual in their continual emphasis on what I call "localizing" the EU. As the EU navigates the continued traditions of the nation states, it is framed as complementary to, not in competition with, national identities. This deracination and localization does produce a certain type of legitimacy for the EU, but it is a strikingly banal authority compared to those political forms that came before. And it is therefore not well fashioned to stand up to the anti-EU populism that is sweeping Europe, as its citizens struggle to overcome the harsh economic and social fallout of the Eurozone crisis. The cultural mechanisms at work creating the innovative, but unloved, imagined Europe and its accomplishments and shortcomings are the subject of all that follows.

Training in international relations did not fully prepare me for where this project would go. I draw widely and rather indiscriminately from scholarship in political science, sociology, anthropology, comparative politics, art history, urban planning, cultural studies and history, as well as international relations. I apologize ahead of time to those disciplines for what is, I am sure, a highly idiosyncratic reading of their literatures. I am less interested in disciplinary smackdowns and adherence to specific traditions, however, than in understanding the curious case of the EU in terms of its evolution of governance. Nonetheless, I hope the reader will be open to my approach and find the journey worthwhile.

This book could not have been written without the monetary, intellectual, and emotional support of many people and institutions. In its very long gestation, I have incurred many debts. I acknowledge the support of Georgetown University and its Graduate Faculty fellowship, and a residence in Paris at Sciences Po and its Centre d'études européennes. Many years of talented and curious Hoyas in the undergraduate seminar, "Imagining Europe" made unlocking the puzzle that is the EU all the more enjoyable. Along with teaching, my day job while writing this book has been as Director of the Mortara Center for International Studies at Georgetown. I thank our donor Virginia Mortara and her family for making possible our vibrant and engaged scholarly community. Adam Olszowka, Eva Zamarripa, Halley Lisuk, and especially Moira Todd all supported this book, and me, way beyond the call of professional duty. Trellace Lawrimore stepped in at the eleventh hour to help with the manuscript preparation with admirable precision and dedication.

John Peterson, Kristine Mitchell, Frédéric Mérand, and Virginie Guiraudon carefully read individual chapters, while Abe Newman heroically read the penultimate draft of the manuscript. They all have my sincere gratitude for their expertise and kindness. They saved me from various egregious errors, but all remaining shortcomings are of course my own. Vincent Pouliot, Dan Kelemen, Henry Farrell, Chuck Meyers, and Charles King always remained encouraging even when this project seemed terminally overwhelming. The work and friendship of sociologists Michèle Lamont and Frank Dobbin transformed my way of understanding politics, for which I am very grateful. Versions of this book's argument, some very early, were presented at many seminars including Princeton University's Center for International Studies, University of California at Berkeley's Center for German and European Studies, the PIPES seminar at the University of Chicago, the Dickey Center at Dartmouth University, University of Wisconsin's Department of Political Science, the Institute for Global and International Studies at George Washington University, Johns Hopkins Department of Political Science, Yale University's International Relations seminar, the University of Pittsburgh, the University of Ottawa, the University of Oregon at Eugene, McGill University, George Washington University's West Europe seminar, and the Penn-Temple European Studies Colloquium (twice). I thank the organizers and participants for helping to move my thinking forward with their comments and ideas. Toward the end of the project, I was very fortunate to have Adrian Favell, Ian Manners, and Marty Finnemore, all of whom know a thing or two about the social construction of political life, serve as my discussants at various conferences. I also thank two sets of anonymous readers at Cambridge and Oxford University Press for their careful reading, and Dominic Byatt for being a wonderfully supportive editor throughout the process.

I would be remiss not to give a shout out to my colleagues in the Department of Government and the School of Foreign Service at Georgetown University—a more friendly, smart, and sensible group of academics you could not hope to find. Carole Sargent and the members of Georgetown's Book Lab deserve special thanks for getting me through some very rough patches. For generosity of spirit and intellect through the years, one could do no better than friends like Sheri Berman, Dan Drezner, Charlie Kupchan, Nicolas Jabko, Dan Nexon, James Vreeland, the late Carol Lancaster, Marty Finnemore, Julie Lynch, Anna Gryzmala-Busse, and Debbi Avant. Over a Campari and soda at Leopold's Kafe, Roland Stephen helped me to see a better structure for the book, long walks with Sarah McNamer in Rock Creek Park bucked me up at crucial points, and conversations with Matthias Matthijs made studying the EU more fun than it should be. Over the years, Abe Newman and David Edelstein's enthusiasm for this project never flagged, even when mine certainly did.

At home, my sons, Theo and Henry, were amazingly supportive and never complained once about their mother's preoccupation with writing, or the time away from everything else that writing demanded. Most importantly, however, this book could not have come about without my luck in marrying the right man, Tomás Montgomery, who continues to astonish me with his ability to be the perfect husband.

Chevy Chase, Maryland
September 2014

Contents

Contents

1

Introduction

How do political authorities build support for themselves and their rule? Doing so is key to accruing power, but it can be a complicated affair. In this book, I show how social processes can legitimate new rulers and make their exercise of power seem natural. Historically, political authorities have used carefully crafted symbols and practices to create a cultural foundation for rule, most notably in the modern nation state. The European Union (EU), as a new governance form, faces a particularly acute set of challenges in naturalizing itself. I argue that a slow transformation in the symbols and practices of everyday life in the EU have built a cultural infrastructure for governance that has helped make the EU a "taken for granted" political authority.

Consider the border between France and Spain, on the coast of the Bay of Biscay in the Basque region. Where Hitler once met with Franco to plead for Spanish support against the French in World War II, there is no longer any physical experience at all of a boundary between the two countries. The old booths housing border guards have been torn down, and cars whizz by without stopping. Elsewhere around the world, policing of borders is an unquestioned prerogative of states, and passports invented in an effort to exert social control over a population seeking to cross national boundaries. Those days seem long gone for those countries of the EU that have dismantled their borders. All 28 member states now share an EU burgundy-colored passport that people flying back from abroad wave at customs officers as they line up in a special queue for "EU Nationals." Moreover, when going out for a night of Spanish tapas in San Sebastián, the residents of Biarritz along the French coast do so without the need to convert francs into pesetas to pay for their *boquerones* and *vino tinto*. Instead, they use euros, the common currency shared by the majority of the EU countries. A single currency has historically been closely linked to state building, as political elites sought to centralize control over the economy and polity. Yet today, despite a series of financial crises that have dragged on since late 2009, 19 member states put authority for their money in the hands of the EU and its Frankfurt-based European Central Bank, and many young people are growing up knowing only a common currency.

I argue that we need to consider how these and other changes generate cultural processes that create the EU as a political authority and subtly reorient citizens toward Europe. Daily life in Europe is repeatedly shaped by or imprinted with the EU, in symbols and practices sometimes obvious and at other times very much under the radar. Pick up an object such as a hair dryer or a cuddly plush toy and there will be a small tag printed with a "ℭ" logo (standing for "*Communauté Européenne*") indicating the product meets EU safety standards. Italian lawyers have had their work routines changed dramatically by the wholesale reorganization and resizing of their law firms toward Brussels, as EU law comes to dominate national legal systems. A family in the Netherlands with an aging parent may now share their home with a healthcare worker from Romania, thanks to the European single market for labor. German firms have recalculated their business plans in response to surprisingly tough sanctions set by the EU in 2014 against Russia after Putin's military interventions in Ukraine. In these and many other ways, the EU is changing the basic foundations of day-to-day life, and in the process reframing as European what used to be solely understood as national political prerogatives. The consequences of EU symbols and practices even extend outside the boundaries of Europe, as the EU's foreign policies and its diplomats construct the EU as a sovereign actor among states, signing international treaties and sending ambassadors to foreign capitals.

These EU programs are important in themselves for quite down-to-earth reasons, as they create winners and losers and redistribute wealth and power. But they also engage important social processes and construct a cultural infrastructure for governance. I define culture as a process of meaning making, shared by some particular group of people, by which they make sense of their world. Dense social interactions help to drive our interpretation of the realities around us, shape how we see, what we value, and thus our very identities. Culture is not intrinsic or monolithic, however. We all belong to different overlapping sets of cultures, and these cultures infuse our sense of self and form our multifaceted identities.

If we think of culture not as something we are, but as something we do, we can start to understand how such a cultural infrastructure, and the identities it engenders, matters for governance. By changing the lived experience of what Europe is, the symbols and practices at work in Europe today make natural a deepening of political power at the European level, while constructing "Europeans." These cultural processes work to create the EU as a social fact, that is, a widely shared intersubjective understanding that seems to exist on its own, separate from us, even as it relies on our collective agreement for its existence. The EU is no different from a long line of new political authorities that have used similar strategies to shore up their legitimacy, most obviously, nationalism and the "imagined community" of the modern nation state. And like these earlier authorities, the power of social control exercised by the EU through these symbols and practices can be highly consequential.

Yet the EU is not simply a supersized nation state. Instead, the EU's cultural infrastructure is rooted in a specific type of banal authority, which navigates national loyalties while portraying the EU as complementary to, not in competition with, local identities. The labels, mental maps, and narratives generated by EU policies are often deracinated, purged of their associations with the powers of the nation state and instead standardized into a seemingly unobjectionable blandness. Consider the following. The euro's paper currency displays abstracted bridges and windows instead of images tied to a specific person or place. Rather than building one monumental national capital in Brussels to symbolize and practice EU governance, European institutions and their mostly unremarkable buildings are flung far across the 28 member states, with the European Parliament even moving, vagabond-like, between cities. The creation of a new single diplomatic voice for Europe has been labeled the "High Representative for Foreign and Security Policy" rather than a European Foreign Minister, symbolically watering down the impact of this potentially pivotal new job. Moreover, the symbols and practices of Europe are often "localized" by nesting them in the member states: the standardized EU passport is issued by each country with its own national crest and the words "France" or "Czech Republic" beneath the EU label. Euro coins balance standardized European symbols and maps on one side while a Celtic harp graces euros originating in Ireland, Queen Beatrix is on Netherland's coins, and Cervantes on Spain's.

These examples and many others all point to the historically distinct qualities of the EU's polity. The EU has effectively used the tried and true political technologies of what I call labeling, mapping, and narrating to create social categories and classifications to govern Europe's people. But the legitimation that is accrued through the EU's tempered symbolic and practical activity is an unusual and relatively thin one. While cultural processes may have made the EU a natural part of the political landscape, folded into national political identities, the EU is often met by indifference by its citizens, rather than with affection. Unlike the historical project of nationalism, the EU's efforts therefore may have built-in limits to the development of a single, stand-alone European identity.

In the chapters that follow, I investigate a wide swath of EU policymaking to demonstrate these dynamics: the use of the EU's public architecture, arts, and popular entertainment to reinforce a particular vision of its political legitimacy; the ways in which the legal category of European citizen and policies promoting the free movement of people change the experience of Europe; and the cultural impacts of economic symbols and practices in the single market and with the single currency. I also examine EU diplomacy and foreign policy, the most difficult area for the EU to finesse its tempered sovereign status but one where symbols and practices have nonetheless helped to legitimate its particular brand of networked human security and diplomacy.

I find a series of deliberate and surprisingly successful policy actions on the part of European officials to naturalize the EU, but also some less successful attempts to create a sense of a unique European identity. In addition, some EU policies targeted toward more material results have had important but unintentional cultural side effects, generating habits and representations that normalize the EU as a new emergent political form. These dynamics are at work even in areas not strictly under the EU's official purview, such as the Union of European Football Associations (UEFA) football leagues and popular entertainment such as the Eurovision Song Contest. A blurring of the lines between the EU and "Europe" buttresses the effort at expanding the taken-for-granted authority of the EU.

My scholarly focus on cultural and social processes may seem trivial compared to the need to analyze the tough challenges ahead in Europe. EU mandated economic austerity programs have brought drastic cuts in public spending, high unemployment, and hard times to many citizens. Deep divisions exist among national leaders about the future direction of the EU, and a possible exit from the EU by the United Kingdom looms. But I believe there is a real payoff from understanding the nature of the social processes legitimating the EU. My perspective helps to explain both Europe's past integration successes, and its potential limits, by situating the EU in terms of larger macrohistorical trends of legitimation and identity creation in political life.

The accomplishments of the EU in promoting democracy, political stability, and economic prosperity in the aftermath of two bloody world wars and a Great Depression remain nothing short of astonishing. I argue that the EU's particularly banal cultural infrastructure has been an important contributing factor in the evolution of the EU's surprisingly robust governance system. However, when today's economic and political crises ratchet up demands for institution building and social solidarity across European publics, and more visibly reveal the winners and losers from European policies, my account predicts that the EU's particular type of banal authority may falter as a legitimating device. Beyond these policy implications, my theoretical specification of the mechanisms at work constructing and stabilizing political entities as social facts, giving them a taken-for-granted status in political life, constitutes a step forward for our study of political authority and collective identity. Often invisible, but far from unimportant, the classificatory mechanisms of naming, mapping, and narrating that I theorize in the EU case provide a conceptual framework for understanding the exercise of social power more broadly, beyond Europe, by any would-be political authority.

The euro crisis that began in late 2009 made the EU a focus of unprecedented political and partisan debate. The European Parliament elections of 2014 and very public national maneuvering over the nomination of new top leaders in the EU seemed to usher in a new era of open contestation in European politics. When we situate the EU in terms of the broader history of political development—be it the Holy Roman Empire, the medieval era's Italian city states , the Hanseatic League of Northern Europe, or the sovereign nation state first consolidated in sixteenth-century France—such contestation is very much to be expected. Arguably, it is a welcome and necessary part of any democratic system. But the cultural infrastructure and linked European identity that have been built to support the EU are straining under the weight of these new demands. Unlike some of the EU's historical precursors, the EU has not been designed to inculcate a passionate sense of European belonging and identity, but rather an implicit and passive acceptance. This book helps us to understand both the surprising legitimation of the EU as a new emergent actor, as well as the potential limits of the cultural processes that have produced it.

The EU as an Emergent Political Authority

Is the EU worth considering as a legitimate political authority at all? I am making some strong claims about the transformation of political power toward the EU level. Political authority can be conceptualized as the process of creating social control and compliance (Hurd 1999). While coercion or immediate material payoffs can bring about adherence to rule, force and self-interest alone will not be sufficient to create robust political order, either domestically or internationally. Legitimacy, in the sense of a claim to a culturally accepted principle or value that shores up the right of that political authority to rule, is necessary as well. Legitimacy is a subtle form of power that rests in a political authority's ability to create consent for its governance while also appearing to transcend that particular political actor. The terms by which political legitimacy is established vary with historical context, as demonstrated by the transition beginning in late eighteenth-century Europe from the norms of dynastic rule to today's democratic sovereignty (Bukovansky 2002).

How should we think about the EU in terms of political authority and legitimacy? To the casual observer, the EU looks to be more prone to squabbling and deadlock than legitimate rule. The periodic EU summits of national leaders seem to be better at producing nice photo-ops in historic places than anything enduring. The EU's single currency, the euro, has been blamed as the vehicle for the financial crises that swept much of Southern Europe and Ireland, and the austerity policies that followed have been blamed for slow growth and high unemployment. Any social solidarity that might have existed among the European publics seems irreversibly frayed. Can we really take the EU seriously as a political authority, one that we can fruitfully compare to earlier moments of profound political transformation and reorganization?

I argue that the answer is a resounding yes. From traffic laws to food safety, to healthcare rights to internet privacy, to busting up large corporations in anti-trust suits, the EU increasingly and profoundly shapes public and private life in its 28 member states and beyond. It does so without recourse to coercion and intimidation but rather with the consent of the governed. As a system of supranational governance began to be built at the European level, and as the EU's membership extended from the original six signatories of the 1958 Treaty of Rome to today's 28 member states, European institutions, administrative bodies, legislators, judges, and policymakers have come to do more and more of the work of governing Europe. A brief outline of these shifted capacities might help to persuade those unfamiliar with the ins and outs of the EU that it indeed has substantial policy capacity. This transfer of power to the European level, beyond immediate national control, raises the issue of what legitimates the EU as a new political authority—the focus of this book.

Historically, the EU has played a key role in market regulation, agriculture, trade policy, and monetary policy. Most prominently, the Single European Act of 1987 and its subsequent legal extensions revolutionized the original market integration project of the early Treaty of Rome, bringing down barriers to trade in Europe and standardizing rules on everything from electrical outlets to roaming tariffs on mobile phones to financial reporting to public procurement rules (Egan 2001; Kelemen 2014). The EU also has exercised a heavy hand in shaping member state monetary policy, first indirectly through its longstanding exchange rate regime and, since 1999, directly controlling participating members' money supply through the European Central Bank and the euro (McNamara 1998). A significant majority of national laws across the 28 member states are subject to the supremacy of decisions by the European Court of Justice, from fair wages for women to the mutual recognition of food standards to competition for public works projects (Stone Sweet 2004, 2010; Schmidt and Kelemen 2013).

Less well known, perhaps, is that the EU has now moved beyond strictly economic policy areas. Although social policy has historically been jealously guarded by national actors, the EU has begun to actively shape welfare and social safety nets across its members (Caporaso and Tarrow 2009; Conant 2010; Anderson 2015). Citizenship and interior affairs have likewise been penetrated by EU programs (Shaw 2008; Olsen 2012). In the area of the environment, the EU has formulated and passed some of the most extensive policies designed to stem global warming (Delreux 2011). Public health, education, and cultural programs have also become part of the EU's policy portfolio, including the Erasmus student exchange program that promotes movement of students throughout the EU (Mitchell 2014). Economic development initiatives and targeted programs have significantly affected the development path of longstanding member states such as Ireland and Portugal, as well as the newer member countries in Central and Eastern Europe. Importantly, however, although its policies redistribute wealth and opportunity, the EU does not have a formal system of direct taxing and spending, or debt creation at the European level, as is routine for all nation states no matter how federal or decentralized.

On the world stage, contrary to the conventional wisdom that the EU lacks foreign policy power, the EU signs treaties alongside sovereign states, negotiates in high level talks such as with the US and Iran over nuclear issues, litigates against nations such as China in the World Trade Organization, and has coordinated robust collective sanctions on Russia. Many observers note that the EU's influence in the world lies in its institutional and distinctive non-military and non-coercive character—in particular the spreading of its norms and values (Manners 2002, 2006; Smith 2003; Meunier and Nicolaidis 2006). The EU has had tremendous influence on many of its neighboring states, most often through the lure of EU membership, and as such has accomplished enduring regime change through institutional and legal channels (Jacoby 2004; Vachudova 2005). In the military sphere, the EU has deployed troops, police forces, and crisis management personnel to more than a dozen conflicts, and has taken over the responsibility for providing security in Bosnia-Herzegovina from the North Atlantic Treaty Organization (NATO) (Mérand 2008; Norheim-Martinsen 2013). Once again, however, in contrast to traditional nation states, the EU does not have its own European army under a hierarchical command, but rather networks the member-state militaries together for its limited joint EU actions.

The main EU institutions that are responsible for this deepening of the EU's policy capacity are the European Commission, the European Parliament, the European Council, and the European Court of Justice (Peterson and Shackleton 2006; Hix and Hoyland 2011). The European Commission is made up of a "college" of national political appointees who serve as commissioners, as well as a standing bureaucracy divided into functional policy bureaus or directorate generals. The commission can initiate policy proposals and implements policy decisions. The European Parliament, made up of European Members of Parliament elected in EU-wide contests every five years, has notably strengthened its role over the past decade, with the power to amend, veto, and advise, and the authority to oversee EU institutions and censure the commission. The European Council is the intergovernmental arm of the EU, being made up of representatives of the national governments. Finally, the European Court of Justice, sitting in Luxembourg, acts in concert with the national courts to uphold EU law and has proved an important actor in the integration process through its interpretations of the EU's laws, or *acqui communautaire.*

These extensive and penetrating governance regimes emanating from the EU level have created what many refer to as a "European constitutional order," where states and their citizens appear to be bound together institutionally in ways far surpassing traditional international organizations (Weiler 1991). Constitutional orders are marked by the binding of members to ongoing governance and a shared commitment to the broader project of the polity, in contrast to international treaties signed by sovereign states in pursuit of specific interests (Ikenberry 2001). Over the decades of the EU's history, adherence to the web of laws and institutions described above has developed to the point where the EU can be described as a legitimate political authority. Importantly, this political order has been underpinned by a host of cultural changes that, in a series of subtle and underappreciated ways, have called into being a sense of Europe as a cohesive, bounded territory.

Has Anyone Asked This Question? How Others Study Europe

How have other scholars addressed the emergence of the EU as a legitimate political authority? Simply put, few observers of the EU have focused on questions arising from this transformation. Many political scientists see the EU as an international organization, an example of institutionalized cooperation in the same category as the International Monetary Fund or the Food and Agricultural Organization. From this perspective, the EU is an intergovernmental grouping of states that come together to cooperate, but whose national sovereignty is not significantly compromised. The EU is a sensible institutional solution to the challenges of world markets, pushed forward in part by private interests—banks and firms intent on creating a big European market for their products (Sandholtz and Stone Sweet 1998; Mattli 1999). Others have argued that the EU is best understood as an intergovernmental solution to more security-related concerns or balance of power dynamics (Rosato 2011). For many years, the dominant scholarly view was that EU cooperation is best explained by understanding the material interests of the participating states and their relative bargaining power in EU negotiations (Moravcsik 1998). Political authority does not arise as an issue, as the source of the EU's legitimacy is similar to that of international organizations: democratically elected national leaders have decided in considered and thoughtful ways to delegate various economic, security, or welfare responsibilities to the European level (Moravscik 2002; Pollack 2003). One group of scholars, the neofunctionalists, pushed the logic of their theoretical insights to encompass the development of a governance regime with truly supranational character-istics, but still remained conceptually rooted in international relations and its foundations in state sovereignty (Haas 1964; Burley and Mattli 1993).

Other EU scholars have moved beyond an emphasis on material interests alone to explain the path of EU integration, focusing instead on the role of ideas and norms in shaping new political dynamics. Shared ideas about monetary policy have been identified as critical to exchange rate coopera-tion in Europe and the creation of the euro (McNamara 1998; Verdun 1999). Similarly, ideational approaches have been helpful for questions about the overall blueprint for European integration and its trajectory (Parsons 2003). In these accounts as well, however, the EU remains a case of international cooperation, not a political authority in its own right. These theorists also focus on ideas as a property of specific actors, instead of theorizing social pro-cesses in terms of overarching social structures or cultures surrounding actors. The ideational approach thus leaves much to explore regarding the cultural basis for the development of political authority in the EU.

Political authority is more at issue in the large literature that directly asks whether or not, or what kind of, European identity is developing in Europe (Herrmann, Risse, and Brewer 2004; Fligstein 2008; Checkel and Katzenstein 2009; Risse 2010). This useful work sees the development of a European identity as a key underpinning for the EU, creating a *demos* or public that is invested in a common fate. Some of the early scholarship on identity was hampered by its assumption, reflected in the rank ordering required of cer-tain Eurobarometer survey questions, that European political identity is only meaningful if it replaces national identities. This overlooked the possibility that the EU is an emergent political form that seeks to navigate enduring national affinities and evade direct competition with the nation state, while still developing a European identity. Neither does asking people to rank order their identities allow for national identity to be intertwined with a European identity, where being Spanish, for example, is itself intrinsically defined by also being European. If identities are not static but rather contextually acti-vated, studying identity solely with surveys may be empirically misleading (Abdelal et al. 2009). Fortunately, scholars have recently moved away from simple dichotomies of national versus European identity and developed more satisfying theories and fruitful empirical strategies for studying identity (Bruter 2003, 2005; Diez Medrano 2003; Hooghe and Marks 2004; Risse 2010).

In this work, I will argue that there has emerged a common—but not single—European identity. But in the next chapter, I elaborate more fully on why a focus on identity alone does not fully capture the social dynamics of European life. Instead, a broader focus on culture can better illuminate the EU's political foundations (Bellier and Wilson 2000). The type of cultural transformation that I argue is occurring in Europe is often implicit, not explicit, and may involve people not even factually knowing the role the EU is playing in shaping their daily lives even as they are part of a common community. It is thus not easily captured by a focus on identity alone.

While certain scholars have noted these dynamics, stating that "What has struck me most about the creation of a European society is the degree to which people are unaware of it" (Fligstein 2008: 2), the literature has not provided a fully developed analytic framework to understand the puzzle of seemingly weak European identity despite deep European governance and authority. One exception is Laura Cram's work, which offers a sophisticated and empirically robust set of findings on the implicit nature of EU identity and its particularly banal imagined community (Cram 2001, 2006, 2009, 2012). In addition, prescient early studies of the role of culture in the political construction of the EU also include Shore (2000) and Delanty (1995), although they have a more normatively skeptical view of the EU's efforts than I take. My emphasis on historicizing the EU and exploration of the specific mechanisms constructing a cultural infrastructure for European governance complements these accounts.

Comparative Political Development and the EU

Part of the challenge of specifying how the EU's political authority is legitimated rests in the difficulty of conceptualizing what, exactly, the EU is. As Ruggie has noted, the EU is challenged by its very novelty: it is a social fact without the vocabulary to identify it as such (Ruggie 1993: 140). Some authors have focused more on the unique qualities of the EU's structure, offering alternative and innovative templates such as "multilevel governance" to try to capture the dynamics of EU politics (Hooghe and Marks 2001; Bache and Flinders 2004). Others have more explicitly drawn comparisons with historical forms of governance, challenging us to draw out the differences and similarities with past political orders (Ruggie 1993; Caporaso 1996; Marks 1997; Bartolini 2005; Marks 2012). A few scholars have begun explicitly to compare the EU to historical processes of state formation or state building, without assuming that the EU will or should evolve into a state (Sbragia 1992, 2004, 2005; Ansell and Di Palma 2004; Kelemen 2007, 2014; Mérand 2008; McNamara 2011; Menon 2014; Börner and Eigmüller 2015). Within this approach, work on comparative federalism has provided an alternative way to study the EU that sheds new light on its dynamics (Goldstein

2001; Nicolaides and Howse 2001; Borzel and Hosli 2003; Kelemen 2004; Fabbrini 2005).

State building has been one of the central axes of investigation across all of the social sciences and humanities and forms the core of the comparative political development field, therefore offering a rich set of insights about the European experience. A well-developed set of literatures probes the multitude of ways in which states have developed the capacity for rule, the causal factors behind the drive toward consolidation at the level of the nation state, and the contestation and creativity that has marked the process of state formation (Tilly 1975; Poggi 1978; Skowronek 1982; Evans, Rueschemeyer, and Skocpol 1985; Bensel 1990). The contested exercise of political authority has been a crucial part of the often tumultuous building of state capacity at every step of the way, from France of the seventeenth century to the consolidation of the American state during the American Civil War to the revolutions of the Arab Spring states today. It is critical, however, when using the state formation literature, to disaggregate the specific processes at work rather than using the literature as a yardstick by which to measure the EU's "stateness." Similar processes may be occurring in Europe today as in the past, but the form and content of the governance they support may differ in important ways from the historic evolution of nation states. There are elements both old and new in the EU as a form of political organization, and I hope that by using some of the vocabulary of the past, we can better see these changes and continuities.

The field of comparative political development, of which the state-building literature is a subset, is eclectic and spans a diverse set of studies. But it can be characterized as sharing an insistence on the importance of historical processes, identifying specific sequences, and configurations of governance and rule, that have consequences for what comes afterwards. A substantial literature has looked at the evolution of political forms in the Western world. Most of the work focuses on the rise of the nation state as the triumphant political entity that arose, out of a cacophony of different types of governance systems, to become the worldwide standard by the beginning of the twentieth century (Spruyt 1994). The gradual emergence of states as the main way to organize political life on a large scale occurred in fits and starts, following multiple paths. Rather than unfolding in a cohesive act of historical innovation, the nation state morphed from its earliest forms in the centralizing French state of the sixteenth century onward to the burst of state formation that swept across Germany, Italy, and elsewhere in the second half of the nineteenth century, to the wave of postcolonial states created after the world wars, to the velvet revolutions of 1989 and beyond. The rise of nation states had profound but often discontinuous effects on the people living under this new form, and on the relations across these new political units. This uneven and bumpy path to political consolidation provides a useful analog to the EU case, both in specifying the causes of political development and in reminding us of the conflict-ridden and contingent nature of these processes.

Scholars have identified three big logics at work in pushing forward the development of the nation state: security and coercion, markets and efficiency, and social logics of community building. All three logics can help to illuminate the particular nature of the EU's political development, and demonstrate the value of comparison to underline the similarities and the differences in the European political project. First, theorists of comparative political development have demonstrated the historical importance of war, changes in military technology, and shifting security threats in pushing forward the transformation of political forms (Downing 1992; Porter 1994). From this perspective, the functional demands of war fighting, such as revenue extraction and logistical complexity, create strong incentives for motivated elites to consolidate and centralize administrative powers and to move from personalized, traditional forms of politics to bureaucratized, rationalized, and impersonal ones (Hintze 1975; Porter 1994). Just as important, the perception of a security crisis has often been crucial in overriding the objections of societal groups and local officials to the transfer of power away from local authorities. These dynamics are captured in Charles Tilly's succinct phrase: "War made the state and the state made war" (Tilly 1975: 42; Tilly 1990). It is this "Westphalian state" that would eventually emerge as our most familiar model where "monopolies of legitimate violence, rational bureaucracies and centralized policy-making authority correspond to territorially exclusive political orders" (Caporaso 1996: 34).

This storyline touches on certain facets of the EU's development, but in very different ways from the historical cases referenced in this literature. It was the shadow of war, not its crucible, that sparked both the early European integration project and its later deepening. In Europe, the desire to minimize the potential for a revival of hostilities among the great powers was a critical original motivation for European integration after World War II, expressed in the European Coal and Steel Community (ECSC) in 1952 and the 1958 Treaty of Rome (Dinan 1994: 9–38; Trachtenberg 1999). The continued deepening of the EU project over the following decades has been understood by many as an attempt to solve the "German problem" by binding Germany tightly together with its former enemies in a quasi-federal union with a single currency and the rest (Sandholtz 1993; Dyson and Featherstone 1999).

Yet the particular historical configurations of the EU's faint and attenuated security pressures meant there has been no coercive displacement of rulers through warfare itself. The EU's unusual development as a peacetime, voluntary entity among political units of equal legal status is reflected in its unique institutional form. The governance system of the EU has slowly evolved over its more than half a century of existence into a very powerful generator of rule, but it has done so without a monopoly on the legitimate use of physical force within its territory, as in Weber's classic description of the nation state (Weber 1918/1991). Neither has the EU gained power over taxing and spending as fiscal policy remains, arguably with somewhat disastrous consequences, at the level of the nation state (McNamara 2011). The lack of direct experience of war suggests why the EU has had to consolidate its powers through institutional, legal, rational-bureaucratic, and symbolic political authority.

The second major logic at work pushing political integration, according to the literature on comparative political development, is economic. There are significant market advantages that come with political consolidation and the territorialization of regulated spaces. Scholars have emphasized how increasing marketization of local economies and the development and routinization of long-distance trade caused a new merchant class to push for centralized political authority in the form of a territorial sovereign state, to stabilize and regulate these new markets (Spruyt 1994). As economic activity becomes more integrated and complex, societal actors make claims on the state to stabilize and regulate markets against the volatility inherent in their growth (Poggi 1978; Skowronek 1982). Rules are drawn up, usually with the aid of federal level courts, to enable markets to function. The historic reciprocal relationship between market construction and polity construction has been identified as emblematic of the need for authoritative governance structures to sustain markets (Polanyi 1944; Ruggie 1982; Fligstein and Stone Sweet 2002).

With market logics, the parallels between historical cases of state building and the EU are easier to see than in the security realm. A key goal of the EU's founding constitution, the 1957 Treaty of Rome, was the creation of a single European market with the protection of the "four freedoms"—the free flow of people, goods, capital, and services. The 1986 Single European Act, which strove to remove all barriers to commerce across the EU by 1992, was a milestone in the achievement of this goal (Sandholtz and Zysman 1989). Private commercial interests actively promoted the European single market and European political elites saw substantial gains from consolidation of European markets (Green Cowles 2012). The European Court of Justice was critical in the creation of the European-wide market through its interpretation of the EU's treaties (Burley and Mattli 1993). Decisions such as the 1979 Cassis de Dijon judgment, which reinforced the principle of mutual recognition of national product standards across the EU member states, gave political ammunition to supporters of integration, rejuvenating EU harmonization policy and spurring the development of the Single European Act (Alter and Meunier-Aitsahalia 1994). In addition, interested European political actors strategically used the market as a frame to overcome resistance to the centralization of authority that such rule making and market governance entailed (Fligstein and Mara-Drita 1996).

The final set of logics identified by comparative political development scholars as crucial to the consolidation of political authority rests in the social realm (Weber 1976). In addition to political–military and economic dynamics, important social logics are at play in legitimizing the accrual of power to new authorities, and creating a foundation of community and solidarity to support the new entity. A central example of these dynamics is found in the rise of the nation state, particularly its consolidation into its modern form in the second half of the nineteenth century, and its dependence on the development of nationalism. Nationalism can be understood as a set of social logics that naturalized and legitimated state power, sometimes with pernicious effects. The rise of the nation state occurred in tandem with the sociological building of a polity that various literatures on nationalism have conceptualized with reference to the building of "social imaginaries" (Taylor 2004), the generation of "national myths" (Hobsbawm 1990), or the rise of "imagined communities" (Anderson 1993) to underpin the new scaled-up polity nation state. Political authorities pursed a wide variety of policies to address the social challenges of state formation, to turn "Peasants into Frenchmen" in the words of historian Eugen Weber's study of nineteenth-century France (Weber 1976). Many of the social mechanisms at work were banal and inconsequential, rooted in administrative activities of classification and categorization, but they acted to construct social reality for their subjects in ways that, if successful, shored up the power of new political authorities. New states used symbols and practices to create Belgians, or Scots, or Indonesians, lumping together previously disassociated peoples in a new social group and binding them together in a constructed national culture that created a sense of national identity (Trevor-Roper 1983; Hobsbawm and Ranger 1983). The modern state has continued to impose political authority through its control over social representations of citizenship and political community, which if successful, become taken for granted and are not viewed as exercises of state power (Bourdieu 1991).

There are some echoes in the EU today of the friction-filled process by which individuals shifted their identities to incorporate a sense of a larger political space and community, although the particular content differs dramatically from the state building described above. The EU has been extensively studied in terms of the material interests at work in the security and economic realm, but its social basis has been far less investigated. To most people, a European level nationalism, a separate and strong European identity, seems elusive at best, and a naïve fairy tale at worst, when infighting among the EU member states appears drawn on firmly national lines. The proud, centuries-old traditions of the European states themselves, with their different languages and traditions, seem to preclude a shared sense of Europeanness or European culture at all. Yet we will see that the EU has both successfully borrowed from the nation state's social formation toolkit, while adding its own twists to the cultural infrastructure of nationalism. Unfolding over the following chapters is a story of how the EU's political culture navigates on top of the nation states, filling the cracks in between the national identities with its own unique imagined community.

A Cultural Infrastructure for Governance

Historically situating the EU in terms of the literature on state building and comparative political development as I have done above focuses our attention on the following questions: How is the EU socially constructed, or not, as a legitimate actor in Europe and the world? What has changed in the daily life of Europeans that shapes the way people think about and experience the EU and its powers? What are the mechanisms at work creating, or not, an imagined community of Europeans? Can this cultural infrastructure legitimate the EU's deepening political authority?

My theoretical guides for this project include French sociologist Pierre Bourdieu, for his focus on symbolic power and the nation state (Bourdieu 1991, 1998), and the seminal sociologist Émile Durkheim and his intellectual progeny, who explain how reality is collectively socially constructed (Durkheim 1939). But I also pay attention to agency and bottom-up experiences of culture, that is, the potential for people to push back, subvert, and ignore the efforts of political authorities to themselves reshape the culture of everyday life (Scott 1985; Wedeen 1999; Hobson and Seabrooke 2007). In this approach, this book joins newer literatures on the EU that are influenced by the transactionalist ideas of Deutsch (Deutsch 1953; Favell and Recchi 2009; Kuhn 2015), work investigating the reactions and attitudes of Europeans as complex, multidimensional, and marked by indifference to the EU as well as by politicization (Duchesne 2011; Duchesne et al. 2013) and cultural and historical sociological approaches to the politics of the EU (Bellier and Wilson 2000; Mérand 2008; McNamara 2010; Saurugger and Mérand 2010; Favell and Guiraudon 2011; Adler-Nissen 2014).

Instead of a narrower focus on identity, therefore, my framework investigates how political authorities "create the given," or the assumptions taken for granted in our lives, and how that should be considered a vital source of power (Gramsci 1971; Lukes 1974; Gaventa 1982). Consider this: a focus group of lower middle-class Britons convened in 2006 was asked by scholars to discuss the EU in a free-form interview. They ended up spending a long time discussing whether Britain should join the EU, although at the time the

UK had actually been a member for over three decades. The extraordinarily complex nature of the EU's governance system, the fact that not all countries have adopted all EU policies uniformly, and the notion that to many, "Brussels" is far away and foreign, make it easy to take the respondents' confusion as indicative of a complete lack of any European identity at all. But that would be a mistake, as there are subtle social dynamics at work creating a cultural foundation for the shift in authority to Europe, even as they differ importantly from the traditions of nationalism.

The next two chapters elaborate my theoretical argument, sketched out in the opening to this chapter, about the social processes naturalizing the EU and the role of its particular cultural infrastructure in that project. I argue that there are several specific political technologies, investigated in the pages to come, that help us to "imagine" the EU. I identify political technologies of labeling, mapping, and narrating that create the EU as a social fact, in ways quite similar to earlier episodes of political development and state building. Labeling affixes names, classifying and categorizing as European things that were formerly disparate and variegated. If words call into being what they seem merely to represent, the pervasive use of labels throughout the administrative and bureaucratic activities of the EU are a source of important symbolic power (Searle 1969; Butler 1993; Scott 1998; Loveman 2005). When people refer to the "European economy" as a bounded and politically relevant entity, it naturalizes the European project in practice. Using symbols and practice to map political entities in the minds of their citizens is a second strategy that has historically been used to create legitimacy (Jenson 1995; Wintle 1996). This process of locating Europe involves visual representations such as a stylized map on the euro, or manipulating the built environment through architecture or urban planning to infuse a sense of place, or policies promoting travel and mobility within Europe, reshaping the lived experience of what constitutes one's community. Finally, narrating is a third tool used by political authorities to frame history and events to their purposes—in this case, to make the accrual of power to the European level a palatable and natural shift. The modern nation state used the new mass print capitalism and obligatory primary and secondary education systems to inculcate national narratives (Weber 1976; Anderson 1993; Zerubavel 1997; Hein and Seldon 2000). Likewise, when the French Revolution is taught as a European event, or the establishment of European Battlegroups are promoted as a guarantee of human security rather than traditional militarism, a narrative about the EU is being created for political purposes. We will see in the chapters to follow that the EU has repeatedly attempted to craft a narrative frame to legitimate itself and its unique governance form (Della Salla 2010; Sternberg 2013).

I argue, however, that the EU is quite distinctive from earlier political entities in the way it uses its administrative powers of classification and division of the social world. As its policies label, map, and narrate, creating a cultural infrastructure for governance, a pattern emerges of EU symbols and practices that seem to intentionally "deracinate" and "localize" the EU. Deracination is what I call the process by which the EU's activities are presented in highly abstracted and technical terms, not rooted or emotionally anchored in the nationalistic ties of the member-state citizens. Localizing is a characteristic of the EU's cultural infrastructure that nests national and local meanings in broader EU symbols, naturalizing the notion of European authority by surrounding it with accepted loyalties and affinities. We will see a pattern of deracination and localization in symbols and practices in areas as diverse as the single market, foreign policy and the framework for European citizenship. The overall effect is to create a more banal political authority than an impassioned or actively engaged legitimacy (Billig 1995).

This book makes a case for putting the study of culture back into our analyses of politics. Remember that culture is defined in this book as the social environment that produces a shared process of meaning making, as people interpret the world collectively, but in ways that differ across various groupings (Lamont and Molnár 2002; Wedeen 2002; Pouliot 2008). We each belong to multiple cultures, not just one, be it the tight culture of our immediate families, the broader culture of our profession, our religion, or our political communities. Political actors actively use their powers to try to shape the culture within which such meaning making occurs. But in addition to intentional activities, policies and governance activities pursued for other reasons throw off symbols and practices that reshape the culture of those living under them. Culture is never static or fully under the control of any individual or group, rather it is inherently dynamic, created through the interactions of individuals who generate larger social structures.

Studying Cultural Processes

We can probably all agree that cultural processes are likely to shape the way we see and act in the world. But studying culture has often been a minefield for political scientists relatively unschooled at grasping these social dynamics. While the study of constructivism in international relations offers some help, I build most directly on those scholars of political culture, such as James Scott and Lisa Wedeen, who have found ways to empirically sort out the relationships at work in national settings (Scott 1985, 1998; Wedeen 1999, 2002, 2008). I also borrow from other disciplines, particularly sociology and anthropology, for help in capturing the cultural dynamics central to the path of European political development. My empirical research surveys a wide range of areas of daily life in Europe, and catalogs the ways in which the particular cultural infrastructure naturalizing the EU's political authority is being built. In looking across such disparate areas as architecture and popular entertainment, European citizenship and mobility, the single market and the euro, and foreign and security policy, clear patterns emerge. The content of the symbols and practices I catalog depicts a European imagined community that uses many political technologies of state and nation building, but sharply contrasts to these earlier episodes in the efforts to portray the EU as complementary to, rather than competing with, national identities and power. My empirical evaluation uses cultural materials across everyday Europe as data, and leverages historical comparisons, particularly with similar projects of nation and state building, to understand what the EU is, its role as a political actor, the nature of European identity, and the robustness of its political community.

My analysis therefore rests on a close reading of a wide variety of phenomena at the intersection between EU governance activities and the daily experiences of Europeans and those outside the EU who interact with it. In this, it is an anthropological, interpretative effort rather than the traditional hypothesis-testing exercise familiar to political scientists. I make a series of causal claims about the importance of the cultural infrastructure, but not in a traditional "if x, then y" formulation. Such a law-like claim would be inappropriate for the historically contingent and socially malleable nature of the processes of cultural generation that I study. Each chapter opens by explaining the role that culture plays in the specific empirical area, and its political consequences. I then demonstrate the ways in which the EU has used the political technologies of labeling, mapping, and narrating in an effort to legitimize itself, and create Europeans. I also pay attention to the cultural dynamics that are generated unintentionally as side effects of materially focused policies, and illustrate how non-EU activities also can change the cultural background in which European lives unfold. My goal is to isolate a pattern of representation and everyday practices unfolding across seemingly different areas of European life, and to link it to the particular political authority that the EU embodies.

The symbols and practices that construct the EU and Europeans, I argue, are not merely window dressing or an inevitable by-product of material interests. Rather, there is real work being done by the EU's processes of categorization, classification, and division. Material power and instrumental interests will always be central to political life. But states are not only coercive entities who tax, police, and administer, but they are also "pedagogical, corrective and ideological organizations" (Gorski 2003: 165–6). Material and symbolic power go hand in hand in history, as legitimate authority is a crucial component of the modern state (Weber 1918, 1947). We should therefore not be surprised that they also matter in the EU. The crafty balancing of national affinities with European, the layering and nesting of European symbols and practices within the national and local, reflects deeper truths about the nature of the EU as a new political authority and allows us to better understand the constraints and possibilities of its governance.

There are some things that this book does not do, however, but which would be extremely helpful to sort out in future research. First, this book does not parse out variations in the reception of the symbols and practices I catalog, but rather looks at overall trajectory of historical change. I try to pay attention to moments of contestation over symbols and practices, but much more focus is needed on the systematic variation in contestation over their reception and adoption. The actors in this story are EU officials, national leaders, non-governmental organizations, firms, and civil society, but I do not develop arguments about the ways in which nationality, social class, or other distinguishing factors systematically track outcomes. Fortunately, there is growing work that does examine the sociology of European integration through close empirical study of cross-national variation (Diez Medrano 2003; Schmidt 2006, 2008), variation by social class (Favell 2008; Fligstein 2008) or by both (Duchesne et al. 2013; Kuhn 2015). But much more work needs to be done. It would also be illuminating to study variations in these processes across polities in Europe that are not members of the EU (such as Norway or Switzerland) or polities on the edge of "Europe" (Turkey or Ukraine). Such finer-grained analyses would be a welcome way to deepen and further specify the larger argument I am making about the sociology of European political development.

Conclusion

On a Saturday in early spring 2014 at the Privoz fish market in Odessa, Ukraine, a heavyset blond woman scales a fish behind a counter while shoppers browse an array of seafood and condiments. A young man unobtrusively walks between the crowd, carrying a large double bass. He sets it down and draws his bow across the strings, playing a series of quiet, low notes. Two cellists and a bassoon player soon join him among the food displays, and the music floats up as the notes gradually weave together to form Beethoven's transcendent "Ode to Joy." Delighted smiles spread across shoppers' faces and smartphones come out, as violins and drums add into the mix and, finally, an entire chorus breaks out singing Schiller's words of brotherhood and celebration.[1] No ordinary flash mob, the Odessa Musicians for Peace

---

[1] <https://www.youtube.com/watch?v=rwBizawuIDw&noredirect=1#t=26>.

and Brotherhood chose the anthem of the EU to underline their aspirations for freedom, liberty, and a turn to the West over Russian domination. This was not the only episode of its kind. A few days later, dozens of musicians simultaneously began playing "Ode to Joy" at seven airports across Ukraine. Organizers called it a tribute to those who had died fighting for Ukrainian freedom against pro-Moscow forces, and a celebration of the signing of economic accords with the EU (*Express Tribune* 2014).

While the EU anthem may be an uplifting symbol for Ukrainians, the symbols of the EU do not always poignantly convey solidarity and peace, or act as a beacon for inclusiveness. A few months before the scene at the fish market, Greek college students gathered in front of the Old Royal Palace overlooking Syntagma Square in Athens. Here, at the site of the Greek Parliament, the students torched blue and gold EU flags in protest over deep cuts in education funding following EU-mandated austerity policies. Beyond Athens, anti-EU demonstrations in Dublin, Lisbon, Madrid, and Rome have all used the symbols of the EU not to celebrate the EU's values, but to protest them.

These examples serve to remind us that studying culture is not about fairy tales, nor is it the opposite of studying power politics or material interest. Symbols and practices are subject to strategic and instrumental motivations, just as with all political activities. They can be a potent power resource. But there is also agency, human creativity, and imagination at work, making culture a difficult variable for those same political authorities to control. There are winners and losers from cultural constructions of European authority. The failure of the European Constitution and its Christian preamble shows how a narrative viewed by some as binding people together simultaneously can be seen as damagingly exclusionary by others.

The next two chapters parse out a theory of culture and political authority and specify the mechanisms at work in the European case. Chapters four through seven evaluate a range of different empirical areas: public architecture, arts and popular entertainment; European citizenship and mobility; the single market and the euro; and European foreign policy. I show how everyday practices and the symbolic representations that surround European citizens reverberate back and create cultural foundations for rule. The final chapter offers some thoughts on the key challenges facing the EU and how the cultural infrastructure of banal authority I identify in this book will impact how those challenges are addressed in the coming decades. In reading this book, it is my hope that readers will come away with nothing short of a new way of seeing the EU and the transformations in governance it embodies.

2

Constructing the EU as a Social Fact

Introduction

To understand the mechanisms at work naturalizing the European Union (EU) as a legitimate political authority, this chapter first outlines the importance of what I call "cultural infrastructure" to legitimating political authority. I spend some time explaining what culture is *not*, in order to tackle the many misconceptions about, and misuses of, the term. I argue that we should understand culture as a dynamic process of meaning making among a specific, delineated group of people. I explain how identities both derive from and help to create interacting cultures, and argue that we all hold multiple identities simultaneously. Having established the theoretical groundwork, I then move to politics, examining how political actors have generated particular types of cultural infrastructures to create new identities and legitimate their power. I draw on concepts including imagined communities and social imaginaries to describe the causal impact of nationalism and other myth-making endeavors, and use them to set up the puzzle of the EU as a new emergent political form requiring social support. I link the success of these legitimating projects to the ways in which social facts are constructed, as phenomena that depend on intersubjective agreement but are made to seem like concrete, objective facts. I locate key mechanisms of social construction in the realm of symbols (as collective representations) and practices (as lived experiences, performances, and interactions with the material world). Both symbols and practices can shift our underlying assumptions about the world in subtle but consequential ways. The conclusion opens up the question of the specific political technologies and meanings involved in the EU's constructing its particular cultural infrastructure, which is taken up in Chapter 3.

Cultural Infrastructure and Political Identity

The EU is a new emergent political form, just as the Holy Roman Empire or the Hanseatic League or the modern nation state all were at one point in time, and the EU likewise has its own trajectory of political development. Rather than seeing the EU only as an assemblage of laws and institutions designed to manage cross-border regulations over quotidian things like cheese or hair dryers, we should consider the EU in terms of historical trends in governance and political development. As elaborated in Chapter 1, when we see the EU this way, as a new polity with claims on its "citizens" and vice versa, it begs a series of important questions that otherwise would not be asked. The most central of these questions is: why is the EU accepted as a new actor and legitimate site of political authority by people both inside and outside of the EU? While it seems obvious and natural that this is so, it was far from preordained that it would be. The stresses and strains of the Eurozone crisis have certainly revealed the shortcomings in the institutional framework for the EU. But we should also look at the more subtle cultural dynamics at work that sustain the EU's political authority in order to understand the EU's potential fate.

Although *cultural infrastructure* is often ignored by those who focus on institutions or political tussles and bargaining in the foreground of crises, I argue that such infrastructure is necessary to support the claim of legitimate authority generated by the EU. Other elements must also be in place to create the conditions for governance, notably a sense of the security benefits to be gained from integration, economic logics that provide incentive for it, and functioning political institutions to support it. But in addition to these widely recognized drivers for political integration, a cultural infrastructure is necessary for a new emergent political form to take hold and stabilize. Culture helps to constitute and naturalize what people view as the appropriate locus of political authority, and it also helps to construct what Benedict Anderson termed an "imagined community" that has the potential to glue people together in a political union, whether robust or weak (Anderson 1993). But what do I mean by cultural infrastructure?

The Missing Piece of the Puzzle: Culture

Culture has often been viewed by modern political scientists as a quagmire of intractable phenomena, or dismissed as a mask for other, more important, dynamics. Although many will concede that political culture and identity may be important, there often is resistance to integrate it into our studies of political phenomena. Scholars interested in explaining the development of the modern nation state have tended to stress the capacity for warfare and coercion, and for economic redistribution and regulation, rather than the capacity of the state for symbolic power in the cultural realm (Loveman 2005: 1652). Others who advocate for the role of culture have actually set back its study by approaching culture as unchanging, static, and primordial. Samuel Huntington's "Clash of Civilizations" thesis is one prominent example (Huntington 1993). For Huntington, culture can be boiled down to an immutable religious affiliation. We are born into our culture, and die with our cultural identities intact. Culture is a property of the actor, in this view, and all those within a delineated culture share that property. Much of the early work on political culture likewise understood nationalist identities of Kurds or Germans as part of the essential DNA of a citizen. But whereas some argue that historic ethnic hatreds are intrinsic, unchanging, and insurmountable, work in comparative politics and sociology has moved away from this view, arguing instead that culture and political identity are continually constructed, dynamic, and contested. Nonetheless, the tendency of non-specialists to see culture as fixed has persisted.

Following these larger trends in political science, culture has taken a back seat to other logics in scholarship on the EU. The two dominant international relations theories explaining Europe's evolution, intergovernmentalism and functionalism, have largely been focused on material incentives, interest groups, relative power, and bureaucratic dynamics to explain the path of integration (Haas 1964; Hoffmann 1995; Moravcsik 1998). To be sure, some scholars have integrated aspects of social logics into their accounts to parse out the dynamics behind the EU's history (Stone Sweet, Sandholtz, and Fligstein 2001), while a newer literature on the EU has emphasized a social constructivist approach to symbolic representation and ideology, framing, and ideas (McNamara 1998; Christiansen, Jørgensen, and Wiener 2001; Parsons 2003; Checkel 2007). But these approaches have tended to shy away from confronting directly the concept of culture, offering explanations that more narrowly focus on ideas and socialization rather than the larger social structures that surround actors and infuse meaning into their daily lives.

There are a few innovative studies that have argued for an explicit cultural approach, but these early studies have tended to focus mostly on the malign effects and cynical calculating of actors promoting a "European culture" as a way to mask the negative distributional impacts of European integration (Delanty 1995; Shore 2000). These scholars rightly see the exercise of power in the actions of the Eurocrats as they seek to create a sense of European identity, and call attention to the normatively questionable process and outcomes at work. However, they overstate the degree of centralization and top-down work being done in the construction of European culture, and thus offer too narrow an understanding of how culture is constructed, hampering our efforts to understand the forces pulling the EU together, or apart. In contrast, my model of these cultural processes sees a central role for European elites across a broad spectrum from public to private actors, but does not see the creation of the "taken for granted" backdrop of European governance as under the control of any one actor or agent.

Closer to my approach is a nascent literature in EU studies that investigates various aspects of the process of European integration with reference to the concept of how collective imaginaries might matter for political development in the EU. Most prominently, Laura Cram (2001, 2006, 2009) has done path-breaking data collection and analysis on European identity. Ian Manners's (2011) inventory of European symbols and their power, and a recent special issue of *Journal of Common Market Studies* on the role of myths in the construction of the EU are important initial contributions to this conversation (Della Salla 2010; Manners 2011). My focus here on the various political technologies that construct Europe as a quotidian social fact offers a complementary view to this emerging literature.

Despite this excellent work, the broader international relations community has yet to take a sustained look at the potential importance of culture to the EU's overall development. Many scholars and observers of Europe who are not working in the constructivist area see culture as a deeply problematic idea not amenable to analysis. So how should we understand the role of culture in the evolution of Europe?

Defining Culture as a Dynamic Process of Meaning Making

The challenge of talking sensibly about culture should not be underestimated. When I give talks on the topic of European integration, many in my audiences intuitively feel that the multitude of languages and long national traditions will make any European culture or collective identity impossible. Although it is undeniable that the EU faces distinct challenges, I counter this view by reminding them that all nation states have faced strongly entrenched local or competing transnational identities. Simply put, all nationalism is invented, and requires that human beings dynamically re-create their loyalties again and again over time. For example, a long and arduous state-directed process was necessary to create French national identity, even extending to the stamping out of local dialects and the introduction of a standardized French across late nineteenth-century France (Weber 1976). To grasp the potential and limits of European identity, we should set aside the view of culture as a fixed and unchanging thing or the totality of values of a society.

The simplest way to make this clear is to define culture as a process of meaning making, shared among some particular group of people. We can think about meaning making as "a social process through which people reproduce together the conditions of intelligibility that enable them to make sense of their worlds" (Wedeen 2002: 717). Clifford Geertz's famous quote is helpful here: "Believing, with Max Weber, that man is an animal suspended in webs of significance he himself has spun, I take culture to be those webs" (Geertz 1973: 5). Think about the ways in which 19-year-olds file into a room, take their seats and open their laptops. An older person, dressed in professional clothes rather than the jeans of the younger people, enters and comes to the front of the room, and starts talking. The young people sit quietly, not interrupting, not getting up or moving around the room. What is happening? Is it a religious event, a performance, a form of punishment? In the culture of the Western university, this behavior is all made intelligible. Culture, as a set of social institutions, makes natural and taken for granted the authority position of the professor, at least in terms of general practices of the class, if not more subtly subversive actions (such as checking Facebook rather than taking notes). While there are functional reasons for the deference to the professor, as the students presumably want to get good grades, it is culture that routinizes and naturalizes the practices, roles, and identities of all in the room and makes them intelligible. A university setting in Doha or Shanghai will likely have a different set of shared understandings that structure the interaction in the classroom from those in Rome. The point is that throughout our day, whether it be in families, schools, terrorist cells, law offices, or army units, we rely on a series of quotidian practices and symbols to stabilize our interactions. They are so prevalent that they become completely commonplace and taken for granted, unremarkable except perhaps when we move into a different setting and we are jolted into seeing all of the previously invisible rules and roles from our new perspective as an outsider.

Indeed, although it is very difficult to see culture when it is all around us, it is vital to recognize that such routinized and widely shared sets of understandings are crucial in stabilizing our social, economic, and political institutions (Thomas et al. 1987). In this, culture becomes a social structure, dynamic, and subject to change by the agents or people within it, but structural just the same (Sewell 1995). By seeing culture as practices of meaning making, we are able to probe into the ways in which actors are making their worlds intelligible and manageable, in both emotional and cognitive ways (Wedeen 2002: 720). Instead of trying to fathom what is inside the head of an actor, as is implied by the scholarly work on the role of ideas in policymaking, focusing on symbols and practices allows us to empirically observe and study culture, revealing the political work being done by culture in particular social settings. This approach also opens up the potential to study more precisely the conflicts, cleavages, and power involved in the construction of cultures, and how symbols can be used as resources in those conflicts (Swindler 1986). The relative position of the teacher in different settings is both revealed and constituted by her placement in the space of the classroom and by the deference, or not, afforded to her by the students, and can be read as one marker of the broader set of political and social dynamics at play.

Seeing culture in this way, rather than fixed and immutable, allows also for instability, contestation, and human agency. Because we must practice the ways of a particular culture, and people within that culture must interpret the symbols used, there is an inherent dynamism and potential for nonconformity or noncomprehension. Symbols have multiple, sometimes conflicting meanings in different settings and for different people. A seemingly straightforward symbol such as an American flag can mean one thing to one person, such as freedom and the long tradition of liberty stretching back to the founding of the United States. For another, it could mean government oppression of individual rights in the wake of 9/11 and pervasive National Security Agency (NSA) surveillance. Culture is structural, in that we navigate inside these various communities of shared symbols and practices, but the structures are changeable and malleable as we create, interpret, reproduce, and subvert them (Geertz 1973; Crane 1994; Berezin 2006). We are active agents, creative and causal, but we also navigate a world full of social institutions that structure what we see around us.

So how does my particular approach to culture relate to the puzzle of the EU's emergence as a political authority? As we will see, there are a range of very old and pervasive technologies for the construction of symbolic and practice-based infrastructures to support particular political regimes and particular political authorities (Ruggie 1993). Emperor Maximilian spent a fortune on public art with the goal of solidifying his position at the center of the Holy Roman Empire (Silver 2008), while in twentieth-century Italy, Benito Mussolini used modernist versions of classical architecture as part of a comprehensive propaganda strategy aimed at reinforcing his fascist rule (Braun 1989; Vale 1992). Symbols and practices have been used to create social facts and engender new identities, as will be explored below, and the "naturalizing" and historicizing of this process to make it appear inevitable and unremarkable is part of what consolidates power in authorities' hands. Understanding what culture is, and is not, is an important first step in evaluating the ways in which the EU may, or may not, be establishing itself as a legitimate political entity and political community.

Culture and Political Identities

If cultures are not primordial and static but rather are the dynamic structures within which we interpret and make meaning of our worlds, then each of us also carries a unique cultural identity that is infused with the variety of all of these different experiences and commitments. We are not of one culture, but of many. One aspect of our cultural identity rests in the political. How do political identities get created, and how do they transform or morph over time and place? As with culture, a mistake often made about identity is the notion that we have only one, single political identity. This is very important, because if multiple identities can coexist, it opens up the possibility that the creation of a European identity may not automatically be in a zero-sum battle, but rather may vary in the ways that identities relate to each other. The identities might be nested, parallel, hierarchical, conflicting, mutually exclusive, or synergistic, to name but a few relationships. If we unpack the idea of identity a bit, we can see this more clearly.

At any point in time, each of us is situated in many different cultures. I think differently about the world because of my identity as a professor of political science, sharing commonalities with other academics. But I also see and participate in the world as a mother, as an Episcopalian, as a Washingtonian, as a Foreign Service brat, as a yogi, and so on. Each of us, anesthesiologist or poet, Parisian or Prussian, are shaped by the unique set of individual intersecting cultures to which we belong. No one single identity (as a lawyer, as a Basque) is paramount all the time, but rather different contexts and situations activate different parts of who we are, even as each identity in turn simultaneously generates different social structures or communities. Not only do variations occur, then, in each of our combinations of these different groupings, but variations occur over time, as well as place. For example, the standard assumptions we share today, such as "knowing" the world is made up of atoms even though most of us have no direct experience of the scientific validity of this statement, are temporally specific understandings of the way the world works, part of modern culture—not universal through all time (Zerubavel 1997: 7). The way we experience the world has been filtered by such assumptions, and they have varied strikingly, and will continue to do so, depending on the historical moment or geographic setting.

Anthropologist Bradd Shore talks about moving to Samoa as a Peace Corps volunteer in the 1960s, and becoming viscerally aware, through the many misunderstandings that took place in his daily life, of the ways in which his frame of mind clashed with local frames. He writes that his experiences there demonstrated that far from meanings being ready made, both he and the Samoans, in trying to understand each other and in going about their daily lives, were engaged in culture as dynamic meaning construction, "an ongoing process, an active construction by people, with the help of cultural resources," the on-the-ground, shared sets of understandings and cognitive shortcuts that every group of humans has (Shore 1996: 7).

When considering the role that an emergent European political culture may play in the construction of the EU, it is particularly useful to remember the following insights: first, that each of our own identities is as individual as a fingerprint, because try as we might, no one replicates our exact muddle of various intersecting social identities. Each of our identities is rooted in a series of larger social groups, but these groups do not submerge or blot out our individuality, but rather allow us to be both part of larger cultural frames but not absolutely beholden to them. Second, those unique fingerprints are actually not fixed, but rather are always in flux, as different identities are activated and come to the fore in different circumstances. What this means for the question of European cultural identity is that national and European identities are not mutually exclusive. Rather than having a hierarchy of political identities that holds over all time and place, a Swede, for example, may feel her Swedish identity come to the fore when traveling in Europe, her Stockholm identity in Sweden, but may feel European on a visit to the US. Moreover, her identity as a Swede may be "Europeanized" such that the two identities are synergetic rather than competitive.

In the case of a nascent European identity, this perspective helps us to understand polling data that has emerged when people are asked whether they feel European. Simply put, it is a mistake to evaluate European identity solely in terms of a self-declared sense of being European, definitively ranking higher or displacing a national identity—of being Italian or Romanian, for example. To do so locates European governance squarely in the model of the sovereign nation state, a recent historical mode of politics that sits uncomfortably with the reality of the European experiment. As Neil Fligstein has persuasively argued, the group of people in Europe who identify themselves as European first and their nationality second is quite small and mostly limited to highly educated, wealthy, mobile people who benefit from, and experience, "Europe" on a daily basis (Fligstein 2008). Adrian Favell's important work on the relatively small number of highly mobile Europeans, whom he calls "Eurostars," reinforces this notion that European identity is confined to those who are so cosmopolitan as to put their European identity above any national commitments (Favell 2008).

But if we take a different view that does not ask people to rank their identities, we might have a more robust appreciation for the process of identity formation in the EU. Thomas Risse proposed the helpful metaphor of a marble cake to describe this type of interacting identity, in contrast to nested identities (say, Sicilian within Italian) or cross-cutting identities (both Catholic and Sicilian) (Risse 2003). Although marble cakes can be delicious, the different flavors vary depending on where you cut into it and, using this metaphor, our identities are likewise less predictably located. Similarly, the intensity and configurations of different social and political identities are likely to vary with different local and national settings. Rather than being fixed in a rank hierarchy, identity is always contingent and experiential as it is an inherently social phenomenon (Berezin 2006). It is rooted both in the social structure of the situation (thus contingent) and in the emotional response of the individual (and so involves particular experiences and the responses they provoke, a felt attachment).

Think about how families have a collective shared identity that interacts with each member's own unique identities (as a daughter, as the youngest, as the "responsible" one) to generate a multifaceted identity that nonetheless has something meaningful in common with others in the family, even while distinctively individual. Similarly, while the people of Europe are not becoming the same, or converging on one single monolithic identity, a cultural sense of being European may be an additive element that interacts with national identities, in ways that vary across individuals and groups, and across time and place.

The relationship between our different types of identities, and the broader cultures within which they are situated, may be relatively harmonious when the various identities can be fashioned so that they do not directly conflict with each other. When my identity as a mother conflicts with my identity as a scholar, however, as when I have both a scheduled lecture and a child sick at home, tension arises as to which identity will win out and direct my actions. In the chapters to follow, we will see how European identity has been consciously and unconsciously shaped across many different policy arenas by actors explicitly seeking to deal with this potential for conflictual identities. One important strategy pursued is to embed national narratives within and congruent to Europe, rather than placing them in opposition to it. An example of this is the change in the way that the French Revolution is framed in high-school history books. Influenced by a European association of high-school history teachers, many EU member-state students now learn about their own national histories in the context of pan-European issues, so that the French Revolution is now taught as a "European" event (Soysal 2002). When this happens in France, it plausibly strengthens French children's European-level identity while not necessarily diminishing their Gallic identity.

When, however, there is a direct and incommensurate clash between the national, regional, or local-level identities and the European level, the tensions between these different political and social commitments will be much more difficult to resolve. This is evident in the foreign policy realm, for example: how can the EU have a legitimate foreign policy if it is not a sovereign state? The identity conflict may come to create problems for the balancing act across these different social identities and political commitments. As we will see, many of the arenas where the EU is crafting a European cultural infrastructure therefore shy away from these most passionately held beliefs and focus instead on more mundane, commonplace iterations of European identity. In the case of foreign policy, as detailed in Chapter 7, dealing with these tensions has meant redefining foreign policy to emphasize human security while nesting EU activities firmly in the national militaries and avoiding any reference to a European-level army. While avoiding some conflicts, these types of strategies may create important limits for the overall construction of political authority in the EU. Next, we further unpack how culture and identity play out more specifically in Europe.

Creating a Cultural Infrastructure for a European Polity

Creating new political affinities is always an uphill battle. The construction of a new political community has always required a significant shift in citizens' vision of the appropriate polity: its scale, its membership, and its meaning. In many instances, this shift occurs with coercion; in other instances it is more voluntary. But in all cases, it involves the creation, through symbols and practices, of a perceived and experienced bond that can glue individuals together in a shared culture and shared identity. If culture is, as argued above, a dynamic and experiential process of shared interpretation and meaning discernment, then these processes will be engaged to build a cultural infrastructure to support, or not, the new political authority, and legitimate, or not, its rule. This cultural infrastructure has been conceptualized by scholars in several ways, as "social imaginaries" that constitute collective societal understandings (Taylor 2004), as a series of myths fabricated to support political integration (Hobsbawm 1990), as an "imagined community" of national citizens (Anderson 1993), or as "collective imaginaries" (Bouchard 2013). Ambitious empirical work across a variety of historical cases has emphatically made this point. To note but one example, an astonishing study of the development of Scottish national sentiments based on the notion of the Highland traditions has likewise traced many of the purportedly ancient Hibernian traditions (Scottish clans with distinct tartans made into kilts and so on) to a combination of creative hucksters in the early nineteenth century and romantic leanings on the part of various members of Scottish society (Trevor-Roper 1983).

The notion of an "imagined community" first explored by Benedict Anderson (1993) in relation to the rise of the modern nation state is a particularly useful starting point for thinking about the challenges faced by the EU and the politicians, policymakers, private sector actors, and everyday citizens who are defining its powers and purpose. According to Anderson, in an imagined community, members have a shared conception of an embodied political space and a sense of belonging, despite never knowing each other personally. Whereas in early forms of political organization, such as the village or tribe, it was possible for all to have some personal connection to each other—if not directly, then indirectly through a cousin or other clansperson or neighbor—as the nation state developed on a larger scale this personal connection became impossible. Therefore, some new ways of creating the bonds of community had to be forged to hold together the newly enlarged national polity by creating a sense of belonging among its citizens.

Political scale helps us in thinking about what the EU is, or isn't, as a political entity. The challenges that the EU face are similar to those of the emergent nation state, where the new bond was an *imagined* one, as citizens will never meet but nonetheless feel connected, as "in the minds of each lives the image of their communion," forming the basis for national identity (Anderson 1993: 6). Because, for example, the political relationship that an Italian in Sardinia shares with a family in the mountains of Trento cannot be directly and personally experienced, it has to be filtered through a common set of ideas and experiences of being Italian. How can a Salamancan in Spain feel one with an Andalusian from Seville? This relationship, being abstract and not personal, requires imagining, and therefore has to be represented symbolically.

Moving beyond Anderson, we can see that this symbolic representation also is joined to shared practices, so that "thinking" is reinforced by "doing." There is a growing literature in international relations, drawing on a broader practice turn in philosophy, political theory, sociology, and the humanities that emphasizes the role of practices in shaping social and political orders (Pouliot 2008). As is discussed more fully below, rituals, be they very clearly linked to explicit political identities or more diffuse, provide a way to put into action shared symbols, even though they are experienced in parallel rather than interactively. For example, an English family in London might sing 'God Save the Queen' outside Westminster Abbey after the wedding of Prince William to Catherine Middleton, while a Welsh family does the same at a viewing party in Cardiff, putting the symbol (the national anthem) into practice (the singing at a communal event), even though physically apart.

Much of the literature on nationalism and its rise in nineteenth-century Europe focused on the forced replacement of local political identities, as the former were seen as dangerous competition for political loyalty by new rulers. The difference between the historical path of nationalism and the EU's efforts at constructing a collective identity is stark. The cultural infrastructure that is being built in Europe explicitly promotes the notion that its members can have multiple identities and belong to multiple cultures, harmoniously albeit with some frictions where they overlap. Remember that cultural communities exist in many spheres of social life beyond the nation, be it across supporters of FC Barcelona, fans of Beyoncé or orchid fanciers, and they overlap and intersect with political identities. Even though recent history has seen the rise of an exclusive commitment to one political order, prior to the nation state, imagined communities existed across multiple forms of political authority, rooted in religion, church, and royalty, and having sometimes vibrant transnational qualities (Nexon 2009). In contrast to medieval and early modern political forms, the imagined communities of nation states are politically defined as inherently limited, bounded, and sovereign. The very rise of the nation state was predicated on the idea of sovereign territoriality. Whereas the imagined communities of the Holy Roman Empire allowed for cross-cutting loyalties and political communities, the nation state delineated a stark boundary of "us" versus "them" in political authority.

Unlike the more limited claims that orchids, Beyoncé, or Barcelona's soccer team might make on their supporters, modern nation states have required high levels of commitment, sacrifice, and loyalty from their citizens. The task of transforming the earlier basis of legitimacy of other entities, such as churches and kings, into a new, national level of political authority was immense. To meet this challenge, political actors within the nation state laid down a series of new symbolic technologies, abstracted away from tangible and physical relations toward new, intangible ones (Ruggie 1993). They also took advantage of exogenous changes in technology to shore up this new community. Many of these transformations involved a revolution in cultural conceptions of time and space to create new ways of thinking necessary to support the "imagined community." The rise of print capitalism and mass media forms such as the newspaper and the novel were instrumental to the development of the political technologies of the construction of nationalism (Anderson 1993).

A variety of symbolic political innovations arose under the nineteenth-century nation state. The creation of new national monuments and rituals, such as the Tomb of the Unknown Soldier, provided a sense of nationness without specificity as to the particulars of who is, or is not, part of the community (Anderson 1993: 9–10). The development of the technology of the national census allowed the categorization and classification of this new group of citizens in a universal form while giving the state tools to extend its bureaucratic power (Starr 1987; Loveman 2005). Expressions of community, such as the museum and the map, were elevated to the national level and arts, artifacts, and boundaries all become part of the larger project of the nation state. These political and social technologies gave people a sense of community beyond their local villages and towns, forever changing the scale of polities.

These accounts of the rise of the nation emphasize the particular political tools, symbols, and technologies intentionally welded by motivated actors, alongside broader structural changes that provided fertile ground for the reorganization of political identities. They should therefore make us wary of assuming the "intrinsic" or essential nature of member-state nationalism as a bar to any such development at the European level, but also make us see that nationalism is not easily malleable or readily replaceable. The obstacles to a sense of a common European political community may be plentiful and real, but to understand the potential and the challenge we need to turn our attention to the question of the actual processes by which such imagined communities arise, or fall apart. The first place to start to understand the underlying mechanisms by which such imagined communities are constructed is with an investigation of social facts.

Social Facts and Invented Realities

The concept of imagined community is extremely helpful in conceptualizing the cultural shift that enables the scaling-up of political authority as the territorial size of a political entity expands, and therefore in explaining the EU's remarkable, if contentious political development. But it does not provide a story of the specific social processes by which the shift occurs. The basic mechanism at work in creating a cultural infrastructure for Europe can be understood better by considering the concept of the "social fact."

Social facts are those invented realities that are purely subjective but take on the qualities of objective, material reality because of their widespread, taken-for-granted hold on a population. Social facts are ideas so obvious that most people think of them as *objective* facts, forgetting that these facts are dependent on shared understandings for their existence. Social facts are key building blocks to our daily lives. They constitute the cultural landscape that we act within by institutionalizing meaning construction within stable, intersubjective understandings that form the foundation for modern life. The production of social facts is happening all around us, all the time, yet the more successful this production is, the less likely are we ever to remark on it.

Paper currency is a nice example. A piece of paper with a euro symbol on it takes on the status of money because we all act as if the paper is valuable itself, rather than merely being a representation of value. If one person stops believing that a 50-euro bill is worth more than a 5-euro bill, it will have no impact on its status as a social fact. However, if there is a widespread rejection of the value of the 50 versus 5 symbol on the euro bill, the social fact will break down, and monetary chaos or inflationary spirals will ensue. Durkheim describes social facts as ways of thinking and acting, collective beliefs and practices that derive from membership in particular societies, or substrata of societies. Over time, through repetition, these social facts come to constitute a reality in their own right, quite distinct from the individuals who produce them (Durkheim 1939: 7; 1973; Durkheim and Mauss 1963). Durkheim emphasizes the coercive, if subtle, structural power that these social facts exert. These taken-for-granted things that we "know" without consciously thinking come to have, in Durkheim's words, a "constraining" effect on actors. In the case of the EU, if it is taken for granted as a social fact, its fundamental existence as a political actor is not contested, although its policies and programs may be.

Remember that collective political entities, be they states or the EU, have to be reified before they can be actors and sites of legitimate authority. In other words, they must be represented through images and symbols, and constructed in practice, because they do not actually exist as full-blown entities separate from the humans who generate them. If successful, this process makes the EU into a taken-for-granted "social fact." If I alone stop believing in the EU, who cares? My position does not negate the EU's existence. However, the socially constructed nature of the EU as a human institution means that it is always contingent on our thoughts and interactions, rather than being logically inevitable or given through "natural" processes, such as those that make the sun rise in the morning or narcissi bloom in April. Our shared conventions take on a status between the purely subjective or the purely material and objective, as people act "as if" these social facts existed separate from the individuals who create them. So, we can easily talk about "the stock market" and its ups and downs, even as it has no actual physical manifestation separate from our collectively believing it exists. Stock certificates certainly exist as pieces of paper, but only have meaning because they are situated within a stable series of understandings, or conventions, that give them legitimacy as representing shares in a company that can be traded or cashed in. In the US financial crisis of 2008, when Bernie Madoff's Ponzi scheme was revealed and publicized, the value of his clients' (imaginary) portfolios collapsed, driven by a change in intersubjective understanding. The monetary realm can readily be seen as one based on legitimated social understandings, sometimes quite robust and at other times quite fragile, but such social facts are all around us once we start to look.

Searle elaborates on the notion of social facts by explaining that while there are brute facts in the world (such as the distance of the sun from the earth), there are also social or institutional facts (Searle 1992: 27). These institutional facts, such as the fact that John Kerry is as of this writing the US Secretary of State, require particular human institutions for them to be meaningful—in the case of John Kerry, the system of US government. Marriage and football are examples of social facts: without a shared understanding of what these things are, they would not exist. While your marriage certificate exists on paper, the legal contract and its recognition are reliant upon human institutions to support it—or not, as in the case of same-sex marriage in much of the world. Football as well is reliant on a set of socially shared and agreed-upon rules to exist. These sorts of variations, Durkheim points out, provide methodological leverage on the study of such facts as social phenomena (Durkheim 1939). Likewise, while the actual earthly terrain of the continent and islands that make up the EU exists as a brute fact, the EU itself is a social fact, invented through our intersubjective understandings.

The challenge for those real-world actors, be they Eurocrats or national elites, attempting to establish the EU as a social fact is to make it seem unremarkable and natural, even as it may be actually quite novel and revolutionary. Bourdieu has called this the ability to "construct the given," that is, to make natural and unremarkable certain categories and actions that reinforce and legitimize political agency (Bourdieu 1991: 170). For Bourdieu, this is a potent form of symbolic power, just as for Durkheim social facts imply a coercive quality. We should keep this point in mind in the coming chapters as we survey the foundations of symbols and practices creating the EU as a social fact. Indeed, when those invested in its creation are successful, the EU is naturalized as an actor such that we don't even think about this process of actor creation, nor do we question the construction of an imagined community of European citizens, who must locate themselves inside this pervasive mental framework even absent a European nation or template for the EU's unique polity. EU scholars have recently demonstrated the traction that we can get by close attention to the role of socialization, to identity change, to discourse, and to similar dynamics in the EU (Christiansen, Jørgensen, and Wiener 2001; Herrmann, Risse-Kappen, and Brewer 2004; Checkel 2007; Schmidt 2008; Checkel and Katzenstein 2009). But there has been less attention to these quite fundamental social dynamics that create the EU itself as a social fact, and allow for the transfer of political authority to its center.

Despite the novelty of the EU, and despite competition from other actors, the EU is a stable social institution granted a high degree of legitimacy in terms of its daily activities. Notwithstanding its many fissures and the continued strength of national identities, it is undeniable that the EU is a political authority of prodigious capacity, one whose intrusiveness in almost all areas of policymaking continues to grow. The EU as a social fact has two faces, both critical to the emergence of the EU as a new governance form. One is inward, toward the EU's citizens and national actors, in the domestic political realm. The other is outward, to the rest of the world, in a process of global actor construction in the international realm (Meyer and Jepperson 2000). As the EU is fashioned as an emergent political actor, it is gradually embedded in networks of relationships, which generate expectations from within the EU (in the form of its own citizens and national governments), and from without (in the form of diplomats, intergovernmental organizations, nongovernmental organizations, and firms). A profound change has occurred over time as the EU evolves further toward being recognized and treated by nation states as a legitimate political authority with representational powers and sovereignty in formal and informal international organizations and regimes, as will be explored in Chapter 7.

Although social facts by their very nature appear natural and unremarkable to us, in truth, a tremendous amount of heavy lifting has to occur to establish them as such. For a new political actor to take on a "taken-for-granted" status, social and political space needs to be reconfigured through cultural processes. Symbols and practices are the means by which social facts are constructed through the broader dynamic processes of meaning creation that constitute cultures. Below, I distinguish the specific mechanisms at work.

Symbols and Political Authority

Political authority has always and everywhere been built in part on symbolic power (Edelman 1964, 1971, 1988). As long as humans have organized themselves into groups, there have been politics at play, and with that, the creation and manipulation of symbols and symbolic power. As Michael Walzer has written: "Politics is an art of unification; from many it makes one. And symbolic activity is perhaps our most important means of bringing things together, both intellectually and emotionally…" (Walzer 1967). Walzer notes that as religious symbols unite man with god, political symbols have the potential to unite man with man, and with something greater than any individual man—a collective political entity. This is particularly important because, as Walzer notes: "The state is invisible; it must be personified before it can be seen, symbolized before it can be loved, imagined before it can be conceived" (Walzer 1967: 194).

As Walzer's quote reminds us, political communities can only be made visible through their symbolic representations, as they are social, not physical phenomena of the natural world. But this process is not neutral or automatic. Powerful actors have sought to gain legitimacy through the creation and manipulation of symbols to represent themselves, as becoming a taken-for-granted social fact is part and parcel of the process of authority creation. Scholars have documented the many ways that the rise of the nation state relied on cultural foundations as well as material capacities (Crane 1994; Steinmetz 1999). Bourdieu reminds us that while the nation state centralized and exerted control across a host of policy arenas, it also was an impressive "symbolic accomplishment" as well (Bourdieu 1984).

Likewise, the EU can only be symbolized, because even as various aspects of the EU come to have concrete form, such as the European Parliament building, in its entirety as a political actor the EU does not have material presence, but exists only in our imagination. The same is true, of course, for the United States, or Italy, or any aggregate political actor. Symbolic representation does the work here, because, in very simple terms, symbols signify. Representations of Europe, such as the euro, signal the presence of the EU, and serve as its constant reminder. But these symbols do not simply represent, they also empower, creating the EU as a political entity in an act of imagination. In economic theory, there is little difference between having individual national exchange rates simply irrevocably locked in value with each other, versus consolidating into one physical currency. But in terms of the symbolic work that the euro as a single currency does for political life, there is a large difference. Although since 2010 the economic effects of the sovereign debt crisis have dominated public discussion of the impact of the euro, there have also been important if not always visible impacts on the social infrastructure or underlying cultural landscape of Europe, as will be discussed in Chapter 6.

While we tend to dismiss symbols as inconsequential, as "only symbolic," they generate and reproduce understandings that provide social focal points around which material interests then form. Counting people in a census, redrawing maps, creating national heritage museums, undertaking land surveys, or creating tax registries each represent and generate understandings, adding to the "grammar" of a political authority by providing a way to visualize what it is (Anderson 1993; Scott 1998; Loveman 2005). Such administrative practices on the part of the state "actively constitute the subjects in whose name it claims to exist legitimately" (Loveman 2005: 1653). National educational systems in particular impart particular ways of understanding the world so as to shore up the authority of the state through symbolic representations of society. These modern developments in governance have both material and symbolic consequences, as they increase policy capacity and the ability to refashion expectations through symbolic manipulations. Likewise for the EU, symbolically representing the "ever closer union" of the people of Europe, as first stated in the Treaty of Rome, is a foundational and elementary step in creating a body politic.

These processes of symbolic representation do not by themselves create unity, or loyalty, or emotional attachment. Instead, symbolic representation creates a unit, a vessel for discourse, reference, and discussion. It then may or may not create loyalty and attachment. These processes also reframe the political universe around the new political authority, shifting if not displacing the preexisting understandings. Symbols are cultural forms that embody meaning, both reflecting but also shaping broader social and political structures. But they are neither separate from, nor reducible to, broader political dynamics and power relations. Agents may actively push back on the deployment of symbols—rejecting, resisting, subverting, or creating counter-symbols. The blue and gold stars of the EU flag may be viewed with approval when flying above a new economic development project in Croatia, but might be trampled on by students in Greece who are angry about economic austerity policies. Thus the broader cultural infrastructure of symbols is reproduced over time, but rarely without adaptation, sometimes morphing into an altogether different set of social structures. But how, exactly, do symbols work to do this?

Collective Representations

Symbols seem very slippery in contrast to traditional forms of material power and capacity. A useful way to think of them is as a vital part of the collective representations that form the bedrock for any culture (Durkhem 1973). Whereas many international relations scholars, including myself, have located the power of social phenomena at the level of individuals who hold particular world views or ideas that influence outcomes (Berman 1998; McNamara 1998; Blyth 2002), if we focus on *collective* representations beyond the level of the individual, we can see culture as doing powerful work in politics. These collective representations are located in external processes of symbolic activity, where certain symbols—be it specific linguistic terms such as the acronym "WMD" (weapons of mass destruction), or images, such as the Statue of Liberty or the pagan goddess Europa—come to signify a host of particular values and understandings. These symbols are a sort of shorthand that has a specific meaning for the particular cultural community where it is in play (but completely different meanings in others). So labeling something a WMD may be a call for action on the part of US neoconservatives after 9/11, but to American liberal democrats may be a symbol of the dangers of scaremongering.

Symbols are consequential when they help to constitute what they purport to merely represent. This constituting or instantiating reality is a powerful causal force, but it is not automatic, as human beings are not "cultural dupes" but rather thinking agents who may actively push back on, rather than accept, the symbols generated by political actors. Yet if accepted, a certain set of symbols create cultural repertoires that act as a shared language or set of experiences to create medium for connection across individuals (Swindler 1986). They serve as public "vehicles of meaning" (Swindler 2002: 313), although they may be read very differently depending on the particular perspective of different audiences, be they individuals, ethnic or national groups, and their location at a particular time in history. Think of the meaning of the value of the euro in international markets. The very strong euro may be a symbol of strength when it climbs against the dollar, and a source of pride and material benefit for Europeans crowding the mid-town Manhattan Apple store to buy devices made cheap by the dollar-euro exchange rate. In other eyes, the high value of the euro may be seen as a drag on efforts to restart lagging economies as exports from the economically distressed Eurozone become more expensive to consumers abroad. The Stability and Growth Pact that guides fiscal policy in the EU can be read as a symbol of sobriety, of the influence of the conservative German macroeconomic policy over the profligate PIIGS (Portugal, Ireland, Italy, Greece, and Spain), or it can be seen as an unwelcome symbol of austerity strangling growth and employment in Europe. It is important to assess what is persuasive in a particular historical moment, among particular social groups, in order to understand how a symbol will resonate. While pushing forward European integration in the name of the market may have gained political traction in the 1990s (Jabko 2006), after the financial meltdown and Great Recession of 2008, such a rhetorical strategy may falter. The point is that symbols are not infinitely malleable in all political settings, but rather they always interact with existing raw materials and prior understandings, and must be filtered through the prism of political authority.

Because symbols have this quality of calling into being what they purport to only represent, the representation of authority through symbols has been a required route for new political actors, as a necessary but not sufficient precursor to gaining legitimacy. Symbols can give social shape to a free-floating idea. Publicly shared symbols actively constitute social and political groups while they simultaneously constrain and give form to individuals (Swindler 2002). Symbols provide a way to give a proto union of people a shape, an image, as there is no "palpable shape or substance" to polities in and of themselves (Walzer 1967: 194). Symbols are a precursor, in this view, to interests and strategies, as culture is the larger context of meaning within which interests can be formulated in the first place.

For our puzzles about the emergence of the EU as a taken-for-granted authority, we will focus on locating culture in collective representations to decipher the meaning of the symbols that EU officials and programs are wielding in the public sphere, and European citizens' absorption or rejection of them. Many of these symbols are deployed directly by the EU itself, as we will see in the chapters to follow. But these symbols are not only found in the specific offices charged with education and culture, but rather occur unintentionally as side effects of all of the parts of the EU's governance activities, from the European Central Bank to the European Food Safety Authority. These activities change the cultural setting, subtly refashioning the backdrop within which politics unfolds. Other important symbolic activity occurs in arenas outside the direct control of the EU as well, in social groups and non-governmental organizations (NGOs), national education settings, privately owned media, or market actors such as multinational corporations. These dynamics have combined to make the emergence of the EU seemingly boring and mundane, camouflaging its world historic significance through the silliness of EU film festivals and bumper stickers with EU logos, while entering into the everyday lives of Europeans and those around the world who interact with the EU.

Practices and Political Authority

Symbols represent the world around us and, in so doing, make it comprehensible—but in different ways to specific social communities, or cultures. But meaning is not only created through our thinking, our cognitive engagement with the world, in images, words, and thoughts. It is also created through practice. Practice—our day-to-day experiences and actions as humans—is what solidifies and makes real those constructions, or contradicts and inverts them (Wedeen 2002; Pouliot 2008). Europe can be represented as a borderless entity on the back of a euro note, but when a French citizen travels from Forbach, France to the neighboring town of Saarbrücken, Germany without having to show identification or have any other experience of a border crossing, that moment becomes part of that person's lived experience of what "Europe" means. Instead of only considering what we think *about* (symbolic representation), we should also understand what we think *from* (Pouliot 2008). Drawing on Bourdieu's idea of practical reasoning can provide a way to understand the processes of authority construction of the EU by highlighting common-sense and inarticulate grounds for action (Bourdieu 1998). Humans reason in multiple ways simultaneously—cognitively, practically, and emotionally—and to fully understand the evolution of the processes undergirding the development of the EU, we need to focus on how practice might matter, and how it interacts with the material world.

Making the Practice Turn

Sociology has recently taken a "practice turn" that can provide a very helpful set of mechanisms for understanding the construction of the EU as a social fact. Culture, as discussed above, can be thought of not only as Durkheim's collective representations, but also as arising from the ongoing, repeated, and patterned actions of actors themselves. In this way, it moves from a sole emphasis on social structure to human agency, providing a more dynamic and satisfying theory of action. The touchstone for scholarship on practice is found in the work of Pierre Bourdieu (Bourdieu 1977, 1980). For Bourdieu, culture is conceived of "not as a set of rules, but as deeply internalized habits, styles, and skills (the "habitus") that allow human beings to continually produce innovative actions that are nonetheless meaningful to others around them" (Swindler 2002: 314). Bourdieu assumes that people continually and actively re-create culture through their own strategic use of culturally privileged skills. But he further makes the point that because such cultural capital is unequally distributed, structures of inequality tend to be reproduced over and over in these practices.

Practice has also been theorized by French sociologist Michel Foucault, who refocused the study of culture to institutionalized practices (Foucault 1977). He has argued that the ways in which systems of categories and distinctions are enacted and made real in institutional practices profoundly shape how history unfolds. For Foucault, institutions use power to enact rules that construct human beings and the social world they inhabit (Foucault 1983). Whereas, for Durkheim, practices and rituals demarcate cultural boundaries and make symbols real, Foucault focuses on how institutions do this cultural work. He also reminds us of how power is implicated in these processes, as the practices generated by institutions such as the nation state enforce or reinforce particular social systems with particular distributional and power asymmetries.

The practice turn has also come to the constructivist approach in international relations, as different theorists have taken up various and sometimes competing arguments about how practice matters (Guzzini and Leander 2006; Pouliot 2007, 2008, 2010; Neumann 2002; Mitzen 2006; Adler and Pouliot 2011). The most relevant to this book's investigation of the EU comes from Pouliot, who argues that we should spend more time considering what people do (Pouliot 2008). Pouliot emphasizes the routines that become a "way of life," and cause actors to be thinking "from" a certain situation rather than thinking "about" it (Pouliot 2008: 257). This can be a powerful way to naturalize certain interactions as the habitual and taken-for-granted way to go about daily life. Thinking "from" a sense of European political identity is a much more powerful and ingrained dynamic than thinking "about" political community and identity. As discussed in the following chapters, across a broad range of activities, new European practices are reshaping political life. From this practice perspective, crossing the French–Spanish border with no passports or experience of it as a border becomes a deeply engrained pattern of behavior that changes the backdrop of discussion about European governance. Even if it does not make that governance unproblematic or uncontested, it changes the basic felt assumptions under which the discussion occurs.

Performativity and Material Culture

Practice also matters for the construction of the EU in several other ways. Processes of performativity, and practices in relationship to objects, or material culture, help us to understand the cultural infrastructure for new emergent entities such as the EU. Performativity occurs when actors engage in social processes of knowledge creation that *create* the phenomena they seem only to describe (Callon 1998; Barry and Slater 2002). For example, consider the role played by finance economists in developing the economic models that created derivative markets. Their theories of pricing these exotic financial instruments were used by market actors, such that the theories were "an engine, not a camera" generating or calling into being those markets rather than merely neutrally describing them (MacKenzie 2006). The economic theories and models of derivatives were "performed" by private actors and thus made real through their practices, making a distinctive and traceable difference in the outcomes of those markets. So, economic markets can be thought of as performing economic theory in conjunction with academic theorists' work, "understanding, analyzing, and equipping markets" (Callon, cited in MacKenzie 2006: 16). For the EU, parallels can be drawn to the early role of academic theorists in providing the ideas behind the functionalist stories of integration, which predicted that increasing integration in one area, say liberalization of trade, would create functional pressures for spillover into other areas, such as the regulation of those newly integrated markets, and eventually end up inexorably pushing forward political integration. The "founding fathers" of the EU "performed" these ideas in creating the original institutions and treaties of the European Coal and Steel Community (ECSC) and the European Economic Community (EEC), while simultaneously validating them. Both the single market and the single currency projects had extensive theoretical underpinnings from European academics whose work likewise played a crucial role in bringing them to life.

Another avenue for practices of performativity is in language. Just as symbols construct what they purport merely to represent, particular forms of communication call into existence that of which they speak. Utterances that "do something" can be thought of as "performance" utterances or speech acts (Austin 1962; Searle 1969; Butler 1993). Here, words do not simply report on separately existing phenomena but rather create and call into being those phenomena. Phrases like "I apologize," "I name this child Henry," and "I bet you five dollars" all are examples of speech acts. When someone uses the Basque name Hondarribia, rather than that town's Spanish name Fuenterrabía, they "perform" Basqueness and create it as a social fact, despite efforts to stamp out such Basqueness after World War II. Similarly, when people use phrases such as "the European economy" or "European foreign policy," they contribute to the construction of those phenomena as social facts through performativity.

Practices create social facts in another way: when they become concretized and have physical expressions. Archeologists and anthropologists have long studied "material culture," or the role of objects in both reflecting and shaping cultures (Hicks and Beaudry 2010). Here, symbols—and the ideas, values, and emotions contained within them—can be physical objects that actors interact with in practice. In essence, symbols are made "real" by being embodied in objects that actually become part of people's lives in a practical way. The euro is the most dramatic example of this process—as the single currency, for better or worse, makes concrete the imagined community it constructs (Castano 2002; Risse 2003; Herrmann, Risse-Kappen, and Brewer 2004; Kaelberer 2004). The social construction of cultural artifacts "is at the same time the materialization of a practice that enables particular kinds of agents to intervene productively in the world of things" (Brain 1994: 193). Symbols become concretized in practice and provide an opening for actors to subvert, tweak, and morph the practice, which may then boomerang back to reshape the symbol. In sum, practice dynamics have the potential to routinize the novel form of governance that is the EU, even as they do not protect it from contestation or derision.

Conclusion

This chapter has laid out the argument for the centrality of a cultural infrastructure for governance in the EU, just as with all newly emergent political forms throughout history. This cultural infrastructure is critical to the generation of the EU's status as a taken-for-granted social fact, as a political authority whose actions may be questioned but whose reality is never in doubt. Symbols and practices, in my account, together provide a potent way to call into being a political authority and create an imagined community of its citizens.

The EU has developed without the bloodshed and overt strife that permeated earlier episodes of state formation, where figures such as Bismarck led all-out wars against recalcitrant subnational entities. Even if national loyalties and political affiliation remain robust, and the EU commands only faint loyalty or is even the object of derision, it is striking how much has been accomplished with minimal political strife. Vast areas of national political economies are now ruled by the EU, and social and foreign policy are being encroached upon, but without the violence or political suppression that has occurred in other instances of political consolidation. In fact, until the Eurozone crisis, there has been remarkably little widespread questioning of the EU's emergence. How can this be?

Chapter 3 details the mechanics of the particular political technologies that the EU has used to create its cultural infrastructure and establish itself as a social fact with subtle, rather than openly contested, powers. Those technologies have layered the EU's symbols and practices on top of, around, and in between the European nation states. This has allowed the EU to be politically under the radar of most citizens, and thus diluted potential resistance, even as the EU makes decisions over critical social values, with huge distributional consequences. The EU has had much less overt politicization over its development in comparison with historical episodes of political development. Yet the tensions in the distinctive cultural infrastructure of the EU are growing. Economic malaise, social disruption, and a sense of political stagnation are putting pressure on the cultural infrastructure of the EU. It is to the EU's particular political technologies and their cultural expressions that we now turn.

3

Technologies of Cultural Construction

Introduction

Throughout history, crafty political actors have deployed a variety of tried and true political technologies to accrue legitimate power to rule, to naturalize themselves as the rightful successor to competitors, past and present. How do these mechanisms work, or not, to produce a sense of community and along with it a new political identity to serve as a basis for governance? And what particular spin has the European Union (EU) put on these processes to establish itself as deeply as it has, despite being challenged by its status as a unique political form without any exact peer in the international system? This chapter lays out the specific technologies of cultural construction that create the EU as a social fact, natural and taken for granted, even if its own actions and policies are contested. These processes are not always directly under the control of the EU, however, but rather implicate a host of other actors and groups, in society and in national governments.

I argue that diffuse processes of labeling, mapping, and narrating are making meanings and shaping interpretation of the daily experiences of Europe in politically consequential ways. *Label*s as a form of naming can be a powerful tool for actors. Labels are always politically fraught as the act of labeling implies the power to describe things as "this," but not "that." For example, calling the geographic area near Jerusalem by the label "Judea and Samaria" carries with it a claim about the legitimacy of Israeli settlements, whereas using the term "West Bank" does not. Calling something European flattens out difference by uniting, rhetorically at least, many into one. Labels act to categorize, and allow for classification and enumeration. Think of the work of meaning that is done through a census, which labels, counts, and classifies, and as James Scott says, makes "legible" a people so that the state can govern, and exercise its power (Scott 1998). All of these labeling activities shape our perceptions of the world around us in acts of creative imagination.

Symbols and practices that serve to *map* a citizenry are likewise an important political technology. The way that authorities socially construct their geographic dominion through physical and virtual mapping processes is also consequential for the consolidation of political power: the drawing of the lines of a map of Nunavut out of the Northwest Territories in Canada becomes a political act, just as the erasure of the felt experience or practice of borders inside the EU creates new political claims and meanings. Where we imagine ourselves located in the world, how we are anchored in space and place, and the way we feel boundaries can all matter for legitimate governance. This chapter will also focus on the political technology of *narrating*. Political actors attempt to narrate our lived reality with frames, myths, or histories to underpin their authority or channel action. The success of those narrations can vary widely, and are never fully under the control of the actors who manufacture them. Nonetheless, the stories that people tell about their communities are a key part of the cultural infrastructure for governance. The material world always has to be interpreted, and the ability to determine which stories are told about that world is a source of power. All of these three political technologies—labeling, mapping, and narrating—can be powerful tools for actors seeking to legitimate themselves.

Each new political authority sets its own distinctive stamp on these processes, and the EU is no exception. But the EU faces two key challenges. First, the EU has no template from which to borrow authority, being the only political form of its kind. Without a vocabulary to define itself as an appropriate locus of governance, the EU faces an uphill symbolic battle. Second, unlike previous new political actors, the EU has not overtly sought to definitively replace existing sovereign authorities. Instead, the EU must navigate the European nation states, trying to create a narrative that allows the EU to be seen as complementary to, rather than in competition with, the member states. Rather than a wholesale replacement, the EU is penetrating into the cracks below, above, and in between the nation states to build its own social reality and cultural infrastructure for governance and authority. To navigate the nation state, I argue that the EU uses a strategy that seeks to "localize Europe," to embed Europe within the national settings in symbols and practices. The Europe being generated by the official EU policies, by civil society, and by market actors, uses symbols and practices in ways that seek to simultaneously appropriate the classic tropes of the nation state, while recontextualizing them to appear complementary, rather than confrontational. If successful, this allows for the simultaneity of both national and local identities with Europe, as certain practices, experiences, emotions, and ideas are standardized into being European, while nested within national and local identities.

Deracination is the other distinctive cultural strategy that, I argue, the EU has used to naturalize its authority. Rather than embrace a nineteenth-century-style nationalism, European elites have attempted to render what are usually passionately contested and deeply held political commitments into dispassionate, technocratic, experts-only exercises in governance. These strategies of deracination standardize while stressing the abstracted, technocratic nature of various policies and EU activities, so as to minimize the potential for the encroachment of the EU cultural infrastructure on the more intimate, emotional attachments of nationalism. The euro is framed as a simple technical fix to meet the needs of the single European market, not a wholesale giving up of national sovereignty over fundamental economic policies. The images on the euro are abstracted, not rooted in any specific historical moment or geographic context.

Together, strategies of localizing and deracinating Europe create a particularly "banal authority" to underpin the European project. When successful, Hungarian, Scottish, or Spanish identity, for example, becomes complementary to, rather than in conflict with, European identity, and the EU's legitimacy is solidified rather than contested. But these successes are not guaranteed, as the mask covering the deeper, inherently contentious aspects of governance in the EU is likely to fray under stress.

The rest of the chapter lays out the nitty-gritty of these cultural processes by focusing first on the role of categories and classification in social and political life, then on the specific tried and tested mechanisms of labeling, mapping, and narrating used not only by the EU but by other political authorities throughout history. The final section of the chapter argues that there is an important historical break, however, in the particular mode of cultural infrastructure being built in Europe, one that can tell us much about the challenges facing the EU.

Categories as a Source of Power

We use categories all the time. Categorization is central to our existence as thinking, social beings. Classifying things in terms of typologies—be it dogs, democrats, or one-percenters—is one of the central ways in which we make sense of the world around us (Lakoff 1987; Douglas and Hull 1992; Zerubavel 1997). We do it constantly, separating the world into "this, but not that." We tend not to realize how pervasive the process of categorization is, except perhaps in a case of unwarranted stereotyping, such as profiling by police or airport security agents. Yet the way we construct categories, and what we put into them, is an inherent and constant part of our daily lives that has important political repercussions. Categories and classification have long been tools of political authorities seeking to govern over fractious and unruly peoples.

Sociologists have dissected the ways in which these categories matter, arguing that much of how we interact with the world is guided by a sense of ideal types, or "typifications" that we use to make sense of things, to reason about what our preferences are or what we should do (Berger and Luckmann 1966). Cognitive psychologist George Lakoff's work demonstrates the "imaginative aspects of reasoning—metaphor, metonymy, and mental imagery" rather than seeing reason as only rooted in objective realities, as many political scientists may assume (Lakoff 1987: xi). Reason instead is anchored in bodily experience and meanings, and does not descend from the heavens, fully formed and universally the same across all times and places. Instead, our very notion of what constitutes logical rationality is rooted in specific cultural contexts that generate the categories our reasoning ultimately rests on.

Lakoff notes that just as a certain aboriginal tribe has a linguistic category, or label, that groups together "women, fire and dangerous things," so we have categories of things that do not objectively seem to go together, but rather vary dramatically depending on the historical or cultural context. Think of the way contagion spreads across financial markets. A close look at the economic fundamentals of the various countries swept up in the Asian financial crisis of the 1990s suggests that investors may have been fleeing national bond markets or foreign currencies because financial market actors lumped them together as being part of a geographic location (Asia), rather than assessing their relative financial soundness. More recent empirical work on financial markets finds that market actors' assessment of sovereign debt risk, which determines the price at which governments borrow internationally, is shaped more by the particular ways in which countries are categorized together by investors, rather than by a country's actual economic fundamentals (Brooks, Cunha, and Mosley 2014). Likewise, membership in an international organization, the "company states keep," has more causal impact on investment outcomes than can be justified by any material facts beyond the perceptions generated from that categorization (Gray 2013).

This sort of mental shorthand, the classification of the world into categories even when they may not be objectively correct, is important for creating stable social structures shared within communities, be they neighborhoods, country clubs, drug cartels, or corporations. All these communities rely on a series of shared and stable social assumptions about the world, sometimes to the detriment of efforts to evolve toward more equality, inclusiveness, or efficiency.

Categories are also important in constructing our own individual identities, our sense of self, and our roles in the various social circles that we live in. We learn to order the world as we grow up, largely as a part of a particular culture. Those "taken-for-granted" categorizations that we unthinkingly use throughout our day are built up over time in specific cultural settings. In a Danish family, fried dough with powdered sugar is put in the category of breakfast, while for a Korean family, pickled vegetables are the natural food to greet the day. In the US, the federal government is assumed to play a role in the provision of national security, but not a universal healthcare system or nationalized daycare for young children. In France, however, it is unremarkably part of what it means to be a state to have nationalized medicine and government-subsidized crèches.

The construction of categories engages power in extremely consequential, if often overlooked, ways. The modern nation state has attempted to monopolize the "power to name, identify, categorize, to state what is what and who is who" (Brubaker and Cooper 2000: 15; see also Bourdieu 1999). Foucault's idea of "governmentality" rests in part on this symbolic power of classification and identification (Foucault 1991). The impact of categories on social orders is significant, as categorization in society has been shown to have persistent effects in maintaining social inequalities (Tilly 1998). Loveman notes that it is through practices of categorization and the regulations that flow from those practices that political actors, such as modern states, "not only naturalize certain distinctions and not others, but they also help constitute particular kinds of people, places, and things," a potent form of power (Hacking 1986; Loveman 2005: 1655).

Counting by political authorities can be another process of social power enabled by categorization (Starr 1987, 1992). The modern nation state has been a veritable treasure trove of classification and counting, as Max Weber first described in his work on rationalized bureaucracies almost a century ago (Weber 1922, 1946). These administrative activities are so pervasive that we tend to think of them as entirely natural for political authorities to undertake, and beyond reproach. Yet the project of moving authority to the nation state was immense, and involved the legitimation of new, disconcerting ways of counting, such as individual accounting rather than taking stock of family or group units (Ruggie 1993). When existing authorities or institutions already have purview over census practices, for example as with birth and death registries kept historically by local churches, the state needs to either co-opt existing authorities or more forcibly wrest away functions to the new political actor. James Scott's simile of "seeing like a state" well captures the notion that much of present-day governance activities are efforts to make "legible" its population, with concrete practices that empower state control over its citizens (Scott 1998). The instruments used to do so are not on the face of it threatening, resting as they do in the realm of boring bureaucratic behavior such as the property register, census, gross national product, and mortality statistics. Yet counting is crucial to creating winners and losers across a range of policies. The measurement of inflation or unemployment in a particular manner may strengthen the hand of price stability advocates or growth advocates. Macroeconomic statistics are defined and measured quite differently across different national agencies, and the construction of those ways of counting is not an apolitical exercise. As we will discuss in the ensuing chapters, the EU has followed this historical pattern of extending its reach to encompass many counting activities traditionally held only by states, such as data collection in the Eurostat agency, Eurobarometer surveys of the EU public, and multiple other EU agency activities. But the EU has done so in purposefully banal ways that attempt to mute challenges to its authority and mask the power latent in these administrative practices.

The political technologies of categorization described above are all things taken for granted today as being appropriate and natural activities on the part of states, the EU, and even international organizations such as the World Trade Organization or the International Monetary Fund (Barnett and Finnemore 1999). But they were all once viewed as deeply controversial and highly political.

Such classifications and categories can help to constitute identities in potentially important ways. We usually think of categories as merely describing something that already exists. But think of the introduction of the category of "Hispanic" on the US census in 1970, which actually played a part in encouraging the emergence of a new political interest group not previously self-identified as such (Petersen 1987; Goldberg 1997). The work that such categories do can even extend to violence, as when the Belgian colonial government issued identity cards to Hutus and Tutsis in Rwanda, and subtly enabled the politically motivated public reconstruction of ethnic identities that was necessary for the horrific genocide that eventually occurred (Malkki 1995, 1996; Loveman 2005: 1655). Categories do not "cause" outcomes such as these, but they are an underappreciated mechanism that enables political action. We now turn to three specific political technologies of categorization—labeling, mapping, and narrating—that have shaped the path of political authority in the EU, drawing out important similarities and differences with the last important emergent political entity, the nation state.

Labeling Europe

Naming can profoundly institutionalize a particular way of seeing something (Austin 1962; Searle 1969; Austin et al. 1970; Butler 1993). Think of the norms in some cultures around the question of whether a wife should take her husband's last name. For some, the name joins a couple together as one, for others, it reinforces gender disparities and the subordination of a wife's identity into her husband's. Regardless of which side of the debate you are on, or whether the decision is automatic or agonized over, it indicates the power of naming. We need language to simultaneously make sense of the world and to call it into being, as our discussion of the creation of social facts established in Chapter 2. Remember that language is a series of symbols that convey meaning only in particular cultural settings. The word "duck" is nonsense to a Spaniard just as "pato" would symbolize nothing to an English speaker. Yet language also has a practice element to it. Using a certain term such as "European economy" both signifies something as well as creating or reinforcing it as a legitimate category. Using it over and over, who uses it, where it is used—all of these practices will matter for whether it is ultimately viewed as legitimate and comes to be taken for granted or not. Naming is a way to make one from many, placing disparate entities under a new, standardized category that then takes on a life of its own—be it short- or long-lived, consequential or not. But that entity cannot exist in our minds separate from the symbolic and practical activity of naming, and therefore the ability to determine names is a powerful political resource.

Language helps typify the world, classifying situations, objects, and people into normalized and generalized phenomena. So words such as "cash" versus "credit" or "subprime mortgages" all can be understood as typifications, creating categories of understanding through standardization. However, understandings vary widely across cultures, and in time and place, even as the actual language stays the same, as today we think about subprime mortgages differently than a bank loan officer might have in 2004.

These typifications are ubiquitous, and can do important work in lumping together things that may in fact be relatively diverse, smoothing out the differences under a common label. Naming something "European foreign policy" does not suddenly make the EU an effective actor in the world. But through labeling it does create a new category that establishes the potential for political action. This potential is made possible by the introduction of a label that can become a resource for political actors, for both friends and foes of a European foreign policy. Both official EU labels, and those that arise unintentionally through everyday use, as side effects of the changed landscape of governance in the EU, act to unite the disparate and fragmented collection of actors that make up the EU into a single unit or category, linguistically and in practice. The new legal category of "European citizen" or the EU logos found on car license plates does not determine that the EU will be a robust or legitimate political authority, but these typifications create the conditions of possibility for such processes to unfold.

Mapping Europe

Another set of important political technologies building the cultural infrastructure of the EU are those that redraw boundaries, map Europeans, and reorient political authority geographically. Using symbols and practice to locate political entities in the minds of citizens is a strategy that has historically been widely used to create legitimacy (Jenson 1995). Here, powerful actors have sought to redraw in space and place the lines of legitimate political community, using language, imagery, and practice alike. In an act of reinvention, the Western plains are categorized as the "American frontier" in the nineteenth century as part of the project of expansion of the US territorial rule (Limerick 1988; Turner 1994). The mapping and renaming of aboriginal territories in Canada has shaped the collective political identity of those groups (Jenson 1995). Likewise, in an effort to shore up the legitimate authority of the Archbishop of Canterbury Cathedral over the Anglican church, the cathedral is metaphorically "placed" in the imagination of its followers at the center of the geographically dispersed, worldwide Anglican Communion. On the floor in the nave of the Canterbury Cathedral, a mosaic of the Anglican Compass Rose with arrows to the four points symbolizes its geographic centrality even as the physical reality may be very different. As with categories, the work that is being done centers on our imaginations—what borders do we draw around our felt lines of political community? Where do we locate political authority spatially—is it centralized as with Paris's Isle de France, or decentralized as with the EU's placement of governance headquarters in Strasbourg, Brussels, Frankfurt, and Luxembourg? Like many other political authorities before them, EU officials have thought carefully about the ways in which the architecture of its official buildings creates a sense of place, but has chosen to embed these within the national settings in an interestingly centrifugal way, as we shall see in Chapter 4.

The process of redrawing legal borders, boundaries, and territory to reflect political rule has been important to governance and political authority throughout time. It had its apogee in the rise of the territorial nation state. But every political community has to translate its legally specified, physical presence on the ground into some sort of set of representations and practices that allow its subjects or citizens to imagine and situate themselves within it. We can think about this process as involving both a sense of space and place (Tuan 1977; Thrift 2007). Space implies the creation of boundaries and the laying out of a grid of relations vis-à-vis other political authorities, generating relative locations of governance, and sites of legitimate authority on some broader, abstracted plane. Place implies the specific environment of authority, both built and natural, for example found in things like architecture or landscapes that are grounded in particular meanings, memories, and significance for those living within.

The creation and use of maps captures some constructed essence of place and space, reimagining space and people's sense of boundaries while acting like a logo to remind people of the claimed coherence of a geographical entity. Maps also embody a "classificatory grid" (Anderson 1993). Maps of Europe, over the centuries, have been important visual representations of what Europe is, where it begins and ends, what is its center and what is its periphery (Wintle 1996). Theological and metaphysical representations of Europe in medieval times had less regard for geographic location than for spiritual location, with Jerusalem, for example, at the center of maps of Europe (with Christ hovering above), replacing the earlier Greek and the Ptolemaic versions (Wintle 1996: 70). During the Renaissance, as man came to be seen as the center of the universe, and navigation and mathematics evolved, maps as we know them today came into being. But even then, "all sorts of cultural aspirations and statements" persisted (Wintle 1996: 71).

The effort to map the EU in space and place is particularly challenging, as the EU must depict itself as distinct from but made up of persisting national territories. We will see in the chapters that follow the creative ways in which the EU tried to strike this balance, particularly with regard to the iconography of the euro notes and coins, which present a variety of different visions of where Europe begins and ends. Substantive policies that created the single market, or the euro, or the free mobility of Schengen, as we will see, also contribute to the creation of the sense of a European space, a bounded political entity. When the EU developed common border policies, complemented by extensive internal policing-security cooperation, it created a new model of non-exclusive territorial sovereignty (Christiansen 2005), one that in turn generated new symbols and practices that shaped the environment for its authority.

Narrating Europe

Once named and mapped, representations also call out for content, bringing in the third mechanism of meaning creation through symbols and practices: *narrating*. Here the work of culture is probably the easiest for most people to see without looking too closely—we are all aware of the ways in which actors, private or public, are motivated to "spin" things to create a particular perspective on what is happening at any moment in time. Political entities, particularly the modern nation state, have their own version of spin. The modern nation state arose in concert with mass print capitalism and brought with it the first systematic, centralized efforts at primary and secondary widespread education (Weber 1976; Anderson 1993; Zerubavel 1997). These new technologies allowed political actors to shape the narrative by which young Italians, Japanese, or Argentines, for example, are taught about the history of their country, and thus became a cornerstone for nationalist projects (Hein and Seldon 2000).

Narrating a political entity's past occurs not only in the formal setting of teaching history in classrooms, or in non-fiction historiography, but across a broad range of cultural materials—in painting, music, opera, novels, and even comic strips. It might even be in the choice of a school's colors, such as the blue and gray of Georgetown University's sports teams—the colors of the warring sides of the American Civil War. Narratives are everywhere, as is demonstrated in the story of reconciliation between the American North and South implied in Georgetown's choice of colors. For some scholars, these narratives are most powerful when they take the form of political myths, collective stories that are told and retold about the polity and make it comprehensible in some way, and for some purpose. Studies of the role of political myths in the EU have pointed out the ways in which history and storytelling has made commonplace the notion of the EU as a beacon for democracy, as a normative power that rejects a long history of geopolitics in favor of humanitarian goals (Della Salla 2010; Bottici and Challand 2015).

The narrating of what Europe is has been going on since at least the Middle Ages (Padgen 2002, but also see Swedberg 1994). The EU has repeatedly tried, like all political authorities, to brand its image, to load public symbols with a certain type of content, and construct a potent narrative (Della Salla 2010; Sternberg 2013). Yet, as in other areas, the EU is challenged in creating its narrative because of its continued coexistence with its member nation states. Pursuing slogans such as "united in diversity" in an effort to parse the potential contradictions of the EU's cultural infrastructure, EU elites have been crafty in their efforts, as we will see below, but also have badly overestimated the leverage that EU identities have on the average European. Strategically, the linkage to already legitimated tropes—neoliberalism, democracy—have been a key part of the EU's symbolic power efforts. At the same time, there is always the risk of diluting the message of what the EU is, by building it too closely on top of existing national tropes—and evidence abounds that many Europeans greet the EU with indifference more than anything else (Duchesne et al. 2013).

Localizing and Deracinating: The EU as Banal Authority

We have spent much of this chapter considering how political entities and actors might use various strategies of social construction to legitimate themselves, with less attention to Europe's specific experiences than to the broader historical record. The administrative practices and symbolic power leveraged to achieve legitimacy and create a "taken-for-granted" or "natural" authority over a people spans many examples throughout history, and arguably reached their apotheosis in the modern nation state.

The EU has pursued strategies that mark it as quite distinctive from prior governance forms, however. I argue that two elements of the EU's development are critical for its legitimation project: strategies of localizing, and strategies of deracination. As we will see, while they have provided an exceptionally successful foundation for decades of gradual political integration in Europe, the type of loyalties and identities they engender have serious shortcomings as a foundation for the evolution of the EU toward a more deeply integrated federal system of governance.

Navigating the Nation State: Localizing Europe

The EU's cultural infrastructure must carefully navigate the preexisting loyalties and identities of the existing nation states even as it creates a political community at the European level. The chapters that follow will demonstrate that the EU's efforts at labeling, mapping, and narrating have sought to recontextualize national symbols and practices so that they appear in a different light and take on a modified meaning. Authorities seek not to strip out the original national identities and associations but rather to reorient the EU's symbol and practices so that they are no longer necessarily viewed in opposition to a potent longstanding national identity. Standardized European symbols and practices are often localized within national cultural tropes. For example, an EU program officially anoints one European city per year as the "European Capital of Culture." In so doing, the historical richness of a city such as Antwerp is projected outward into Europe as part of a shared cultural heritage, not one tied exclusively to Belgium. The goal is to resituate member-state affinities within a broader frame of Europe, allowing for both the universal (EU) and the local (Belgian), not replacing but complementing deeply held identities. In this way, elements that are part of the daily national culture—that is, the symbols and practices that make meaning within the local political community—are reclassified from purely national, to national but somehow simultaneously embedded within "Europe."

Multiple modes of symbolic representation and practice follow this logic. The primary language adopted by the EU for its legal actions uses the term "EU directives," rather than calling the rules "laws," a conscious decision to avoid direct conflict with sovereign nation states but instead nesting the EU rules within the national rather than competing with it. While English is the overwhelmingly dominant language in practice across EU administrative offices, all of the 23 EU languages are celebrated as putatively equal in the official communications of the EU. The euro is a poster child for the careful balancing of national and European symbols. While the euro's paper currency is standardized and uses only carefully abstracted, generic European images, each participating member state issues its own euro coins with standard European imagery on one side and national symbols, such as King Juan Carlos or the Irish harp, on the other. The national governments all use a standard EU passport design, although the passports themselves are not actually issued by the EU. They use a common color (burgundy), with the EU name appearing in the national language (*Europese Unie*) at the top of the passport, but also with the national symbol and name, such as the Dutch royal coat of arms and *Koninkrijk Der Nederlanden*. So, we have both a deft co-optation and standardization of a core national symbol, the passport, while leaving control over passport issuance to the national authorities and setting the EU symbols side by side with the national ones.

A second way that the EU has localized while categorizing its states together within the EU frame is by explicitly promoting "universal," purportedly ahistorical, values that are widely shared among liberal democracies in the modern age. Making the EU centrally concerned with issues such as human rights, democracy, and economic efficiency, in this view, therefore does not demarcate the EU as distinct or grounded in any particular national political culture (Soysal 2002). Liberalism, with its emphasis on individual rights and its deep roots in Western Enlightenment thinking, is instead refashioned as universalism in this strategy. The motto of the EU, "united in diversity," reflects this approach as it (paradoxically) stresses both commonality and a unified, singular identity as well as diversity and pluralism. Some scholars have therefore argued that the EU should be understood not as a form of national identity, but in terms of civic identity, in a departure from more traditional forms of ethnic or cultural identity (Sassatelli 2002). The result is what some have termed a post-nationalist EU. However, it is evident that the EU also appropriates quite traditional symbols and political technologies (passports, citizenship, paper money), and familiar and conventional expressions of state or national authority (Manners 2010). The question is whether ideas such as "united in diversity" can be made intrinsically meaningful despite their banality, or whether it is enough for the EU to function as an empty frame within which many multiple cultures flourish without eroding the whole.

These brief observations get to the point that Europe's cultural construction does not have the EU replacing preexisting political authorities as occurred with the historical rise of the nation state. Tellingly, when the EU appropriates national symbols more directly, as with the failed effort at a European Constitution in 2005, it runs into trouble, as will be discussed in Chapter 8. EU policymakers must instead find other ways to fit within the existing cultural context of the modern nation state, appropriating and reinventing national symbols, juxtaposing rather than confronting them. The EU and traditional national symbols coexist, but policymakers have attempted to frame them so as not to be in direct competition with each other, their effect additive and positive sum, not zero sum. This creates a European space that does not depend on a unified, collective emotion or "predisposed identity" nor one neatly bounded cultural community but rather an "assemblage of principles and their enactment," such as democracy, progress, human rights, and gender equality (Soysal 2002: 281). The nation coexists with the EU in this space, but it is resituated, reinterpreted, reimagined, and no longer the sole authority.

Deracinating Nationalism

The EU's cultural infrastructure is notable for a second strategy, one that marks it as quite distinct from previous emergent political entities. That is the strategy of what I call deracination. The EU has been successful, in part, in legitimating itself because of the way it has portrayed a deracinated version of governance while pursuing the political technologies of labeling, mapping, and narrating. It is no accident that the British press focuses on things like rules from Brussels on the size and shape of bananas, while sober central bankers rule over the euro, faceless lawyers in Luxembourg shape community law, and the people of Europe doze over the thought of the labyrinthine governance structure that is the EU. Indeed, blandness and integration by stealth is a longstanding EU tradition. The European Court of Justice succeeded in shifting legal power to the EU level in part because of the ability of law to serve as a "mask" for politics, reducing revolutions in sovereignty to dry legalese, impenetrable, and seemingly innocuous (Burley and Mattli 1993). This banality has its pluses and its minuses, as we shall see, but it is clearly part of how the EU has constructed itself as a political authority and social fact of remarkable tenacity. This banality has enabled the creation of a type of imagined communities of Europeans who have taken on ways of thinking and acting within a new European governance scheme that, at the very least, creates a permissive consensus for the historic consolidation of power in Brussels in the decades following the 1958 Treaty of Rome. This "banality by design" helps the EU to navigate the preexisting and robust national communities.

Unsurprisingly, therefore, there is a skeptical literature that has arisen among scholars of Europe that stresses the low self-identification as European that people evidence in interviews and polls (Díez Medrano 2003; Favell 2008; Fligstein 2008; Checkel and Katzenstein 2009). It is clear from this work that people do not have the nationalist fervor or pride in themselves as citizens of the EU that they have as, for example, Swedes or Greeks. I have argued in Chapter 2, however, that displacing national identities is not what we should expect from the EU, so perhaps this yardstick of comparison is incorrect. We need to look at the issue not as European identity versus national identity but at the potential for layering and blended identities, including the creation of a taken-for-granted Europeanness. So, instead of looking for the fervor of national identity as we traditionally think of it, we might look instead for evidence of what has been called "banal nationalism" (Billig 1995), translated into this new, non-state governance form—what I call "banal authority."

A key insight of this approach is that nationalism does not only arise in crisis and conflict, but that nations are reproduced on a daily basis, through banal and mundane ways, and it is those habits of mind and practice that underpin national identity (Billig 1995). Those activities and representations that seem the most clichéd (flags and anthems, for example) matter, for they reproduce national identity in ways that prime populations for supporting their states in more emotional or difficult times, such as war. Established nations continually "flag" or remind their populations of nationhood in a myriad of seemingly innocuous ways: "this reminding is so familiar, so continual, that it is not consciously registered as reminding. The metonymic image of banal nationalism is not a flag which is being consciously waved with fervent passion; it is the flag hanging unnoticed on the public building" (Billig 1995: 8).

This concept of banal nationalism well captures the deracinated, "under-the-radar" taken-for-granted rhetoric and practices that create Europe as a legitimate actor and reverberate back on individual identity in ways not captured in the polls (Cram 2001, 2006). For example, the uncontroversial acceptance of a public EU entity, the Eurostat Agency, commissioning Eurobarometer polls that ask people whether they "feel European," can be argued to have created a chain of representations and practices that creates and reinforces the concept of the EU as a legitimate actor and European as a legitimate category of identity. The work of seemingly mundane, technical bureaucrats and telephone polling agents does not excite the mind in the way that a national day of independence with fireworks and fervent anthem singing might, but it may have important effects in creating the foundation for EU governance, by legitimating a range of statistical and information-gathering activities. Ironically, from this perspective, Eurobarometer is constructing European identity even as it is reporting its nonexistence. So, it is not the degree of felt or activated "Europeanness"—although that is important in other contexts—that matters for this argument but rather the normalization of the EU as a legitimate governor. We are clearly not in a situation where the EU has replaced national identity but, as the following chapters will show, the EU's cultural impact is in its very particular type of "banal" imagined community. Participation in this community involves both active dynamics ("imagine this!") and passive participation (unthinking repetition and habits of practice that reproduce Europeanness). Viewed this way, we might see the puzzle as not that there is so little European identity but rather that there is so much implicit, taken-for-granted Europeanness at work.

It is both a strength and a weakness of the EU that it forges its imagined community with a particularly banal sense of nationalism—a rather blood-less, often highly technocratic, and usually quite quotidian sense of political authority—rather than impassioned, blood-racing heroism.

Conclusion: Not So Fast?

The EU is challenged by its very novelty: it is a social fact without the vocabu-lary to identify it as such. (Is it an international organization? Is it a state? Something in between?) The EU has a much more uncertain ideational exis-tence than the nation state, even as it is experienced in a multitude of every-day ways and has been established as a social fact, as discussed in Chapter 2. However, the EU certainly does not have the galvanizing motivation and constitutive experience of fighting and dying for the homeland that shaped national identity in other historical experiences. Neither does the EU extract revenues and redistribute them as the modern state has to create constella-tions of societal interests with a large stake in the success of the state, although the EU's policies do have less visible redistributive effects.

Yet I am arguing the EU is a profoundly important new political authority, one that governs over its citizens in ways intrusive and far reaching. Its cul-tural infrastructure has been built in ways somewhat stealthily, to construct the EU as localized or nested in national identities and as deracinated or banal and unthreatening. It seems a contradiction in terms, but despite its many other, and often profound shortcomings, the brilliance of the EU as a new political actor is partly in the way it has been able to establish itself as a banal, boring, technocratic entity with seemingly few claims on the passions and emotions of political life. The story of the EU's cultural infrastructure for gov-ernance is one built on the incremental accumulation of small, everyday and seemingly insignificant symbols and practices, layering one on another. EU officials, political elites, market-based actors, and societal groups alike have drawn on time-tested political technologies rooted in the human tendency to categorize the world—labeling, mapping, and narrating the lived realities of life in the EU in the twenty-first century—so as to shore up the cultural infra-structure of governance. When symbols and practices of the EU as a political community, as a body politic, solidify into collective imagination they act to create a social foundation or infrastructure for authority (Walzer 1967: 167). When the symbols and practices are accepted into the public realm and cease to be problematized or questioned overtly, they create "units" of understanding, thought, and feeling, and construct the EU as an actor. Both the internal and external face of the EU are projected and represented in this process, transmitted to multiple audiences within the EU and abroad. In some instances, as we will see in the chapters to follow, these activities have been intentional, conscious, and strategic, but they are sometimes uninten-tional side effects of policies. Regardless, they are never fully under the con-trol of any one actor. Culture can be shaped and manipulated in strategic and self-interested ways, but the structural qualities of the intersubjective, shared social understandings that create meaning in any particular cultural setting can never be simply reduced to any one actor's desires.

I have argued that these developments are constructed in part through strategies of localization that help the EU to navigate robust national iden-tities. For example, when the role of the EU in reinforcing Spain's move to democracy in the 1980s is narrated such as that being Spanish comes to mean simultaneously and inherently being European as well, the EU becomes localized and nested in national cultures. Equally important are strategies of deracination, which make the power shift to Brussels less threatening, by framing Europe in terms of seemingly unimportant things. An EU golf team in the Ryder Cup, for example, or the EU Film Series at the American Film Institute in Washington, DC, or the presence of the European Commission president as a member of the G8 international meetings all seem like tepid encroachments on national symbols and practices, but, I argue, they subtly change the backdrop of politics in ways that legitimate the EU.

In the chapters that follow, the various cultural pathways to European gov-ernance are illuminated, drawing on the framework of political technologies above. But it is also important to ask which meanings, symbols, and practices have become authoritative and which have not. Are there rituals of the EU's imagined community that are rejected or called out as mere veneer for the legitimation of the EU? Do the rejections and push-back in some way rein-force the traction of the EU's political community, or do they undermine it? We will also probe into the politics around the choice of various symbols and the development of different practices.

EU symbols and practices have diffused into everyday life, but they remain phenomena whose importance is difficult to measure. The following chapters therefore begin to establish my theoretical claims by describing the nature of these symbols and practices and the processes themselves. I situate them historically in terms of comparative political development and state-building examples so that we might leverage comparative analysis to learn about the nature of the EU and its particular path. The stories that follow show that the EU has taken on multiple state-like symbols in ways that label, map, and narrate Europe as a distinct and coherent entity, but in its own unique way. We first look at an area easily understood as having cultural implications: Chapter 4, "Buildings, Spectacles, and Songs," examines architecture, popular entertainment, and the EU's anthem. Chapter 5 looks at the realm of citizenship and mobility across national borders, which has long been at the heart of the practice of Europe. Chapter 6 examines how the single market and the euro have created ample arenas for the imagining of Europe, while at the same time raising the stakes for a collective European identity. Chapter 7 turns to efforts to construct a European foreign policy, finding that even in an area jealously guarded by the nation states, the strategies of localizing and deracinating have made some purchase on the construction of the EU as a coherent entity. In this way, my empirical analysis of the pattern of symbols and practices of European politics starts with the areas understood as furthest away from the core powers of the nation state to the areas most directly challenging to national sovereignty, allowing us to see the ways in which the EU legitimates and naturalizes itself across many different governance settings. The contradictions inherent in the strategy of constructing Europe's legitimacy will be explored in Chapter 8, which situates my findings and arguments in terms of the future of Europe.

4

Buildings, Spectacles, and Songs

In September 2012, with the late afternoon golden sunshine slanting over the greens at the Medinah Country Club in Illinois, "Europe staged golf's greatest-ever comeback to win the Ryder Cup" as the UK's *Sun* newspaper trumpeted. When all had given up on Europe's chances against a dominant American golf team, the Europeans surged back and won, delighting those spectators clutching blue European Union (EU) flags. Afterwards, the power-house team of golfers, led by José María Olazába with brilliant performances by Rory McIlroy and others, held the Ryder Cup high above their heads, their necks wrapped in blue scarves sporting the yellow stars of the EU.

The "Miracle of Medinah" will live long in European sports lore. But it should be of interest to us for something else: it calls attention to the ways in which "Europe" is constructed and given meaning. Labeling a disparate group of golfers from the Basque country of Spain, Dusseldorf in Germany, and Northern Ireland, among other places, under the category "Europe" makes a concrete claim about the coherence and felt reality of the EU. The waving of EU flags by the players' wives as they paraded into the country club on day one, and the jaunty matching suits that the players wore, all symbolically proclaimed their standardized similarity as European nationals. The "European" sports fans glued to their screens experienced a moment in which the bonds of fandom coexisted with, even if they could not mend, the fraying of ties brought about by the EU's political and economic troubles. The sports section headlines proclaiming "We are all European now" above photos full of EU symbols drove Nigel Farage, the euroskeptic British UK Independence Party (UKIP) Member of the European Parliament, to complain: "Whenever I watch the television all I see is that wretched EU flag. What on earth has this [golf tournament] got to do with the European Union?" The political possibilities of the tournament did not go unnoticed by Farage, who went on to say "I don't want this being hijacked by an increasingly unpopular EU" (Channel 4 News, October 1, 2010).

The European Commission has spent a lot of time and money on public spectacles and popular entertainment. From noisy and colorful street festivals stretching from the Brandenburg Gate to the Grosser Stern monument in Berlin in celebration of the fiftieth anniversary of the Treaty of Rome, to the annual May 9 Europe Day events across the EU, to the worldwide "Open Days" program that makes EU buildings and embassies accessible to the public, the EU has sought to embody "Europe" in a variety of cultural products and events. This chapter explores some of these activities, both official and those not directly funded or run by the EU but, I argue, engaging similar dynamics. Although some might dismiss these activities as "merely symbolic," the sheer amount of money and effort should make us interested in why they are promoted by EU officials and national politicians. The EU's overarching Cultural Programme for the period 2007–13 spent approximately €50 million annually, with €400 million budgeted in total. The revamped 2014–20 plan rearranges cultural and media programs and ratchets up the budget to €1.801 billion (approximately €300 million annually), an increase of about 600 percent (European Union 2006). Just as with early projects of nationalism in the nineteenth century, these seemingly irrelevant cultural activities reframe the social meaning of the EU and enable its governance. They are stealthy contributors to the dynamics of cultural reorientation and change that are building a new, if fraught, sense of Europe for its citizens. Buildings, spectacles, and songs can do important work in creating the category of Europe, locating it in peoples' hearts and minds, and narrating what Europe means.

These activities did not arise spontaneously from the grassroot desires of individuals or citizen groups, but neither are they completely under the EU's bureaucratic control. Some were the result of a strikingly well coordinated, meticulously planned—if not always successfully carried out—set of policies that were first formally articulated in a little-known 1985 report on how best to strengthen European identity. In many ways, these policies are identical to the catalog of nation-building activities used by states over the last century to consolidate their legitimacy. Yet their particular execution and framing demonstrates the uneasy relationship that the EU has with traditional national political identities in Europe. These cultural programs reveal the ways that the EU is trying to reorder political authority by creating an entirely new European level of legitimate governance, while stepping gingerly over the existing national powers and sentiments.

In these cultural activities, the EU has had a partner in private business interested in selling creative products and experiences. The consolidation of EU media and entertainment markets has created opportunities for a broad reach across millions of potential consumers. European media markets dwarf the EU's official spending on cultural programming, with the major media providers raking in over €15 billion annually (Institute of Media and Communications Policy 2013). The stories I tell in this chapter demonstrate the complex interaction among many different actors—European bureaucrats, media companies, corporations, citizen groups, and national politicians—in the intended and unintended naturalization of the concept of Europe in everyday life in the EU.

It is important to remember, however, that cultural activities are a double-edged sword for any actor promoting them. Simply put, the meaning of specific cultural products and experiences is never under the control of any individual, bureaucracy, or firm. For example, in this chapter we consider the ways in which the built environment has been used to project a particular sense of Europe's political authority, but we must remember that a particular building does not carry inviolate symbolic content. Rather, all symbolic representations need to be interpreted by the viewer, as symbols are not statically inscripted with meaning in their physical representations, but rather must be dynamically interpreted. The new glass and steel tower of the European Central Bank (ECB) may be built to appear majestic and fiercely independent, but in a context of economic hardship and distress it instead may be read by citizens as imperial and unfeeling. There is "work and speculative imagination" that must go on in cultural politics, and we cannot simply read these symbols like "words off a page" (Hubbard 1987: 128). Likewise, the practices engendered by these cultural policies can be subject to multiple interpretations, even by those engaged in them. Although the subjectivity and contingency of these meaning constructions is no doubt a key concern for the EU officials responsible for cultural policies, ironically, it is that dynamic work of imagining Europe that creates the cultural infrastructure for governance among its citizens.

The chapter begins by explaining in more detail why cultural programs and activities—defined as being centered on creative, artistic, leisure, or entertainment experiences—are political. I then turn to an overview of official EU cultural programming. Selective examples of the work done by cultural policies follow, so as to demonstrate how these activities constitute Europe. Architecture and built spaces can be a powerful tool for and expression of political authority. The EU's particular approach to both the aesthetics and the use of geographic space throughout the EU signals how the imaginary Europe being built is one that seeks to cohabit with existing national sentiments. The second cultural arena considered is spectacles, most centrally the Eurovision Song Contest. Private interests mount cultural events, including sporting programs, which categorize participants in a European frame, mapping and narrating the ties that bind, even as they allow for difference. Finally, the last section focuses on the EU's adoption of and efforts at reinventing the symbols of nationhood, particularly in the EU's anthem. Here is where the hard limits of the cultural programming strategies are felt, as the outcry over the official adoption (as opposed to the de facto usage) of the flag, anthem, motto, and national holiday as symbols of the EU demonstrates the limits of the strategies of deracinating and localizing Europe.

Why Are Cultural Activities Political?

Cultural policies and the creative expressions, products, and experiences they generate are perhaps the most visible and apparent symbols of identity, whether existing or aspirational, in Europe. Whereas in the chapters that follow I will likely have to convince the reader of the role of symbols and practices in areas such as the single market or military strategy, policies geared toward the arts and entertainment are self-evidently "cultural" in the sense of engaging the processes of meaning making described in Chapters 2 and 3. But are such arts and leisure policies worthy of serious political analysis? Despite the hundreds of thousands of euros spent by the EU in this area, and the billions of private transactions that constitute cultural product markets in Europe, political scientists studying the EU have largely ignored the realm of explicit cultural policy. Scholars often bracket cultural policies and creative products because they believe that such things are unimportant to politics, occurring in a separate sphere from the contestation over votes, budgets, or traditional power politics.

Shutting the door on cultural activities, policies, and products is a missed opportunity for understanding how political authority and power are constructed, and how shifts and changes in the cultural realm reverberate back on the more conventional elements of politics we usually study. Think of the digital revolution. While the business and consumer applications of the Internet were assumed initially to be the biggest drivers of the online world, it is social media such as Facebook or Snapchat that have arguably been the key elements pushing forward both innovation and usage. Rather than studying culture as something in opposition to the broader dynamics of power and material interest, therefore, we should open our eyes to the ways in which the study of culture interacts with and infuses power and interests (Ikenberry and Kupchan 1990; Nye 2004). Instead of opposing a rationalistic versus a cultural sphere, we should seek to understand how they are interpenetrated. Culture understood as the traditional arenas of the arts, religion, or education has a critical role to play in the establishment and evolution of political orders. Even practices and symbols in the cultural sphere that seem widely disconnected from the pull and haul of EU politics are consequential, in that they both reflect political battles and also form a backdrop for the more vivid debates unfolding over things such as whether the EU should have its own

Eurobond, or in the formulation of a common EU position on sanctions against Russia.

These cultural activities can have an external face outside the EU as well. An annual EU film series at the non-profit American Film Institute in Washington, DC may seem trivial on its own. But when it is but one of a constant series of cultural events offered to Americans and framed by the label EU, it can gradually over time introduce a potentially new baseline for thinking about the EU countries as not only a collection of sovereign states but also an intentionally grouped entity with a common historical and artistic heritage. When the EU member-state embassies have their annual joint European Open House day in Washington, DC and visitors from the US and many other countries troop through their 28 national buildings, each of which flies the EU flag next to its own, the practice and the symbols habituate participants to an EU that is simultaneously strongly united yet also made of distinct sovereign states.

Indeed, for the EU, the seeming innocuousness of such cultural activities is arguably an advantage. Nonetheless, sometimes the creative arts, education, or sporting events can become very hotly contested, when policies around the arts become publicly and explicitly framed as about collective but contested identities. The officially commissioned sculpture *Entropa* by David Černý displayed during the Czech presidency of the European Council in 2009 created an uproar because it depicted crass, negative stereotypes of each EU member state. That controversy highlighted the power of art to arouse impassioned debate, and to offend. Likewise, the objections of Nigel Farage to the branding of the Ryder Cup team with EU symbols is an indication that some political actors do see the potential for these seemingly innocuous activities to subtly reinforce European integration on the sly.

The cultural activities examined in this chapter narrate a story of a Europe that somehow is simultaneously localized, nationalized, and European, all at the same time. The various cultural programs, be they official EU or market-generated, portray a universal Europeanness that is inclusive, open-ended, and one that celebrates the distinct national heritages while claiming them as all part of the broader set of European culture. Whether it is celebrating Prague as a "European capital," choreographing elaborate parties around Europe to watch the Eurovision Song Contest, or stripping the German lyrics out of "Ode to Joy" so that it can be the EU's anthem, the cultural arena is rife with the dynamics constructing the EU as a very specific type of political authority. While many of these efforts have proceeded without contestation and have become part of the taken-for-granted social and political landscape of Europe, some of them have floundered and, in so doing, provide opportunities for us to understand the latent struggles of Europe's integration.

Creeping up on Culture: The EU's Official Cultural Programs

The EU was initially built on the foundation of coal and steel, and centered on the single market and free movement of goods, services, capital, and labor. The original quasi-constitutional document for today's EU, the 1957 Treaty of Rome, can be read to be making an implicit argument about the role of culture in its statement that the goal of the treaty should be to "lay the foundations of an ever closer union among the peoples of Europe," as stated in its preamble. Yet culture and cultural programs are only mentioned in passing. The treaty's Article 7 refers to the goal of national nondiscrimination, which implies that the members of the EU are one community that should not be differentiated, but treated as one. A second reference allows exceptions to the principle of free movement of goods, in cases where a barrier to trade is made for "the protection of national treasures possessing artistic, historical, or archaeological value" (Article 36). The circumspect legal language meant that the EU initially had no formal direct authority for activities in the cultural realm, although there were a variety of ad hoc and ongoing activities. The European Parliament issued a series of resolutions about various cultural affairs, and established committees such as the Committee on Youth, Culture, Education, Media, and Sport, to support the development of European-level involvement in these areas.

However, by the 1970s, there was a stirring of active interest on the part of the European Commission and national leaders on European culture and identity as a way to deepen the integration project. A summit of the European leaders in Copenhagen in 1973, in the wake of the OPEC oil crisis and a sense of drift in the transatlantic relationship, marked the first explicit treatment of the question of European identity. A communiqué issued at Copenhagen begins by stating that "unity is a basic European necessity to insure the survival of the civilization which they have in common," and portrays a European identity that both preserves the "rich variety of their national cultures" while defending the principles and "attitude to life" they share (European Council 1973). Those principles include representative democracy, rule of law, and social justice, "which is the ultimate goal of economic progress," and respect for human rights. Building on the common market and moves to enhanced political cooperation, the communiqué argues for a transformation into a "European Union" before 1980, one open to the world and committed to the Atlantic alliance but playing a stronger role through its new unity and single voice.

In the next decade after Copenhagen, selected EU documents started to reference the need for social cohesion and "collective consciousness" at the European level (Pahl 1991; Shore 2006). In addition to rhetorical changes, material resources began to be directed to cultural matters and a new unit was created to oversee cultural policy in the EU. As with any good bureaucracy, the new cultural officials of the Directorate General for Culture, Youth, and Education began to generate reports to legitimate the expansion of their activities. In so doing, they began producing some pointed revisionist history about the origins of these new European-level cultural programs, framing them as an appropriate response to democratic pressure, in the form of a "widely felt need for greater coordination" on the part of citizens in member states rather than arising from national leaders' views (Shore 2006: 14).

Most remarkable in terms of the EU's comparative political development are the two reports issued in 1985 by the Ad Hoc Committee for a "People's Europe," chaired by Pietro Adonnino. This committee was charged by the heads of state and government at the European summit in Fontainebleau in 1984 with coming up with measures to "respond to the expectations of the people of Europe by adopting measures to strengthen and promote its identity and its image both for its citizens and for the rest of the world" (Council of European Communities 1984). Why so remarkable? Because reading the laundry list of activities that the reports put forward is like reading a clairvoyant's predictions for the future. It also mirrors very precisely the nation-building activities that most modern states have historically followed—but frames them as pushed by grass roots demands rather than constructed from above.

The Adonnino Committee, chosen by the member states and made up of well-regarded senior European officials as well as marketing and public relations experts, spent one report almost exclusively on the importance of strategies to increase mobility within the EU through the removal of the physical and psychological borders between EU states. It also encompassed a list of the various cultural policies and programs directly modeled on the member states' national activities, but moved to the EU level: a European lottery, a European Academy of Science, European sports teams, a new European emphasis in school textbooks, and a pan-European audio-visual area with European television channels and broader Europeanizing of commercial cultural sectors. It further called for the establishment of a series of European cultural programs, such as a European Youth Orchestra, and awarding an annual "European City of Culture." The report suggested inaugurating an annual public holiday named "Europe Day" on May 9, the anniversary of the Schuman Declaration (1950) that founded the European Coal and Steel Community (ECSC). It further proposed spending EU funds to create a series of Monnet Chairs in major universities, named after Jean Monnet, a Frenchman touted as one of the "founding fathers" of the EU, in addition to other material support for the study of the EU as a scholarly object of inquiry. The reports also proposed the adoption of official EU symbols, namely an EU logo and flag, a European anthem, a European passport, and European driving licenses and vehicle license plates.

What is striking reading through the reports today is how many of the specific proposals for strengthening and promoting European identity have become reality, accepted as part of the EU's basic activities, even though they could have been viewed as a radical infringement on the traditional activities of the nation state. That such a comprehensive "to do" list was drawn up in the 1980s, and has gradually come to fruition, demonstrates the remarkable agility of EU officials to navigate national loyalties and project a complementary, not competing, vision of Europe. The adoption of many of the Adoninno Committee's goals was also assisted by support in the 1970s and 1980s from various financially motivated actors who viewed a European cultural market as a potential windfall for their products and economies (Tretter 2011). European heritage tourism was promoted by Italy and France, support for pan-European audio-visual products was sought by EU producers, and British publishers pushed for a robust EU market for their books. The new European Commission attention to the role of European-wide cultural products and services was thus bolstered by a network of interest groups that saw the pan-European cultural market as a new avenue for profit.

The recommendations of the Adonnino Committee moved forward with the signing of the Maastricht Treaty of 1992, which stated: "The Community shall contribute to the flowering of the cultures of the Member-States, while respecting their national and regional diversity and at the same time bringing the common cultural heritage to the fore" (European Union 1992). Today, the EU's official website steps carefully, stating that even with the Maastricht powers: "However, the EU's role is limited to promoting cooperation between the cultural operators of the different EU countries or to complementing their activities in order to contribute to the flowering of the cultures of EU countries, while respecting their national and regional diversity, with a view to highlighting the shared cultural heritage"[1] EU officials have stressed that while they have a "pragmatic" approach to culture, it is not a neutral one (Sassatelli 2002: 440). The stated overall goal is to create a "European cultural space," and variety of "pragmatic" policies such as sponsorship and subsidy campaigns, exchange programs, regulation of cultural goods and markets are in place. All also simultaneously work on the level of symbol and practice to allow people to imagine that European-wide cultural space and experience it themselves.

In the sections that follow we look at three areas that are particularly suggestive of how the intertwining of EU policies and markets for arts, leisure, and

---

[1] <http://europa.eu/legislation_summaries/culture/index_en.htm>.

entertainment products is building a cultural infrastructure for governance in the EU. The architecture of the EU and the physical location of EU buildings around the entirety of the European space reinforce particular narratives about what the EU is and give traction in constructing an imaginary Europe. A range of cultural performances, be it football matches or the Eurovision Song Contest, create common spectacles that tie together far-flung viewers or, sometimes, bring them physically together in the same space. Finally, the EU has also engaged in the building of layers of symbols and practices that directly mimic the nation state, such as a flag and an anthem. These buildings, spectacles, and songs have the potential to demonstrate the nuts and bolts of the construction of an imaginary Europe. We now turn to the representations and experiences in labeling, mapping, and narrating Europe that these cultural programs provide, with an eye to understanding their role in naturalizing European governance and legitimating its political authority.

Building Culture: Capital Cities and the EU

The built environment in which we live, work, and play is one that we generally take for granted on a day-to-day basis. But it is worth considering what buildings do (Gieryn 2002). While they keep the rain off our heads and our furniture, and keep out the cold, they also do much more. Buildings display wealth or social status (think of the royal palace at Versailles or the suburban McMansion home), affirm hierarchies (Don Draper in his corner office in the television show *Mad Men*), or in the case of public buildings, shape our perceptions of public authority and our sense of ourselves as citizens (Glazer and Lilla 1987). Buildings can be thought of as an example of material culture, and architecture as a physical exemplar of the social construction of cultural artifacts (Brain 1994). For the EU, the placement, design, and ordering of buildings—and the cities that they make up—matter, both in their reflection of the EU's politics and in the potential that these built environments have to shape the way people feel and perceive the EU. Buildings, and their placement in space, help to narrate the world, even as they seem but physical entities.

The EU's emphasis on using buildings and urban planning to shape its relationship to those it governs is nothing new. Capital cities and public buildings have long been part of political projects, be it imperial rule or nation building, both as symbolic expressions of power and authority and as methods of control through the built environment (Gordon 2006). Think of Garibaldi's pristine white statuary in Rome and the nineteenth-century monuments, public buildings, and boulevards that were part of his post-unification efforts to remake Rome for modern times (Kirk 2005). Most capital cities in the West reference Rome and Athens in their neoclassical architectural styles, seeking to reinforce the ideals of republican democracy through aesthetic choices, and to shore up legitimacy for their rule by doing so (Bednar 2006).

The EU is therefore no exception in using architecture for political purposes to symbolize and legitimate a capital city as the physical core of a bounded political territory. However, the manner in which the EU has gone about its physical representations and presence is quite different from the Western tradition of capital cities. The EU has shied away from brazen attempts to compete with the monumental and myth-making architecture of national capital cites. The result has been very few iconic EU buildings and no single capital for Europe. Brussels, while the EU's bureaucratic center, is made up of a hodgepodge of administrative buildings, only a few of which are ambitiously designed. European officials have staged elaborate architecture competitions for the design of a few exceptional buildings for which the design process has been touted as an open, transparent, and inclusive public process, rather than an exercise in top-down power. Rather than concentrate all key EU administration in Brussels, the EU has geographically dispersed the physical presence of its governance, with multiple locations throughout Europe hosting EU agencies.

A European Parliament with two rotating locations and a third city for its secretariat? A central bank located a several-hour train ride from the economic and financial policymaking offices of the EU? Is there a method to this madness? I argue that there is, and it is one that demonstrates the unique position of the EU as an emergent political form that must navigate the existing member states and their citizens while at the same time building its own political identity and community.

Brussels: A Contested "Capital" City

Decisions made about public architecture provide a window into the underlying social, economic, and political dynamics in any particular setting. For example, dramatic public protests erupted in late spring 2013 over the plans of Recep Tayyip Erdoğan, Turkey's prime minister, to raze and redesign Istanbul's civic gathering point, Taksim Square. Heartfelt debates over what to do with the former World Trade Center site in New York City demonstrates that public spaces and buildings can become highly charged symbols, and the choices made about them can be viewed as important and consequential for how particular events, polities, or people are remembered. The creation of Brussels as a capital city has been an ambiguous project, contested along the way by the Bruxellois and often clumsily navigated by EU officials. The rather tortured process of creating a centralized location for the EU, and the particular forms of physical representation this has taken, can be read as a reflection of the overall character of governance of the EU.

A long line of scholarship on Rome, Paris, Berlin, and other cities demonstrates that political elites have historically used national capital cities as mythologized and heroic spaces to help legitimate and naturalize the concentration of power at the center of a polity (Vale 1992; Ladd 1997; Lasanky 2005). Napoléon Bonaparte III transformed the Paris landscape to both shape and reflect French nationalism. Baron Georges-Eugène Haussmann's nineteenth-century reorganization of the city plan for Paris was not only an aesthetic exercise, but also part of a larger set of consolidation activities on the part of Napoléon to physically enact authority (Harvey 2003). Bismarck and Hitler, in their separate ways, both used Berlin as a platform for the physical expression of the centralization of German power (Van Der Wusten 2000). In twentieth-century Italy, Benito Mussolini used modernist versions of classical architecture as part of a comprehensive propaganda strategy aimed at reinforcing his fascist rule, borrowing legitimacy from the ancients (Bottoni 1938; Braun 1989; Vale 1992). Pierre L'Enfant was commissioned by George Washington in 1791 to draw up a set of ambitious plans for the upstart American capital of Washington, DC, fashioning it into a classically republican, Greco-Roman city of monuments and wide boulevards.

Brussels itself was not immune to these dynamics. King Leopold II transformed Brussels in the late nineteenth century into a modern city as part of the consolidation of the relatively new Belgian state, with widened roads, new public squares, triumphal arches, and more attractive neighborhoods for the upper-class bourgeois who supported his power (Hein 2004: 135–6). Across the European capitals of Paris, Rome, and Stockholm:

> A whole series of institutions became part of the standard apparatus of a capital city in the second half of the 19th century, e.g. a museum of national heritage, national library, opera and theatre, university, zoo and botanical garden, streets, squares and plazas designed for civic entertainment and the display of self, concentration of the mass circulation and national quality press, opulent railway stations to mark the central position of the city and to provide a festive entry. In cities where there was an opportunity to do this, or where power relations allowed large scale planning, some or all of these institutions were put together in a *Gesamtkunstwerk* [a comprehensive work of art]. (Van Der Wusten 2004: 150, translation added)

Anyone who has been to Brussels knows that there are three pokey little train stations, confusing to visitors although presumably good against foreign invaders. Although one is called Bruxelles Centrale it hardly qualifies as a monumental station along the lines of Union Station in Washington, DC but rather is similar to the two other stations in the city, Midi and Nord.

When we think about the EU as a governance organization, however, this lack of ceremony over a central entry for Brussels fits surprisingly well with its overall cultural strategy of deracination, downplaying the shifts in political power that have occurred with the evolution of the EU. The buildings, the siting of those buildings, and the process of locating the physical governance of the EU all work to symbolically minimize the importance of the European project, and thus limit the legitimacy demands placed on the new political authority. Whereas historical examples of national capitals seem designed to shore up the process of nation building through explicitly heroic architecture and planning, the EU's efforts go the opposite way—minimizing the shifts in the concentration of power toward the European level.

Looking back on how decisions were made by the six original members of the EU's precursor organizations makes it clear that no comprehensive plan for a formal EU capital initially existed. Rather, a series of drawn-out bargains involving the locating of functions in Luxembourg, Strasbourg, and potentially Saarbrücken, intransigence on the part of various regional and national officials, and an emphasis on de facto developments rather than long-range planning all shaped the ways in which Brussels emerged as the EU's informal capital (Hein 2006a). In taking these series of non-decisions, officials backed away from the traditional trappings of national capitals. But their initial urban design non-statement conveys something important about the nature of the EU, just as the more recent efforts to use architecture to make a more visible statement about the role of the EU in citizen's lives tells us about a trend of increasing encroachment of the EU into areas usually associated with nation states (Aureli et al. 2007).

The official EU buildings were originally built with the notion that they were likely to be only temporary office housing for their occupants. The architecture and urban planning in Brussels in what is today known as the *Quartier Europeén* (European Quarter) was therefore undertaken with a view not toward symbolic weight but rather with flexibility as to future use and with potential private employers in mind (Hein 2006a). Berlaymont, the hulking glass building that to this day houses the European Commission bureaucracy, was financed by the Belgians, and then rented to the EU until such a time as the EU might make a decisive move to create a truly European capital—assumed to be probably somewhere other than Brussels (Hein 2006b: 142–4). The European Quarter's construction was undertaken with little local input and often involved the razing of homes and historically significant structures.

Complicating matters, aside from the EU presence, postwar Brussels encompasses its own multilevel and splintered national sovereignty in the Belgian state's three distinct linguistic and geographic political communities—Brussels, Wallonia, and Flanders. All three political communities have their own separate offices and representation in Brussels. In addition, the transatlantic alliance of NATO is also headquartered in the Brussels area. For much of the postwar period, Brussels was overseen by a patchwork of different city planning authorities, making for a decentralized and fractious planning process over these different political entities.

A series of new, more ambitious EU buildings were proposed in the 1970s. But plans became embroiled in fights throughout the next decade as a newly invigorated Brussels grassroots urban activist movement protested plans to raze existing neighborhoods to make way for more EU architecture (Romanczyk 2012). The older EU buildings were viewed as out of scale, and sitting uneasily in their neighborhoods, something rather typical of the overall poor urban design process—as anyone who has walked the grey, monolithic blocks of Brussels knows. The exertion of power implied in the razing of existing neighborhoods and their replacement with centrally planned buildings had created a backlash against the business-as-usual siting of EU governance.

Gradually, the process by which designs were chosen and urban planning carried out began to change in the 1990s, as both the formation of a new governing body, the Brussels-Capital Region, streamlined and focused urban planning, while on the EU side, a growing confidence and awareness was stirring of the potential for buildings to provide a symbolic face for the political authority of the EU (Papadopoulos 1996). The result was a new emphasis on democratic input, with open EU design competitions becoming the norm for any new project. Whereas in the past, huge public protests had blocked various building projects, efforts at upgrading the public relations aspect of EU building lessened contestation. A series of deals, involving the agreement to build a new European Council building to house the executive functions of the EU in Brussels in return for the European Parliament to be sited there too (as well as Strasbourg), moved forward the Brussels EU complex. Today, those buildings include the Commission, the European Council (made up of heads of EU member states and governments, the president of the commission, and the president of the council), the Council of the EU (made up of the national ministers of various functional areas such as finance or agriculture), as well as the de facto dominant seat of the European Parliament.

Overall, however, as with other aspects of the EU's cultural policies, there has been a reluctance to directly copy the potent national imagery of capital architecture or flaunt the notion of Brussels as the EU's capital. The result has been relatively little in the way of iconic buildings that explicitly try to reinforce or concretize the EU's political community. As the buildings stand, and are used by thousands on a daily basis, they do represent the EU in practice even if they do so by default rather than by design. What is represented, according to one scholar, are faceless bureaucracies in unfriendly spaces that the EU employees themselves do not like (Hein 2006b: 142–5). Ironically, the widely reviled Berlaymont has itself become a symbol of Brussels as a

European capital since it was built in 1968 (Shore 2000: 160). Indeed: "it was evidently no small matter to tear down a major supranational symbol. Therefore, today the bulk of EC affairs are conducted out of the Berlaymont and surrounding buildings" (Hewett 2009: 20). Despite asbestos issues and a physical presence closer to a fortress than the warm and fuzzy "united in diversity" official motto of the EU, Berlaymont has endured.

It is only with the more recent EU buildings that a distinctive emphasis has been placed on the urban planning process, and the buildings themselves have been designed with an eye toward literal as well as symbolic transparency (Delanty and Jones 2002). The *Espace Léopold*, the complex of European Parliament buildings centered on the hemicycle that houses the debating chamber of this legislative body, was constructed beginning in the late 1980s with attention to the potential symbolic power of multiple windows and openings. The shift toward more conscious use of the architecture of the EU as an expression of collective identity is evident in some of the other subsequent EU buildings, as larger and more imposing and monumental plans have been drawn up for structures such as the Strasbourg hemicycle and the ECB, and the renovation of the European Court of Justice, as will be discussed below. These large-scale, more visible and prominent projects also have been designed to put a salve on the social exclusion and upheaval that came in the early years of Brussels's development, while simultaneously situating the EU's efforts within acceptable boundaries of the member-state identities. The tensions implicit in the uneasy creation of the new imagined community of Europe have played out in the developments around Brussels as a contested capital of the EU.

Meet the Neighbors: The EU in your 'Hood

Despite the fact that the label "Brussels" is often used in common parlance to signify the EU itself, many important EU agencies are actually far flung around the geographic space of the EU. In contrast to the traditional placement of governance activities in a capital city, the message sent is one of inclusiveness, transparency, and integration with local political communities, rather than a geographic concentration of power (Kelemen 2005). The major EU institutions are located in the core founding states of the EU, in Brussels, Belgium (the European Commission), Luxembourg (the European Court of Justice), Frankfurt, Germany (the ECB), and Strasbourg, France (the European Parliament, splitting time there with Brussels and with secretariat offices in Luxembourg). Worth noting is the acrobatics and expense involved in having the parliament in two separate towns, over 400 kilometers and a five-hour drive from each other. The caravan of movers needed—and the duplication of objects, papers, and offices—all have cost an outrageous amount of money, estimated at €200 million per year (Strasbourg Seat Study Group, n.d.). Of course, this duplication serves a straightforward political purpose by spreading around EU money and making the local populations happy. But the dual address of the parliament and the dispersal of the other major institutions also does something else, both symbolically and in terms of practice. The European Parliament's dual headquarters presents a striking example of "localizing" the EU in national settings, moving outside of the Brussels bubble and physically into the member states.

This practice of localizing Europe is very different from the historical strategy of centralization typically found in national capitals. It is even more felt in the more recent case of the regulatory and administrative EU agencies, which centrifuge out the physical presence of governance across the territory of the EU (Kelemen 2005). Over 40 different agencies work on scientific, technical, regulatory issues, and operations requiring specialized expertise, and these are located throughout every corner of the EU's geographic area. Employees of the European Food Safety Authority agency live in Italian communities outside Parma (appropriately the home of the celebrated Parma ham and parmesan cheese). In this way, they might become normalized as part of the local community rather than the EU being something existing only far off in a rainy Northern European city. This holds true as well for the fishery experts in Vigo, Spain at the Community Fisheries Control Agency, or the customs and border control officers in Warsaw, Poland at the European Agency for the Management of Operational Cooperation at the External Borders (FRONTEX), or scientists working at the European Environmental Agency (EEA) in Copenhagen, Denmark. New agencies, such as the European Institute for Gender Equality in Vilnius, Lithuania, have notably been placed in the more recent enlargement member states, where they might knit the political authority of the EU into the very fabric of these local communities.

The dynamic of "localizing Europe" could not be more literally executed: instead of a far-off capital city generating all rules and regulations, the agencies become part of the neighborhood, employing local workers while also bringing Eurocrats into the schools, dinner parties, and football leagues of the city where they are located. Placing EU offices physically close to multiple citizens in different settings allows for the projection of power into the many parts of the EU. At the same time, it tames and domesticates that power by making it a neighbor. The EU's regulatory agencies, if mapped, demonstrate a remarkable spatial dexterity spanning across the EU member states in a systematic way. The physical representation and practice of EU governance thus departs sharply from the unitary national state, instead projecting itself as a polycentric, networked political entity. By making the EU literally part of French, German, Italian, and Czech neighborhoods, it becomes more likely that Europe will be seen as nested within, rather than competing with, the national political communities.

Long before the more recent placement of administrative agencies in Parma and elsewhere, the decisions around the location of initial core institutions of the EU, as well as their architecture, engaged similar issues. The earliest expression of this phenomena was the siting of the original EU institutions in Brussels, Strasbourg, and Luxembourg, smack dab on the historically contested border between France and Germany. A "Committee of Experts" commissioned to look into where to put the first major institutions called for them to be located in this area as a way to bridge Latin and Germanic cultures (Demey 2007). Moreover, as Kelemen notes, putting the buildings there can be read as "symbolizing not only reconciliation between the two powers, but also symbolically checking the (still huge) powers of both countries' capitals to ever declare war on their powerful neighbor again" (Kelemen 2007: 60). Rather than putting headquarters in Paris, much less Rome or Frankfurt, the EU could signal a new beginning far from those regimes that were at the heart of the violence and failed polities of World War II.

Strasbourg had the attraction, as well as its location in Alsace-Lorraine, of having a building large enough to immediately host the new European Parliament (EP) at its start in 1958. A large building with a hemispherical auditorium was already hosting meetings for the Council of Europe (an independent human-rights-oriented international organization with a broader membership than the EU). Starting in the 1980s and gaining steam in the 1990s as the EP gained new legislative and oversight powers, some of its members demanded a move to Brussels, where the other major political institutions, the European Commission and European Council, were located. After a series of tussles with France over the siting of the EP, and the unofficial EP use of an international conference facility in Brussels as a way to force the issue, a deal was struck to allow for the EP to do its business in both Strasbourg and Brussels (Hein 2006a). The siting of the EP, along with the other EU institutions, was finally codified in a European Council agreement in 1992, subsequently annexed to the Treaty of Amsterdam in 1997.[2]

---

[2] The Treaty of Amsterdam's protocol reads:

(a) The European Parliament shall have its seat in Strasbourg where the 12 periods of monthly plenary sessions, including the budget session, shall be held. The periods of additional plenary sessions shall be held in Brussels. The committees of the European Parliament shall meet in Brussels. The General Secretariat of the European Parliament and its departments shall remain in Luxembourg.

(b) The Council shall have its seat in Brussels. During the months of April, June and October, the Council shall hold its meetings in Luxembourg.

(c) The Commission shall have its seat in Brussels. The departments listed in Articles 7, 8 and 9 of the Decision of 8 April 1965 shall be established in Luxembourg.

(d) The Court of Justice and the Court of First Instance shall have their seats in Luxembourg.

(e) The Court of Auditors shall have its seat in Luxembourg.

Another major institution, the European Court of Justice (ECJ), has been permanently and exclusively located outside Brussels. Situated from its founding in 1952 in Luxembourg, it also straddles the Franco-German region. As Brussels emerged as the de facto capital city, the ECJ's distance from the rough and tumble of day-to-day EU politics signals to European citizens its presence as an independent, apolitical arbitrator, putatively above intergovernmental squabbles and power grabs. The legitimacy of the ECJ in interpreting EU Treaty law necessitates the independence of its judges, appointed by national leaders but protected from subsequent national influence. The relative physical isolation of the court underlines this principle, as does its location on the Kirchberg plateau, separated by a ravine from Luxembourg City, along with several other EU buildings and, more recently, a museum of modern art designed by I. M. Pei, and a new concert hall. The location of the ECJ elevates it, literally and figuratively, above the fray of EU politics.

The Architecture of Legitimacy?

Beyond the polycentric nature of the EU institutional geography, the architecture of the EU is also suggestive of a particular type of political legitimation. While initially very different from the monumental architecture of historical state-building projects, EU architecture of late is making bolder claims about the meanings embodied in EU buildings. While the early architecture of EU buildings, such as the much maligned Berlaymont in Brussels, reinforced the notion of a very banal type of European authority, starting in the 2000s there has been a distinctive trend toward a more aggressive use of symbolic imagery and space in support of European governance. Recent EU buildings appear to embody a more positive and proactive set of meanings around EU political authority. This increased ambition is very much on display in the renovation of the Luxembourg-based ECJ, undertaken between 2004 and 2007. The renovation, by Parisian architect Dominique Perrault, dramatically changed the design of the building while also enlarging it. Perrault used massive metal webbing in transparent gold materials to both let in and reflect light—sunshine during the day and an artificially produced glow at night—and centered the building on the main courtroom with gathering spaces around its edges. The architectural critic of the UK's *Guardian* wrote that between the ECJ's "pencil-thin gold towers lies a kind of shimmering palace. This is the grand new public plaza, between the towers and the

(f)   The Economic and Social Committee shall have its seat in Brussels.
(g)   The Committee of the Regions shall have its seat in Brussels.
(h)   The European Investment Bank shall have its seat in Luxembourg.
(i)   The European Monetary Institute and the ECB shall have their seat in Frankfurt.
(j)   The European Police Office (Europol) shall have its seat in The Hague.

main building, and its interiors are some of the most extraordinary yet created for the EU." He goes on to say: "With the EU Court of Justice, [Perrault] has shown us how a rational, highly organised and seemingly matter-of-fact building can be dazzling, even romantic. The law has never looked quite so colourful" (Glancey 2008). This reception is a far cry from the early EU buildings, whose anonymity would more likely put reviewers to sleep than stir any critical or positive reception.

The new emphasis on using architecture proactively is also found in another key EU policy institution, the ECB, located in Frankfurt, Germany. Unlike the European Commission, the European Council, or the ECJ, the ECB is a relatively young organization, officially coming into being on June 1, 1998 as per the Maastricht Treaty. The introduction of the single currency and the administrative apparatus supporting the euro was rich in opportunities for shaping symbols and practices to shore up EU political authority, as will be discussed in Chapter 6. But the siting and architecture of the ECB is also an important part of the story.

It was decided very early on to have the ECB located in Frankfurt, Germany, the longtime home of the Bundesbank. The German central bank had been glorified both in Germany and throughout Europe as a beacon of stability and sobriety (McNamara 1998; Heisenberg 1999). Coming off of decades of economic instability and currency depreciation, Eurozone members hoped that some of the Teutonic geography would rub off on the euro. Pragmatically, some ECB employees noted that locating the bank in the often gloomy and unglamorous Frankfurt would encourage more applications from Northern European economists than from the macroeconomically suspect Southern Europeans (McNamara 2001). Originally housed in a series of office towers in downtown Frankfurt, a plan for a new, purpose-built ECB building was eventually put into play. A multistage design competition, in keeping with the stated EU emphasis on transparency, democracy, and civic participation, resulted in the choice of a striking new tower complex, designed by the Viennese architecture office Coop Himmelb(l)au.

Central banks around the world have tended to their images very carefully. The website of the US Federal Reserve Bank of New York describes the bank's Italian Renaissance–influenced building as follows: "The Bank's 20th century American designers, like their 15th century Italian predecessors, sought a structural expression of strength, stability and security. These planners intended to inspire public confidence in the recently formed Federal Reserve System through the architecture." The ECB did not try to mimic such historical styles, however. Instead, the ECB's building, completed in 2014, takes some architectural risks and seems to embrace innovation while still attempting to root itself in a familiar past. The new ECB building is located on the original site of Frankfurt's Grossmarkthalle (the former wholesale market hall) and those renovated 1920s-era buildings remain as the public entrance spaces for the ECB complex. A second building links the Grossmarkthalle to the office spaces of the two polygonal high-rise towers. The towers appear either askew or dynamically in movement, depending on your perspective, and mark a dramatic departure from the staid orthodoxy of German central banking traditions. Green construction and sustainability are emphasized, along with attention to integrating the buildings into the existing urban fabric of Frankfurt. However, the ECB building's symbolism collided with the announcement, at the building's "topping off" ceremony in the fall of 2012, that the project had incurred cost overruns to the tune of 40 percent. Bloggers and news organizations in Europe had a field day with the hypocrisy implied by the ECB's proselytizing of austerity for the economically distressed states of the Eurozone while spending €1.2 billion on its new building. Both the careful orchestration of the ECB's design and the social contestation around its construction indicate a new era of consciousness for the linkages between the EU's architecture and governance. While the EU's architectural efforts hark back to the historical use of public spaces and places by the nation state and earlier forms, they also reveal the ongoing tensions in the siting of EU political authority among and between the European nation states.

A Multitude of "European" Capitals

A final way in which the EU uses the built environment to "localize" its governance through seemingly innocuous cultural activities departs from the relatively straightforward practices described above. Instead, in a deft sleight of hand, the EU has created a program that co-opts existing member-state national capitals and their inhabitants, and symbolically transforms them in a new, meta-narrative, into "European" capitals. In this overt exercise in rebranding, the EU has attempted to recontextualize existing national cities into a broader frame of "Europeanness" through a program entitled the European Capitals of Culture (ECC).

The program began in 1985, at the suggestion of well-known actress and singer and then Greek Minister of Culture Melinda Mercouri. Initially, one city was selected each year to receive the designation of the "European City of Culture," with funding to promote itself as such in advertisements, and through festivals and cultural events, but in subsequent years two or more cities have often been designated. The program is a symbolic initiative that attempts to reimagine cities such as Madrid, Antwerp, or Genoa as simultaneously a city uniquely tied to its own specific national and local culture and history, and a "European capital." The program was initially called "European Cities of Culture," but was changed to the much more symbolically rich "European Capital of Culture" terminology by 2000. The designation has had positive material effects, with one study concluding that this designation had considerable impact on tourism and economic development for those cities chosen (Palmer-Rae Associates 2004).

In addition to these material effects, the relabeling of national cities as European contributes to the construction of the social reality of Europe, while allowing for an ambiguous and fluid content. As discussed in Chapter 3, such categorization can allow for identification with Europe even while remaining ambiguous as to what that might actually mean. A careful empirical study of the process by which the ECC 2000 unfolded demonstrates how the official EU slogan of "united in diversity" is the dominant narrative in the European Capitals of Culture program (Sassatelli 2002). That year, instead of just one city, three Northern European cities (Bergen, Helsinki, and Reykjavik), three Central European cities (Brussels, Kraków, and Prague), and three Southern European cities (Avignon, Bologna, and Santiago de Compostela) were chosen. Aside from the spatially spread-out nature of the cities, little obviously unites them, but the program itself frames them as "European" and thus situated in the same category, ambiguous as it is. Local authorities took up this frame also, with the Bologna representative explaining that all were pulling together to achieve the goal of "representing Italy in Europe, and Europe in Italy" (Sassatelli 2002: 442). Indeed, a quantitative analysis of the websites of the nine programs found that "Europe" is among the most frequent keywords, used almost as much as "culture," "music," and "theater" (Sassatelli 2002: 444). While the impact of this program on the development of one standard "European culture" is deeply questionable, there is no doubt that the repetition of the labeling of a city as a "European capital," as with any ritual, shifts expectations and normalizes what might have been odd or unsettling. The label "Europe" is diffused into the everyday fabric of the cities, in a subtle and banal set of representations matched with various practices celebrating these "European capitals." When a bus in Liverpool meanders through the city with a large banner proclaiming that city to be the European Capital of Culture of 2008, it recontextualizes in the public discourse the place of that northern England city in the historical narrative of European citizenship and political authority. The symbols also present themselves as a political resource for those wishing to push back on the political authority of the EU, however. When Istanbul was designated as a 2010 European Capital of Culture in an effort to extend a cultural olive branch to Turkey (long waiting to join the EU), a grass-roots activist group converted the graphic design into one that used the logo but substituted "European Capital of Fiasco" instead. Using Facebook and Twitter, the group sought to document "the mismanagement of Istanbul's role as European Capital of Culture throughout 2010."[3]

---

[3] See <https://www.facebook.com/2010fiasco>.

Spectacles: The Europeanization of Cultural Markets

Imagine you are watching a gripping film, full of suspense over whether a rogue spy might escape the grasp of her former boss who is out to kill her before she exposes a high-level conspiracy. The heroine flees from Lisbon to Paris, and then to Prague. What you don't know is that the script for the film originally called for the heroine to go from Paris to Marseilles, but the producers secured subsidies from the EU and national governments to put multiple European locations into their storyline. As film critics have often dismissively referred to the result of these subsidies as "europudding" productions, producers have recently shifted into more sensitive and "pan-European" multilingual productions (Kirschbaum 2005). But the joint financing continues. The reason for the EU's interest in the screenplay locations? The official cultural activities of the EU are dwarfed by the size of the European markets for commercial cultural products, making them a very attractive vehicle for the efforts at generating a common European identity.

Unlike foreign affairs or monetary policy, most culture products are produced beyond the policy circles of Brussels or Frankfurt, but they are subtly shaped by EU actions. To buttress and legitimize policy inroads in the cultural realm, EU officials argued for the need to build up European commercial cultural industries, such as the huge and growing audio-visual market, particularly as the single market program proceeded apace in the late 1980s into the 1990s (Shore 2006). With the single market's deregulation across a host of audio-visual areas, a new truly European market for entertainment, sports, and news has arisen, evidenced in the success of the EU-wide 24-hour news channel, Euronews, and the sports news version, Eurosport.

The EU's impact on cultural industries is abundantly clear in an unlikely area: European football or soccer, which has been called the "archetypical example of Europeanization" by cultural anthropologists (Borneman and Fowler 1997: 508). Football is a part of life across the EU countries and the advent of televised matches created an important pan-European viewing market. There has likewise been a dramatic integration in the basic structure of the market for professional football players across Europe. One important push for this change was the ECJ's "Bosman" decision in 1995. Whereas UEFA had a rule that required a majority of the players on the field to be substantial residents of the country where their team was located, the Bosman decision removed these restrictions. The ruling cited the free movement principle for workers in the single market, as found in Article 48 of the EU treaties. This new "free agency" of players made possible the hiring of players from all over Europe and the world, severing the close ties between the nationalities of the players and the location of their club. While FC Barcelona does have many prominent Catalan players, they also have superstar Lionel Messi from Argentina. Since the 1995 change, many football clubs now have a mix of European nationalities, with some prominent players moving among several different nations, such as the English footballer David Beckham's time with Manchester United, Real Madrid, and Milan; or Frenchman Thierry Henry's playing for Arsenal and Barcelona.

European soccer is a mammoth industry, with the top 20 clubs generating revenues of over €5.4 billion per year (Jones 2014). The transition away from nationally based clubs to free agency has transformed the market and brought more revenue to some of the most popular teams that are able to bid for the star footballers. But the impacts have also arguably been felt in the sphere of "imaginary Europe," as the changed practices have erased national borders. Spanish soccer clubs are no longer made up of Spanish players competing with their countrymen for the Spanish title and then representing their club, and implicitly their country, in the European-wide Champions League. Instead, a new border has been drawn by UEFA that encompasses the entirety of the EU as the source for players, although the names, playing fields, and mascots are still rooted in the local football clubs. The result is a much more porous representation of what constitutes one's local team, forcing fans to embrace players with different names, languages, religions, and traditions. This can result in unexpected loyalties and accolades: for example, in the 1990s, Manchester United's venerated "English King of Soccer," Eric Cantona, was French (Borneman and Fowler 1997: 509). The reshaping of local club teams' rosters with players who now represent the mobility and openness of the EU is one more way in which a new mapping of what constitutes everyday life is occurring.

The integration of entertainment and media markets across Europe was linked very early on in the process of European integration to another uniquely European cultural product and leisure-time activity: the Eurovision Song Contest, considered below.

The Eurovision Song Contest

In Eugen Weber's historical survey of the practices that created a sense of French nationalism in the nineteenth century, he calls attention to the decline of the songs, festivals, and *"veillées,"* or evening get-togethers, of French village life, which were replaced by standardized, packaged entertainment from Paris (Weber 1976: 413–18). Today, Europe's packaged entertainment equivalent involves spandex, robot dances, and questionable taste in lyrics and costumes—the Eurovision Song Contest. Watched by 125 million viewers across Europe as well as Asia, Africa, and the Middle East, the Eurovision—tacky and reviled as it may be—is also a widely shared, collective experience. Its theme song is pervasive even outside the contest, as it has been played for decades in advance of various European television co-productions, and German children learn it as a matter of course when they begin piano lessons.

Eurovision's roots were exactly in the sort of project that the European Commission's cultural activities were designed to promote, although the contest has never been formally associated with the EU. Its genesis was originally in the consortium of nationally held media companies, the European Broadcast Union (EBU), based in Switzerland. But from the start, mapping what constitutes Europe has been somewhat problematic in the Eurovision Song Contest. It was started in the core countries of Western Europe, but soon expanded to all members of the EBU (since 1973 including Israel). Mediterranean countries such as Lebanon, Libya, Egypt, Algeria, Tunisia, and Morocco have been invited as members of the EBU, although only the latter has participated in the contest (because of the unwillingness of the rest to broadcast the Israeli performances). The colonial legacies of Britain and France, as much as geography, determine the definition of Europe found in Eurovision.

The EBU secretariat came up with the idea of a song contest among the former adversaries of World War II, motivated by the notion that "light entertainment," as its creators called it, might help to unify Western Europe through music and a competition among nations that did not involve tanks and bombers, but rather spangles and arpeggios. Equally attractive was the chance to promote the new technology of television through a simultaneous live broadcast throughout Europe, a complex undertaking at the time. From the original seven participating states in 1956, the contest has mushroomed into 39 countries in 2013, all members of the EBU. While centered in Europe, the EBU spreads out to North Africa and the Mid-East Mediterranean states as well as into the former Soviet space, thus going far beyond the membership of the EU. Each participating country puts forth a performer singing an original pop song, and viewers vote for their favorite (but are not allowed to vote for their own national song). While nations compete against each other, because they must capture votes outside their own borders to win, there is by definition a pan-European quality to the competition as it crowns the best "European" song.

Despite not being a part of the EU itself, "the ESC [Eurovision Song Contest] is perhaps the largest and best-organized institution promoting a cultural kind of pan-European identity" (Tobin 2007: 28). It is a fascinating arena for dissecting the various strands of national and European identity politics that get played out in the competition, demonstrating the complex cultural dynamics at work, as it both creates a new model of European citizenship while also reinforcing national conflicts and grievances. The song contest and the emotions it engenders demonstrate the simultaneous strengthening of national identity and differences within the larger framework of Europe, so that rather than displacing or competing directly with the nation states, Europe becomes a new layer or context for political community, managing diversity rather than eliminating it. Aesthetic symbolism in musical form, dance, and costumes becomes the focal point for expressing and, perhaps, adjudicating these diversities. The larger communal practice of watching the competition, broadcast simultaneously across Europe, draws together spectators in one moment carefully choreographed by the Eurovision producers. As Katrin Sieg has stated: "the Eurovision Song Contest (ESC) has become a key arena for staging a unifying Europe's capacity to accommodate an expanding range of national and cultural differences, and for imagining Europe as a harbinger of cosmopolitan values, including diversity, democracy, and human rights" (Sieg 2013: 244–5).

One of the standardizing processes at work constructing a pan-European identity in Eurovision is the use of English as the *lingua franca* of the contest: winning songs have been in English more than any other language despite the fact that only two of the participating countries (the UK and Ireland) use English as their national language. In a telling exception, France has always used French (except for using Breton in 1996). Spain's 1968 contestant sang in Catalan, a language at the time outlawed under Franco, so the entry was eventually replaced by the Spanish government. Songs often use nonsense syllables (la, la, la; diggi-loo, diggi-ley) to get around the language issues, but the default is now to use English lyrics (Raykoff 2007: 2).

But while initially designed with the putative goal of being a unifying, nonpolitical event, the Eurovision Song Contest is of course highly political, full of complex cleavages and contradictory messages. As with the Olympic Games or the World Cup, Eurovision creates an international setting for a mixture of national identities and prestige, but in this case, one within the frame of "Europe." Most obviously, countries have used the event to send political messages to each other, as with Greece's withdrawal in 1975 to protest Turkey's entrance into the contest, and the Hellenic song the following year that protested that country's invasion of Cyprus. As per tradition, the contest was held in 2012 in Baku, Azerbaijan after that country won the 2011 competition, but the human rights record of Azerbaijan, and their forced relocation of many from the capital in the name of "beautification," caused controversy and turmoil (similar to that decades earlier when the contest was held in Franco's Spain in 1969).

The political dynamics are more nuanced and potentially more potent than they might be in sporting competitions because of the opportunities for symbolic representation that the contest provides through the songs and performances. And just as the EU promotes its image of "united in diversity," the

Eurovision program has over the years crafted a specific set of convergent pop culture practices that create a particular meaning of what Europe is, albeit ever changing over the years with new members and widening geographic scope. This was evident in the symbolism of many of the national entries on the heels of the democratic revolutions of 1989, which celebrated with titles such as "Brandenburg Gate' and "No more walls." Italy won the contest that year with "All together: 1992," which heralded the soon-to-be-signed Maastricht Treaty dramatically deepening European integration (Raykoff 2007: 4). Since the 2000s, the opening segment in the finals featured video feed of crowds in squares around Europe doing different dance sequences, underlining the notion of the simultaneity of experience and the ability of Europe to come together, while expressing individuality. Eurovision producers created a series of carefully choreographed practices to emphasize and make visceral the sense of collective participation. While this is the result of private activities of the Eurovision producers, it expresses and ritualizes the narrative of localization, of nesting the standardizing experience of Europe within local meanings that, I argue, is the hallmark of Europe's cultural infrastructure today.

Even while the Eurovision Song Contest creates an opportunity for a broad vision of what it is to be European, it also creates the potential for marginalization within the competition and the melodrama of performance and judging. The contest seems to map Europe in terms of the ins and outs. One Romanian quoted in 1993 noted that: "We have always wanted to belong to Europe and the Song Contest is the only part of Europe that functions without political union. For this reason, we want to be a part of this world" (Raykoff 2007: 7). While Romania did eventually join the EU, for other states such as Ukraine there is little guarantee that they will ever see their Eurovision status matched by actual EU membership.

Ode to Joy: Reinventing the Symbols of Nationhood?

To enhance your legitimacy and political authority, why not appropriate the tried and true cultural tropes of nationhood, flags, and anthems crafted in the last few centuries, even as they often hark back to even earlier projections of political authority? This strategy is risky for the EU, as it directly confronts the question of the relationship between the EU and its member states, and the EU and nation states in the international arena. The EU has indeed taken on multiple state-like symbols and practices in ways that label, map, and narrate Europe as a distinct and coherent entity, but in every instance the EU has localized and deracinated them to reduce the sense of threat to national identities that might be implied. For example, it is now quite common for official photos of national leaders, such as French president François Hollande, to have the European flag alongside their national flag on their Christmas cards or when they make important announcements. Pervasive repetition of the juxtaposing of the EU and national flags may create an implicit acceptance of the legitimacy of the EU on par with the national political authority. But it may also serve as an ever present irritant to those who object to the tacit equivalence granted to the yellow and blue EU symbol.

The narrative that underlies the EU symbols and practices is found nowhere more clearly than in its motto: "united in diversity." While other symbols, discussed below, were often borrowed from the Council of Europe, a non-EU human rights–based international organization, the motto is original to the EU and only came into use in 2000. The winning entry in a contest originally organized by a French newspaper for secondary-school students, it was first translated into English as "unity in diversity." The contest snowballed and spread across the then EU-15 member states, involving thousands of entries from schoolchildren, and geared toward the fiftieth anniversary of the Treaty of Rome. A distinguished group, including several former heads of state, chose "unity in diversity" as the EU motto. It was immediately used in the European Parliament and at various high-profile events, eventually being written into the proposed European Constitution, where it was slightly modified into "united in diversity." United in diversity is a telling narrative for the EU, particularly in contrast to *"e pluribus unum,"* or "from many, one," the US motto. It implies a localized Europe, of many different identities, peoples, and cultures of the EU, coexisting in harmony rather than being flattened into one monolithic nation. But even as it projects a strong stance of unity, the motto also is full of tension. It helps us to see how the deracinated and universalized cultural symbols and practices of the EU sit uneasily with the traditional notions of nationalism.

A closer look at the process by which the (unofficial) European anthem was chosen, and how it is used in practice, sheds light on the particular construction of political authority in Europe. The careful navigation of national sensibilities while a narrative is created about the ways in which the EU complements and enriches the nation states is ever present in the contestation over "Ode to Joy."

A Song without Words

Music has been used to political ends presumably since the first person sang a song of praise of a leader or beat a drum in the heat of battle. Charlemagne, who ruled over Europe as the first Holy Roman Emperor in the eighth century, exemplified this. Charlemagne ordered that the plainchant, the central musical element of church services, be codified so as to create a single, universal body of religious music across Europe (Dickinson 1902; Treitler 1984).

87

This was not a simple bureaucratic decision. Instead, the hope was that this standardization would engender a new universal frame to draw worshipers together under the Holy Roman Empire (Clark 1997). In the case of the EU, the choice of Beethoven's "Ode to Joy" (An Die Freude), from his Ninth Symphony, was meant to create a frame for imagined community, just as national anthems have long been de rigueur for new nation states. But what separates the EU anthem from national songs is the careful navigation of the existing symbols and loyalties of the member states. This is evident in the decisions around the choosing of "Ode to Joy."

The original lyrics of "Ode to Joy" are taken from a poem by the German writer Friedrich Schiller. The poem celebrates an Enlightenment-era hope for peace among all mankind, envisioning a brotherhood united in a Kantian perpetual peace. It was originally adopted by the Council of Europe (the broader, non-EU organization concerned centrally with human rights) in 1971 as the unofficial "anthem of Europe." Clark (1997) provides a careful historiography of the debates between the European Commission and its member-state supporters and the (then) new member, the UK, in the early 1970s over the adoption of "Ode to Joy" for the EU itself. The UK voiced its strong objections to the supranationalism implied by the adoption of an anthem, particularly one stressing a universal coming together of nations. The compromise reached was to begin to use "Ode to Joy" informally at events in Brussels throughout the 1970s, without its adoption in any official capacity.

A second key compromise was to adopt only Beethoven's music itself, not the song's lyrics. As music is abstract in nature it is less specifically tied to one country than the words of Schiller, and with no words, the anthem can be played without regard to translation. There is certainly an irony in censoring the words of a song that professes the universality of humankind because they were originally written in a specific national language. If there was a true transcendence of nationalism, presumably the point would become moot. The ironies continue as the standard music arrangement used for EU occasions was originally arranged by Herbert von Karajan, a conductor long tagged as having Nazi allegiances. Indeed, the Ninth Symphony is thought to have been Adolf Hitler's favorite piece of music. Nonetheless, Schiller's words emphasize the collective over the individual, and Beethoven's music incorporates both diversity and harmony (Clark 1997), all in keeping with the "united in diversity" and larger messages that the EU seeks to promote as it constructs itself as a legitimate political authority.

Not surprisingly, given how laden the symbolism was, in the subsequent years the question of whether to officially designate "Ode to Joy" as the EU's anthem unleashed a plethora of political protests. With the reinvigoration of the EU in the 1980s, the European Parliament took "formal note of current practice concerning the European anthem" (Clark 1997: 800) and, in 1988, passed a resolution expressing their hope that a European flag, passport, and anthem would increase European identity and community (European Parliament, June 9, 1988). When the Berlin Wall fell a year later, Leonard Bernstein conducted Beethoven's Ninth in that city on Christmas Day 1989, while in Potsdamer Platz, the wall's breaching had a soundtrack of music that included Pink Floyd, not Beethoven (Singh 2011: 2). While continuing to be used at various EU and other European events, the issue of making the anthem official was taken off the table with the failure of the European Constitution. Nevertheless, the anthem is widely recognized as such, and its musical notes—but not its words—continue to grace public events across Europe.

It is important to remember that the adoption and use of these symbols in official capacities do not by themselves create true political legitimacy or imply the consent of the governed. After all, deeply illegitimate regimes such as North Korea have flags and anthems, and one of the first acts of the terrorist group Islamic State in Iraq and Syria (ISIS, also called ISIL) was the adoption of a black-and-white menacing flag to represent itself. Rather, the point is that these symbols, by representing the EU as an actor, create or constitute it and thus generate the "units" of understanding by which we can love, hate, judge, or negotiate with another (political) actor. They situate the EU as a social fact on par with the nation state, even as it differs in critical ways.

Conclusion

The construction of the EU as a naturalized social fact, a taken-for-granted site of political authority, is necessary for governance. This chapter has added to our assessment of the specific mechanisms by which Europe has been constructed as a political community, albeit one with some very distinctive characteristics. While the chapters that follow will probe into the seemingly more rationalistic realms of citizenship, markets, and foreign policy, and argue that they too are imbued with culture in the form of symbols and practices that construct meaning, in this chapter we have focused on the more traditional "soft" realms of architecture, pop culture, sport, anthems, and flags. Yet here too, there is fertile ground for the work of labeling, mapping, and narrating Europe in ways evocative of the rise of other political forms such as the nation state. What is different is the continual emphasis on the localizing of Europe. By claiming the cultural heritage of Genoa or Antwerp as a "European Capital of Culture," an effort is made to simultaneously balance both the historic affinities of Liguria or Flanders and the ambitions of a broader, united Europe. The EU's strategies also perform the deracination necessary to make these moves palatable to the broader public. Focusing on sports teams such as the Ryder Cup or the Europeanization of football clubs aids in presenting these changes as banal and unthreatening. But we should not dismiss this type of everyday culture as inconsequential, or we risk being hoodwinked by the latent power intrinsic in these symbols and practices.

5

Citizenship and Mobility

Introduction

The 2002 film *L'Auberge Espagnole* opens with a shot of an airplane lifting off a runway and a young man's voice ruminating that "everything started here." Centering on a year in the life of a multinational group of European university students studying in Barcelona, the narrator goes on to proclaim, in French-accented English, that he is "not one but several," to wit: French, Spanish, English, and Danish. The movie can be criticized for the wildly optimistic portrait it draws of one seamless, cosmopolitan Europe. In the face of the social cleavages revealed with the euro crisis—with Germans chastising Greeks for being lazy profligates, and Greeks calling Angela Merkel a modern-day Hitler for imposing harsh austerity measures—the romanticism of these Barcelona students seems naïve and unrealistic. Yet even in the wake of the euro crisis, young people of different European nationalities continue to come together under EU programs to experience each other's cultures and languages. In fact, the Erasmus student exchange program at the heart of *L'Auberge Espagnole* has expanded exponentially in size and funding. Beyond university students, the EU has also championed initiatives to promote the increased mobility across national borders of all Europeans for work, retirement, or for services such as healthcare. These policies are slowly, if unevenly, redrawing the symbols and practices of boundaries within Europe for many of its residents, even despite the "real mess"—in the words of the movie character—that may come along with these experiences.

This softening of felt borders is a startling development given the sovereign nature of political authority in the age of nation states. What might be the consequences of the new symbols and practices of mobility for the broader European project? What are the cultural building blocks, deriving from European mobility, that have worked to relocate Europe as a scaled-up, bounded political entity? The EU's citizenship and mobility policies have mattered in many material ways, but they also have reshaped the social logics under which people live. The daily activities and representations of "EU citizens" as a legal category embodied in a European passport and the technology of travel within the EU, supported by programs that make that mobility possible, all contribute to a reorientation in the EU's "taken-for-granted" backdrop of political authority. These changes have also fed into a historical narrative about a shared European history, one that works to animate the idea of a European citizen. The practices and the representational symbols in play are gradually shaping the cultural meaning of what constitutes Europe and peoples' relationship to it. We will see that specific political technologies of labeling, mapping, and narrating, described in Chapter 3, are at work in creating a new cultural foundation for European legitimacy. These technologies rely on the projection of a deracinated and localized imagined community that naturalizes the EU as a new emergent political authority, but does so in ways that may limit the depth of the transfer of loyalty to Europe. Examining the creation of the European citizen in symbols and practices can tell us a lot about the character of the EU's political development in comparison to the modern nation state.

I begin with a brief discussion of why borders, mobility, and citizenship implicate cultural dynamics, then provide an overview of the EU policy history in this area. I examine the symbolic and practical implications of European citizenship as a legal category with its own European passport, and then explore the reframing of history education across the EU from the nation state to a pan-European view. I turn to look more closely at the practice of mobility first in the Schengen free-movement area, then the Erasmus program, as well as other changes in the everyday symbols and experiences of European mobility. The overall pattern that emerges is of the construction of a particular type of imagined community of Europeans, one both gingerly tiptoeing around the nation state while borrowing liberally from the tried and true technologies of political authority construction.

Why are Borders, Mobility, and Citizenship Cultural?

Issues of citizenship, borders, and mobility are tangled up in cultural dynamics of meaning making. Intensely political, the cross-border movement of people engenders overt contestation across all types of polities. To be a citizen is to be not just an individual, but a part of a social collective, and therefore citizenship directly engages with issues of political identity. Citizenship comes with specific rights and responsibilities that are rooted in the key issues of political life (Marshall 1950; Brubaker 1992; Bauböck 1994; Bauböck and Guiraudon 2009). Citizenship decides who can vote, participate fully in civic life, and live unimpeded within national boundaries. Citizenship, bounded

by territorial lines, is central to our historical understanding of political development and the rise of the modern nation state itself.

In turn, the borders that define citizens are central to the political organization of the modern world. The rise of the modern nation state has been a story
of the rise of a territorially exclusive, hierarchical political entity, defined by
its boundaries (Ruggie 1993; Krasner 1999). Until recently, we assumed that
the political identities of people within sovereign borders were distinct and
exclusive, not shared across nations, and that those political identities are
encapsulated within the legal category of citizenship (Brubaker 1989). Europe
has been making its own internal borders permeable to an unprecedented
extent, in contrast to the hardening of borders that marked the rise of the
sovereign nation state. Both the symbolic representation and the lived experiences of boundaries have changed for many (but not all) of those living
within the EU, shifting the cultural setting for political life in Europe even as
contestation continues over who is being excluded from this newly expanded
Europe.

We tend to think of borders as politically drawn boundaries established by
war or negotiation and subject to formal law. But mental boundaries matter as well (Barth 1969, 2000; Lamont and Molnár 2002). Our mental maps
of the geography of a community are influenced by personal experience, as
daily routines segment the space around us into particular neighborhoods.
There may be sharp demarcations of physical geography (mountains or riv-
ers) or ethnic, racial, or socioeconomic divides. The redrawing of boundaries,
legal or mental, can be used to increase the power of some actors over others, and ultimately reinforces the legitimacy of the actor whose boundaries
are accepted (Anderson 1993; Scott 1998; Goddard 2009). It is these types of
cultural imaginings of Europe that we consider in this chapter.

The wager of EU officials is that the deeply held national political identities associated with citizenship and borders can be made complementary
to a new widened European identity through new symbols and practices of
mobility. So, German or other EU students pay local (Scottish) fees at the
University of St Andrews, thanks to European Court of Justice rulings and the
Erasmus student mobility program, while "EU Nationals" zoom through lines
at Charles de Gaulle airport or other entry points to the EU, flashing their
standardized burgundy passports, territorially locating themselves at the
center with Europe all around them. Just as nation states have worked hard
to manufacture certain historical narratives of their founding, enshrined in
museums and taught in school textbooks, so has the EU engendered stories
about European citizens, albeit always carefully balanced against national
traditions. But before discussing the specific illustrations of these EU dynamics, we start by considering the development of EU citizenship and mobility
policies.

The Evolution of EU Citizenship and Mobility

Mobility was an initial focus of early European integration policy, long before the explicit legal category of "European citizen" came into being. But it took many decades for the legal and political infrastructure to be built to fully support free movement. After the initial introduction of the concept of worker mobility in early postwar European Coal and Steel Community (ECSC) treaties, the 1957 Treaty of Rome more widely promoted the establishment of what were called "the four freedoms"—that is, the free movement of goods, services, money, and people—to create a common market for Europe. To accomplish this goal, the Treaty of Rome conferred on workers "the right to accept offers of employment, to move freely among the member states for this purpose, to reside in any member state if employed there, and to stay in any member state if formerly employed there" (Maas 2007). The European Commission was given the authority to implement these provisions and largely did so within the next decade.

Progress toward more mobility continued over the next few decades, but did so erratically. One key 1976 European Council decision established a practical foundation for later moves to European citizenship by implementing direct universal voting in European Parliament elections starting in 1979. This decision created a link between the public and Europe's legislative body, bypassing the national governments that had previously been intercedents in the electoral process. The decision also subsequently enabled reforms granting the right to vote in municipal and European elections according to one's state of residence, rather than nationality, reframing the linkage between territorial location and citizenship from a national to European-wide scope.

A major step toward the creation of a borderless Europe occurred in 1985, in the Luxembourg town of Schengen, where Germany, France, Belgium, Luxembourg, and the Netherlands signed an agreement, outside the normal EU treaty protocols, to eliminate border controls (Zaiotti 2011). The next big development after Schengen, the Single European Act, came into force in 1992, as discussed in Chapter 6. Encompassing all EU members, the single market provided a blueprint for redrawing the lines of Europe's political community by eradicating national borders for most commercial transactions and exchanges, by constructing a common external border, and by granting free movement rights to workers, retirees, and students. The Single European Act radically pushed the concept of a borderless EU, with free movement for all, squarely into the accepted public discourse, with the European Commission serving as a critical actor in reframing and legitimizing this move forward in European integration (Fligstein and Mara-Drita 1996).

European citizenship was only explicitly created as a legal category in the 1992 Maastricht Treaty. Maastricht spelled out the political status of EU citizens through four sets of rights: free movement rights, political rights, the right to common diplomatic protection when outside the EU, and the right to petition the European Parliament and appeal to the EU's ombudsman. In response to concerns, particularly on the part of Denmark, that EU citizenship might be made legally superior to national citizenship, the subsequent 1999 Amsterdam Treaty contained the following text: "Citizenship of the Union shall complement and not replace national citizenship" (European Union 1997, Art. 8A, par. 2). The 2003 Nice Treaty further moved forward policymaking on citizenship and mobility by easing rules about how decisions on those topics would be made, extending qualified majority voting among the heads of state and government over free movement rather than requiring unanimous support. Yet the most contentious rules regarding passports, identity cards, residence permits, social security, and social protection were still exempted from qualified majority voting.

In the 2000s, the European Constitutional Convention then focused renewed debate on the nature of European citizenship. The convention was viewed by some as an opportunity to further consolidate the idea of a European citizen and give it more symbolic and practical weight, as will be explained below. But the constitution faltered in referenda in France and the Netherlands in 2005, in part because of its overt encroachment on deeply held national symbols and practices, such as citizenship itself, as we will return to in Chapter 8. Despite the failure of the constitution, the EU has gradually secured a rule-based regime that has profoundly transformed the legal framework for travelers, workers, students, and retirees from national to new European boundaries. Moreover, these decisions have accompanied a host of changes in the territorial basis for a variety of social rights such as healthcare, the right to establishment, old age pension, and the recognition of diplomas that the European Court of Justice had asserted over preceding decades (Wiener 1998: 9; Conant 2006, 2010; Caporaso and Tarrow 2009; Anderson and Kaeding 2013). These specific political, social, and economic rights and entitlements are helping to move the EU toward a single political space within which citizens can work, play, study, and retire.

The Construction of the "European Citizen"

The label "European citizen" probably sounds odd and potentially oxymoronic. Aren't citizens only possible if there is a nation state? The assumption is that for citizenship to have legal meaning and bite, it must be within a traditional government setting where there can be real claims on, and protections for, those meeting the requirements of that category. Also, citizenship is generally understood to encompass a deep sense of membership, of meaningful identity attaching to a collective community (Brubaker 1992). Citizenship can also be defined as robust participation and deliberation in the political process, once again surely possible only in a nation state setting (Gutmann and Thompson 2004). Some argue that citizenship should be defined by the right to basic necessities—a life free of poverty, hunger, or homelessness—implying a governance system equipped to offer those things (Marshall 1950).

These conceptualizations of citizenship differ in their emphasis, but all seem to create an unassailable link to the nation state. So how might the EU, then, have citizens of its own? We may say that someone is a "citizen of the world" but that signifies mostly that they enjoy exotic foods and can speak to taxi drivers in their native tongues. Citizen, in that phrase, is a metaphor for cosmopolitanism, but it does not convey real political attachment or legal force. Work on post-national citizenship has pointed to the loosening of the bonds with the nation state and the development of transnational relationships and identities, but they remain the exception rather than the norm (Soysal 1994).

It is surprising, then, that the EU has been developing a framework that instills in its residents a citizenship that does have legal force and meaning in practice (Olsen 2013). This seems to disprove one well-known French academic's dismissive statement some decades ago that "there are no such animals as 'European citizens.' There are only French, German, or Italian citizens" (Aron 1974: 653, quoted in Olsen 2008: 40). And yet in a more recent scholar's words: "Exactly what 'Citizenship of the Union' means in political or cultural terms, however, is still a matter of debate" (Shore 2000: 66). In creating the category of European citizen, the usual EU political strategy of deracinating and localizing EU symbols and practices seems to be upended. Instead, the EU seems to be confronting head-on the conventions of nationalism and state power by directly mimicking the prerogatives of the state. But, once again, we see that the EU's use of the category of citizen is tempered so as to make it complementary to national citizenship, even as the EU attempts a revolutionary reimagining of citizenship itself.

This reimagining is dramatic when compared to the conventions of sovereign states. The EU supposition is that Italians or Slovenians or Romanians, for example, can be simultaneously citizens of their national homeland as well as citizens within a larger, shared European community. In so doing, the EU is attempting to make natural the supranational projection of a category historically reserved for nation states, and use it to legitimate a transformation in power toward Brussels. This use of a legal construction for post-national sovereignty is mirrored at the international level where the EU has been fashioning itself as an actor among nation states in the international law and organization field, signing treaties and assuming a legal personality of its own.

These legal constructions can be thought of as speech acts, as discussed in Chapter 3. Speech acts call into being what they purport merely to represent (Austin 1962; Searle 1969; Butler 1993). The Maastricht Treaty created the legal category of European citizen with the swoop of a pen, but that category only has impact as it becomes a taken-for-granted part of the social landscape of the EU. It is certainly true that Maastricht "aroused neither enthusiasm or anxiety among the newly hailed citizens of Europe, most of whom were either unmoved by or unaware of it" (Shore 2000: 67). But by declaring the people of the EU European citizens, Maastricht created a chain of representations and practices that enable an array of potential consequences.

Some of those consequences flow from the new legal category of European citizen, permeating into the national settings and creating a new cultural infrastructure for discourse and action on the legitimacy of European governance. A gradual development of an interplay of the elements of citizenship, namely membership, identity, rights, and participation practices, dates from the early decades of EU integration (Olsen 2008). In the legal field, a preponderance of data indicates that lawyers and their clients have restructured their relationships and activities toward Brussels, creating a new social layer of legitimation for EU integration through the law (Kelemen 2010). New constellations of actors and coalitions have responded to the opening for political influence through EU citizenship. For example, women's groups have sought to establish their claims to equal treatment within the more welcoming EU treaties. A wave of efforts to organize civil society groups toward the European level have reoriented political action to the EU and, in the process, invented the citizens of Europe through these social processes (Greenwood and Aspinwall 1998; Weisbein 2001; Cram 2006; Greenwood 2011). In some instances, funding from the EU itself has prompted actors in civil society to explore what citizenship means and in that way translate these speech acts into expectations about citizens' own roles (Moro 2012). For example, the European Citizen Action Service (ECAS) promotes an EU-wide network of national civil society groups that seek to increase civic participation in European matters, while the Active Citizenship Network, funded by the EU's Europe for Citizens Program, promotes advocacy for individuals and groups around issues such as patient and consumer rights.

Despite all this meaning-making activity, the majority of Europeans simply do not feel a rosy sense of European citizenship and attachment to the EU. For many years, this disaffection translated into the very low salience of European issues for most voters. More recently, as evident in the 2014 European elections, the EU has increased its salience, but only in ways that affirm voters' distrust and distress with European policies. Nonetheless, the creation of this new category of European citizen matters in subtly changing the backdrop for governance, naturalizing the shifting location of European political authority, even if that authority is critiqued on its substance. The European projection of the category of citizen is not a seamless copy of nation state practices and meanings, but rather is a blurred and weakened version of national citizenship.

As discussed above, European citizenship itself, as a legal category, directly rests on preexisting national member-state citizenship, even as it creates European-level rights. When the 1992 Maastricht Treaty first created European citizenship, it did so with the proclamation that: "Every person holding the nationality of a Member State shall be a citizen of the Union" (Article 8(1)). European citizenship therefore differs from national citizenship in that its requirements are not uniform and set at the European level, but rather vary with the national rules of each member state. So you must first be French, or Slovakian, or British, before you can then be automatically European, with the rights and obligations of both legal categories.

But the problem of what, exactly, a European citizen is, still remains. The European Constitutional Convention debates in the early 2000s laid bare the contradictions and contestation around European citizenship. The introduction of the notion of "dual citizenship" in the European Convention implied that EU nationality would be on par and equal to the member-state nationality. But the push to reclassify EU citizenship caused significant political backlash. The citizenship dimension ended up being part of the negative political debate about European integration rather than being a celebration of new political rights and identities. The proposal for a dual EU/member-state nationality was a break from the tried and true strategy of what I have called localization, of embedding the EU in national categories in a way that avoided full-on confrontation with national identities. This symbolic confrontation of the EU and member-state identities may have contributed to the constitution's rejection in referendums in France and the Netherlands, torpedoing its adoption.

Despite the constitution's fate, the category of European citizenship continues to have significant traction in certain practices across the EU. Many of these changes flow from earlier European Court of Justice rulings on non-discrimination. The principle of European citizenship requires that EU citizens lawfully resident in another state must be treated the same as their own nationals across a range of public activities. This drawing together of disparate nationalities into one European category has erased some experienced boundaries of Europe in unexpected, everyday ways. For example, when residents of Greece enroll at Cambridge University in the UK, they pay the same £9,000 rate that British students pay, while "overseas" students from anywhere outside the 28 members of the EU pay substantially more. Contrast this with the US$10,000 tuition charged to residents of Virginia studying at the University of Virginia, while those living next door in Maryland would pay $38,000 for the same education. The EU's website, "Your Europe" explains why: "As an EU citizen, you are entitled to study at any EU university under the same conditions as nationals."[1]

The implications of European citizenship in practice are likewise found in the EU's rules regarding entrance fees to national cultural institutions (Hoffmann 2011: 1). If you are a young adult resident in the EU (or of Iceland, Norway, or Liechtenstein, which make up the European Economic Area) you can enter the Louvre Museum in Paris for free, just as a French student would, whereas young adults of the same age from outside Europe will be charged €16 to enter. In a 2006 Services Directive, the European Commission declared that the "right of non-discrimination" for European citizens meant that museum fees could not be different based on nationality within the EU, erasing the boundaries among those states (Hoffmann 2008, 2011). In contrast, a visit to see the stunning landscape photography of Ansel Adams at the Oregon Historical Society in Portland by out-of-state students would cost $3.50 each for the experience, whereas it would be free for Oregon students, as there is no similar rule barring discrimination in fees within the federal US system. While these are practical differences, they also create living categories, reframing the question of inclusion and exclusion within the European community, constituting "us" and "them."

European citizenship has real material advantages even as it raises questions about its meaning. Equal access to publicly funded institutions is just one of the more banal practical consequences of the creation of the legal category of European citizen. But these examples indicate what occurs when the category of European citizen is given legal force and then can, in ways large and small, transform social relationships and shift expectations. A perhaps more potent symbol and practice that flows from European citizenship, at least for those who travel internationally, is the European passport, to which we now turn.

The European Passport: Nesting National Citizenships in the EU

Charles de Gaulle Airport, located outside of Paris, is often a chaotic mess, teaming with travelers flying across the Atlantic, or eastward to Asia, or to smaller towns all over France. The passport control areas, as with most international airports, have long lines of people waiting to present their official

---

[1] <http://europa.eu/youreurope/citizens/education/university/admission-entry-conditions/index_en.htm>.

credentials to bored-looking *Police aux frontières* (PAF). But, just as in any international entry point to the EU, one of those lines includes people from 28 nations all clutching burgundy-colored passports. The passports look similar, but are not exactly the same. Almost all the passports feature a coat of arms, but they differ: for example, one is an ornate coat of arms depicting a lion and a unicorn with the words UNITED KINGDOM above it, one has a stylized eagle with a cross in its beak under the word ROMANIA, while another has a picture of a harp and the words EIRE and IRELAND. At the top of each passport are the words EUROPEAN UNION (or EUROOPA LIIT in Estonia, or for the Italians, COMUNITÉ EUROPEA, and so on for each national EU language). The strategy of nesting the EU within national political culture is strikingly evident, as the symbols and practices of border crossing are simultaneously standardized (as the EU citizens all wait in the interminably long passport control lines at JFK airport in New York, flashing their burgundy passports) while still localized with the passports' different national symbols and labels.

Passports are so taken-for-granted today that we forget that they are remarkable exercises of power and political authority. Passports are a relatively recent invention, only dating to World War I, as states sought to monitor and control the passage of foreign nationals. Passports enabled the registration of people and surveillance of movement that deepened the administrative power of the state, establishing discrete, delineated citizenship and cross-national classification and interaction (Torpey 2000). If the passport was important for the historical development of the nation state's power and its "embrace" of its citizens as subjects to a newly empowered administrative realm, what does that imply for the EU passport? Similarly to Scott's (1998) observations about the ways in which the development of registration and tracking devices such as passports and a national census have made their populations "legible," and in so doing built state capacity, we can think of how the EU passport also makes "legible" these new European citizens. The EU passport symbolically projects a political authority bounded not by national territory but by a new, imagined European space. Importantly, however, the EU does not issue the passports itself, but rather member states retain that control, albeit with the standardized EU designs and EU requirements regarding biometric information and other aspects. The EU member states themselves continue to determine who can receive a passport. However, a European infrastructure for the monitoring, surveillance, and control of people across borders continues to evolve with the Schengen Information System and the European Arrest Warrant (Velicogna 2014).

This transfer of authority to the EU was not without contestation, and the evolution of passports toward a common European format has been a relatively slow process, accruing symbolic power rather than full administrative control. In contrast, a centralization of internal policing of European mobility has moved much more quickly to the EU level in response to concerns over terrorism. It is clear from the documents surrounding the development of the EU passport that political elites involved saw the potential for broad political impact. Wiener reports on EU communiqué language that stated: "the fact remains that the introduction of such a passport would have a psychological effect, one which would emphasize the feeling of nationals of the nine Member States of belonging to the Community" (Wiener 1998: 26). The same historical dynamics that pushed nation states to categorize and classify their populations as a way to exert their power have prompted EU policies, although always mindful of not stepping too hard on nation states' prerogatives. Even though not everyone in Europe owns a passport, the EU symbol of 12 yellow stars is now standard on national identity cards issued by EU member states, even as those national cards differ in design and legal status. These shifts in documentation and surveillance up to the European level imply a meaningful increase in social power for the EU and the generation of a new cultural setting for European politics.

Narrating Europe's History

Citizenship implies a shared political history. Fortunately for the EU's project of naturalizing its political authority, we write and rewrite national histories all the time. History is constantly being interpreted and reinterpreted in ways both motivated by specific interested actors and in ways unconscious and unthinking. Nation states may attempt to frame the past so as to create consensus where there is none, or to shore up specific types of national identity, or to legitimate involvement in a war (Zerubavel 1995). Yet the project of inventing a shared history is never easy. One of the main channels for such invention is education, often the site of highly contested, politically fraught battles over attempts to change the way that young people "see" national history (Weber 1976; Frank et al 2000).

Because of the continuing dominant power of the nation state, the EU does not play a prominent role in shaping the content of European education, aside from its activities through the Bologna process to promote student mobility and standardize credentials and degrees. But work done by a variety of civic groups is creating a new pedagogical foundation for the idea of an EU citizen, with a shared history. Networks of nongovernmental groups, such as national and European associations of educators, have led these efforts (Soysal 2002). Historians in the European Association of History Educators (EUROCLIO), or the European Standing Conference of the History Teachers Associations, and other such organizations have been pushing forward new interpretations of the national histories of the EU member states. In these interpretations, national histories are linked together and nested within a larger, common European history. EUROCLIO collects European education statistics, assesses textbooks and teaching, and coordinates curricula, building a layer of institutional support for the reorienting of history to the European level. Supported financially by the European Commission, private foundations, and European corporations, EUROCLIO's mission statement, found on its website, approvingly frames Europe as a principled entity encouraging dialogue, conflict resolution, and human rights.

The efforts of EUROCLIO and many others have had effects. Drawing on an exhaustive group project surveying history texts and curricula across the EU, Schissler and Soysal write that "we observe trends towards a taming of national history" as national events are reframed and recast in a broader European context (Schissler and Soysal 2005: 5). They note that these European trends echo a larger trend in Western education systems to situate national histories in broader contexts of regional or world history, stressing patterns and dynamics that stretch across different settings (Schissler and Soysal 2005: 5). However, the trends in secondary education in the EU are particularly striking in their pointedness, although not all states are on board. For example, the 1789 French Revolution is taught in France as a pivotal event for France, but also a larger turning point for European history with implications for the "broader self-understanding of all of Europe" (Schissler and Soysal 2005: 5). Britain has not revised its history textbooks toward Europe, however, reflecting its euro-skepticism (Haus 2009). As part of the larger trend of the Europeanization of history, specific historical figures linked closely to particular nations, such as France's Joan of Arc or Germany's Bismarck, are demythologized and moved from the center of the national story across many EU states. In their place, other individuals and trans-European groups, such as the Vikings, are highlighted instead as part of a shared European tradition, crossing borders. Soysal notes that in this new historical approach, for example, Alsace-Lorraine is presented not as a deeply contested political place but rather as a "region in the heart of Europe" (Soysal 2002: 275). A French textbook will compare the historical tradition of linguistic diversity in France (for example, Basque, Normand, or Provençal) to the many languages of the EU, the implication being that such diverse cultures and languages are normal and no barrier to political community. Likewise, the Europeanization of Spanish history teaching involves the drawing of parallels between the late nineteenth century and today, as Europe is presented as a modernizing solution for Spain in textbooks from both periods (Luzón 2005). These activities all work to create European citizens with a shared historical background.

Of course, schools are but one site for narrating a shared history. Historical tourism, museums, and archeological digs can all play a role as well. To this end, the EU has funded the reconstruction of a range of historical heritage sites across Europe, partnering with local groups to dig up, renovate, or restore sites and artifacts. Often carried out in tandem with the cultural activities of the Council of Europe, the broader international organization that includes EU member states as well as other European nations, the EU's own activities have added up to €26 million over the period 2007–11. These activities are explicitly framed as "preserving European cultural heritage," strongly emphasizing the notion of a shared—not simply national—history, and culturally mapping Europe for its citizens. Initiatives celebrating a common European history include the Europa Nostra awards for historical conservation, preservation, and research, which recognize and provide monetary awards for projects such as the conservation of the walled city of Nicosia, Cyprus, or a timber building preservation training center in Chichester, England (European Commission 2014a). A revamped 2011 program invites applications for official labeling as a "European Heritage Site," chosen by an independent committee of experts. The first round recognized the medieval Great Guild Hall in Tallin, Estonia, as well as a World War II Nazi transit camp in Hooghalen, the Netherlands. The Europa website information on the program notes that:

> The European Heritage Label (EHL)... will help to strengthen a sense of belonging to the EU, based on shared European history and cultural heritage, with young people as the main target audience. A further goal is to increase cultural tourism which will result in economic benefits. (European Commission 2013b)

Through such programs, the EU is able to present itself as a strong supporter of the flourishing of national and local historical identities while also putatively drawing together Basques and Scots and Greeks and others into a common European heritage. This allows European citizens to share a common history but one with many different chapters, localizing and celebrating the uniqueness of Celtic burial cairns, for example, while claiming them as part of a universalized European tradition. When signage on these treasured local cultural heritage sites displays the EU flag's blue background and yellow stars, it subtly naturalizes the juxtaposition of European citizenship and local identity. The power of labeling, mapping, and narrating as political technologies is well displayed in these EU activities.

The effort to write a new history on top of the old is not uncontentious nor necessarily successful, however. Marine Le Pen, the leader of the vehemently anti-EU French political party Front National, often appears at rallies with a large icon of Joan of Arc above her. Instead of the Europeanization of French history, Le Pen is claiming the symbolism of the Maid of Orléans' battles against English domination. Le Pen uses Joan of Arc not to celebrate Europe but to decry the larger influence of outsiders in French life. The seemingly innocuous European Heritage Label effort has likewise been strongly contested by British members of the European Parliament as a "vain effort to force a common European identity" and the UK has declined to participate, with representatives of the diplomatic service saying the existing UNESCO World Heritage program works well to protect the UK's sites (EurActiv 2011). While the Europeanization of history proceeds, there will continue to be push-back by various groups and political leaders, as the stakes for the rei-magining of a shared history are too high for it not to be otherwise.

Erasing Borders and Branding "Europeans" on the Move

The ability to move freely throughout a territory is a key practical part of citizenship. As Maas notes: "One of the modern state's most notable functions is to facilitate the free movement of people within its boundaries, and the essence of full-fledged state citizenship, as distinct from earlier local citizenships, is its uniform applicability throughout the state's domain" (Maas 2007). While formal European citizenship was only created with the Maastricht Treaty in 1992, de facto citizenship had arguably been growing since the initial efforts to increase labor mobility with market integration decades earlier (Wiener 1998; Maas 2007). For EU citizens themselves, mobility has proved one of the most appealing innovations of the EU. In Eurobarometer polls, when asked the question "What does the EU mean to you?" the majority consistently choose the response "the freedom to travel, study, and work anywhere in the EU" (European Commission 2009: 85).

Schengen and a Borderless Europe?

Borders in many ways "represent the very essence of statehood" as they delineate the physical extension of political authority internally, as well as define the geographic units that make up the sovereign state system and thus the lines that other states should not cross (Zaiotti 2011: 2). The most dramatic dismantling of EU borders is found in the Schengen regime. The first Schengen Treaty, signed on June 14, 1985, codified an agreement to allow the free movement of people and the removal of border controls among its signatories: Germany, France, Belgium, the Netherlands, and Luxembourg. In a carefully chosen symbolic act, the treaty was signed aboard the MS *Princess Marie-Astrid*, a passenger liner anchored on the Moselle River in a section of the water under a three-way legal jurisdiction, the condominium of Germany, Luxembourg, and France (Zaiotti 2011: 4). Today, the Luxembourg village of Schengen on the banks of the Moselle is the site of the "European Museum—Schengen" where the "history and significance" of the treaty are celebrated in a variety of media and installations, according to its official website.[2] Although initially an agreement negotiated directly between the governments, with successive enlargements, Schengen became folded into the EU treaties and institutions, and now encompasses all EU members except the UK and Ireland, with Croatia, Bulgaria, and Romania currently in transition to membership. The European Free Trade Area countries, Iceland, Norway, Switzerland, and Liechtenstein are also part of the Schengen area.

What has Schengen meant in practical terms? If you are on a train traveling from Amsterdam to Brussels, the ride will not be interrupted by something as archaic as border patrol guards coming onto the train north of Antwerp to check your passport. Crossing over from the Basque beach town of Hendaye, France to enjoy tapas in Fuenterrabia, Spain, the passport control kiosk is gone, and cars zoom by where once they had to line up and wait to be checked. Once dismantled, it is hard for most Europeans to imagine such barriers being in place, as movement through most of the EU today conveys little sense of politically drawn borders and state control mechanisms for monitoring the passage of citizens. Instead, the physical experience is of the free flow of people within the Schengen countries, rendering the crossing of national boundaries unremarked and unremarkable, a daily activity for many living near borders, or those traveling for business or pleasure.

In addition to Schengen's transformation of the regulation of border crossing, dramatic changes in the technology, cost, and ease of travel itself over the last few decades have promoted European-wide travel to a wider range of income groups. With the Trans-European Network's high-speed trains now crisscrossing much of Europe, distances have shrunk. Deregulation and the rise of private airlines such as EasyJet and Ryanair now make it feasible for most Europeans to travel across Europe for the weekend, creating the possibility for experiencing the EU's shared space. Just as the building of roadways and train lines in nineteenth-century France helped transform "peasants into Frenchmen," such exogenous changes create possibilities for closer integration of Europe even as they are not determining in themselves (Weber 1976).

Of course, these changes in the legal and felt experiences of borders do not mean that Europe is now a utopia of equal treatment. For one, borders do still exist in very real ways on the perimeter of the Schengen states, most notably for travel into and out of the UK. Passports are checked at entry points there, and various groups of people not perceived as welcome within the EU are excluded from this freedom of movement. Within the EU itself, internal police surveillance strengthens the hand of the state even as borders dissolve (Christiansen 2005). Social borders are intensifying within Europe, in the sense of socioeconomic cleavages; and cultural, racial, and

---

[2] See <http://www.schengen-tourist.lu>.

class delineations are ever robust, particularly for immigrants and minorities (Balibar 2004: 1–10; Fligstein 2008). But even with those important caveats, in very practical and physical ways Schengen has transformed the experience of Europe into a space not delineated by sovereign borders.

Erasmus and Mobility for All?

A host of other EU policies have vigorously sought to promote mobility by reducing the legal and administrative barriers to EU citizens' ability to work, study, travel, or retire outside one's own country. As the opening of this chapter indicated, the well-known Erasmus program enables university students to spend time in another European country, studying side by side with locals as well as with other expats. The program, officially titled the European Action Scheme for the Mobility of University Students, began in 1987 and has steadily grown, providing stipends for student exchanges across national borders and facilitating the registration and credentialing of intra-EU study. By 2014, over 3 million students had taken advantage of Erasmus since its founding (European Commission 2013a: 9). In the 2011–12 school year, more than 250,000 students (and 46,000 staff) studied and worked in another EU country under Erasmus and 2 million more are targeted to do so in the period 2014–21 as the program expands and is extended to student internships, training, and sports exchanges (European Commission 2013a: 8). Joined to the principle of equal treatment that allows any student of an EU member state to pay national fees for their education, Erasmus creates a powerful financial and administrative incentive for student mobility.

The official statements founding Erasmus stress the benefits of a trans-European pool of workers experienced in a variety of economic and social settings, the advantages of creating a "pool of graduates with direct intra-Community cooperation" who can then provide the basis for further European integration, as well as the interaction of students from all corners of Europe "consolidating the concept of a People's Europe" (Council of Ministers 1987: 21–2, cited in Sigalas 2010: 243). The political motivation for Erasmus is also rooted in part in the work of scholars such as Karl Deutsch, who focused on the importance of day-to-day, mundane interactions and communications as forging a sense of shared identity across borders (Deutsch, Burrel, and Kann 1968; Fligstein 2008: 16; Kuhn 2015). The Erasmus experience represents the largest program in the world promoting cross-border study. Although the early rhetoric stressing Erasmus's role in creating a shared European identity is no longer as explicitly stated, it is still found in various speeches and European Commission documents (Sigalas 2010: 244).

A thriving literature has attempted to empirically ascertain whether or not participation in Erasmus, say as a Danish student studying in Florence, changes how that student thinks and feels of themselves vis-à-vis Europe (King and Ruiz-Gelices 2003; Sigalas 2010; Wilson 2011; Kuhn 2012; Mitchell 2012; Van Mol 2013). In an example of selection effects, students participating in Erasmus unsurprisingly have much higher levels of stated European identification prior to their studies than non-Erasmus students. One study of a mix of British and continental Europeans found that about two-thirds of the students starting Erasmus self-identify as both national and European—and that proportion doesn't change much after their Erasmus experience (Sigalas 2010: 256). In a more recent empirical study of change over time in almost 1,500 Erasmus students across 38 German universities, another scholar finds an increase in a sense of European identity linked to contact with other EU students, beyond the initial selection effect (Stoeckel 2014). Likewise, Mitchell's survey work finds a more robust relationship between participation in Erasmus and European identity (Mitchell 2014).

The empirical battles will likely go on, as the study of identity change is very difficult. While the results of the EU's Deutschian experiment are still not clear, the hotly contested European Parliament elections of May 2014 did provoke the organization of a pro-Erasmus interest group made up of alumni and study-abroad students whose website detailed which European Parliament candidates to vote for, in each district, based on their likely support for increased Erasmus funding. While this is but one example, it demonstrates that the program has created a new group of people with a stake in EU politics who are willing to be vocal and participate in determining the future path of the EU.

The hundreds of millions of euros that the EU spends per year to fund the Erasmus program indicates that there is a view among decision makers that it is an important program. The quotes from the movie *L'Auberge Espagnole* that opened this chapter portray Erasmus as a unique moment of finding commonality across European nationalities and, in the process, transforming oneself. The students in the movie are all still very much rooted in their national identities, and in some ways find those identities strengthened by being expats, just as the American Club of Brussels has a thriving business of cocktail parties and outings amongst people who would probably not consider themselves sharing much in common—except when they are abroad together. But in other ways, the students are profoundly changed on return to their home nation.

The push to increase mobility for students and young workers has also involved other EU efforts to smooth out the professional frictions associated with moving across borders. In doing so, they are also creating new standardized practices for young people that recategorize and reframe their experiences in ways that universalize them into "Europeans." In the early 1980s, a network of information centers was set up to advise students on cross-border education and transfer of qualifications. The administrative mechanics are in place to allow for recognition of education credits in the "European Credit Transfer System," a program introduced by the European Commission that requires the study-abroad credits to be recognized across the EU. The Bologna Process, a wide-scale European education reform initiative initially established outside the EU's institutions, has successfully promoted a standardizing of university degrees and credentials across Europe as well, with the goal of creating a European Higher Education Area, reframing the experience and material consequences of education (Terry 2008).

Beyond university students, ordinary people in the EU have a multitude of opportunities to engage in social practices and activities of daily life beyond their national borders. Professionals, be they lawyers or hairdressers, can study and work abroad with their credentials and training mutually recognized across borders. In so doing, they largely need not worry about surrendering their financial benefits or political rights, as the EU legal regime now extends to both. The single market for labor mobility in services sometimes surpasses federal systems such as the US. With the adoption of several new EU rules since the mid-1970s—especially Directive 77/249/EEC on the freedom to provide services, Directive 89/48/EEC on the recognition of diplomas, and Directive 98/5/EC on the establishment of lawyers—the EU allows for lawyers to work in any member state without additional licensing (Hoffmann 2011: 3). Contrast this with the time-consuming efforts required by a lawyer in Massachusetts to pass the New York bar exam so as to be licensed to practice in that state, as the US does not have a standardized federal legal certification.

Beyond lawyers, there has been an effort on the part of the EU to provide accessible formats to capture nationally specific credits, training, and qualifications and "translate" them into a standard format—a "European CV"—in what the EU calls the effort to promote the "recognition and transparency of qualifications." An official 2003 EU booklet entitled *It's Your Europe: Living, Learning and Working Anywhere in the EU* trumpets "The European Union—wide open with opportunities for all" and "encourages you to think seriously about the benefits and personal fulfillment to be gained through living, learning or working in another EU country," adding: "It's no secret: Europe can change your life if you want it to" (European Commission 2003: 3). Whether that is true or not, it is certain that, for students at least, a lot of time and money has been spent in trying to reshape the EU into one space.

An extensive collaborative study of the Europeanization of daily life, EUCROSS, summarizes this changing landscape well:

> Europeans today can travel, work, study and retire abroad freely (i.e. without visas and other state permits), using low cost regional airlines made possible by EU deregulation; they can vote for the European Parliament and local governments

in any member state, regardless of their nationality; they can collect pensions as foreign residents at a local post office; they can buy property security within a mutually recognised legal system; they can shop on line in another EU member state without having to pass through custom offices. (Favell et al. 2011: 5)

But have these opportunities resulted in much mobility inside the EU, beyond the Erasmus students? The EUCROSS survey sample of Germany, the UK, Denmark, Italy, Spain, and Romania finds that indeed there is much more mobility than the conventional wisdom on Europe acknowledges. Their data shows that one in every six Europeans in their sample nations has spent at least three months in another EU country (Salamonska, Bagalioni, and Recchi 2013: 25). Moreover, over half of those surveyed have visited another EU country in the last two years, whether for a vacation, work, or other reasons (Salamonska, Bagalioni, and Recchi 2013: 25). The project also sought to understand the frequency with which EU residents virtually cross borders, by interacting in a non-physical way with others outside their national boundaries. They found that almost three-quarters of their sample connected online or over the phone with "significant others who migrated or with friends they met during their physical trips," while almost one-third of those surveyed engaged in cross-border transactions, either shopping online or transferring money abroad (Salamonska, Bagalioni, and Recchi 2013: 25).

Mobility within Europe is also not always driven by economic reasons but rather a significant portion of those moving across EU borders have done so for romance, leisure, adventure, and lifestyle opportunities (Santacreu, Baldoni, and Albert 2009). In particular, cross-national marriage is becoming increasingly common in the EU as Erasmus and work opportunities bring people together and often result in one of the couple permanently moving to a new EU member state (De Federico de la Rúa 2005; De Valk and Medrano 2014).

Earlier work on the "Eurostar" life rightly reminds us that "nationally specific and locally-rooted forms of urban life in Europe" persist (Favell 2003, 2008). Indeed, informal barriers to long-term worker mobility, from housing and labor markets to family structures and commitments, to the still nationalized social services, continue to keep most people from fully experiencing Europe as a single space. Permanent moves that result in people living outside their country of origin remain low. The reason is simple: most of us are deeply embedded within a series of social institutions and commitments that do not easily or even desirably disentangle themselves. But even as widespread permanent relocation is less prevalent in Europe than in nation states, mobility is part of the lore of the EU, a myth that may be potent even if not acted on (Recchi and Favell 2009). It forms part of the narrative of the EU, and thus the imagined community of Europeans.

Europeanizing the Banal: Labeling EU License Plates

What is the most banal thing you can think of when it comes to the actual practice of mobility? It might be license plates. Necessary, but who wants to think about them? In the recent past, a drive through Madrid would reveal cars with the symbol "M" and a string of numbers on their rectangular license plates, with a decal sticker off to the side with the letter "E." The M signified Madrid, as B would indicate Barcelona and so on. The "E" stood for España. Today, however, cars drive by with license plates displaying the EU flag, blue with a circle of 12 yellow stars, with a small "E" directly below. The local identification of the car has vanished. The shape and format of the plate itself is now exactly the same across all the EU member states (although optional in Sweden and Cyprus). This completes a process begun in the late 1990s with a series of regulations issued by the commission to standardize plates and, in the process, reframe the geography of governance such that each member state is now symbolically nested inside the EU.

Thought about in this way, license plates can be seen as part of the naturalization of European citizens within a larger community. This reclassification and labeling, with the EU symbols overlaid on top of the national symbol, recategorizes drivers, and anchors them in a location that is mapped onto Europe's political authority rather than only local and national levels. In the United States, license plates are issued by the particular state you live in, with images and slogans carefully chosen to project a particular narrative: New Hampshire's "Live Free or Die," Florida's bright "Sunshine State," or Washington, DC's "Taxation without Representation." Seemingly banal, they also do symbolic work in the US federal system (although there is no official USA sticker, as it is presumably not needed as there are relatively few cars on US roads from outside its borders).

Beyond license plates, as of January 2013 all driver's licenses issued in the EU also have a standardized look and format, as well as a standard set of minimum requirements for earning a license. The new license cards have the EU flag in the left corner with the acronym of the issuing member state in the center (such as IRL for Ireland), and on the right the name of the country spelled out in bold on a background of very faint type that spells out driver's license in all the languages of the EU. The symbolic power of categorization and classification that developed with the rise of administrative nation state has shifted to the European level—at least in this seemingly banal area of driver's licenses.

The experience of traveling along the roads of Europe is standardized as well, with rules about right on red, priority to the right, speed limits, and so on gradually becoming uniform, along with infrastructure safety rules governing things such as the design of road tunnels. The signage that accompanies these rules and practices also has been reformed, with European-only agreements within a broader United Nations agreement, the 1968 Vienna Convention on Road Signs and Signals. However, the UK, Ireland, and Cyprus still have one glaring exception to the standardization, of course, which is driving on the left-hand side of the road. If you enter the UK on a car ferry, you immediately know you are in a very different place as you enter the never-ending traffic circles, hoping for the best. This jarring difference is only in keeping with the uneasy relationship that Britain has with Europe. License plates, driver's licenses, traffic rules, and signs are so under the radar that they easily form the everyday, taken-for-granted naturalization processes that provide a foundation, albeit a very banal one, for the legitimation of the EU as a new political authority. Their similarities, and differences, with similar exercises of administrative power on the part of the nation state, tell us a lot about the path of EU development, however, pointing out the ways in which the EU both is developing political authority but always in tandem with the ever powerful nation states.

Conclusion

Citizenship and the mobility of people over borders and boundaries are areas of immense political importance. Mobility helps to construct citizens in social, legal, and material ways. It is no surprise that borders have long been jealously guarded by political authorities intent on securing their citizenry, their economy, and their political power. Despite this, policies promoting the movement of people in the EU, joined with the legal construction of the European citizen, have created a new series of experiences and symbolic representations of Europe. A retired British couple buying a cottage on the Costa Brava, or French students studying in Italy, for example, likely have no political motives whatsoever in making their individual decisions to take advantage of EU mobility and citizenship. Yet a slow process of knitting together the daily lives of people from the 28 member states has transformed the possibilities for interactions across borders. In addition, these processes have been bolstered by the historical rethinking of European citizenship. Shifting historical narratives of secondary-school teachers and other educators across Europe, along with the repetition of EU programs such as the promotion of European heritage historical sites, have helped to construct European citizens as a plausible reality.

We do not have conclusive data on the impact of these dynamics on individual political identity. But the effect of the symbols and practices that are generated through those decisions subtly shift the taken-for-granted realities of people such as the retired British couple and the French students mentioned above. The backdrop of everyday life in Europe has been reframed to label people as European citizens; to locate them in a single political, economic, and social space; and to narrate a common European history. The contestation and pushback that has occurred in that space is part and parcel of the process of naturalization, as the EU comes to the fore as an emergent actor, but one whose legitimation is always tenuous and tempered by the continued material importance and social power of the nation state.

6

The Euro and the Single Market

Introduction

The piece of paper is slightly crinkled, but its bright colors are still vivid in the sunshine. I turn it over, looking at the rose-colored Romanesque archway inscribed on it, the European Union (EU) blue flag floating in the corner and a blurry map of Europe on the reverse side. This euro can buy me a coffee, or a copy of *Hello* magazine, or a Paris metro ticket. Paper money is so much a part of our daily lives that we take for granted that it can be exchanged for goods and services, for *haricots verts* or haircuts. But the fact that this is true should be of interest to us, because it is far from clear how a small bit of colored paper is widely recognized as valuable. This sleight of hand rests on an array of social institutions and political relationships that allow us to trust that paper currency will be recognized as a distillation of value. A 50-euro note is both a practical resource for the person who holds it, and an object embedded in a larger cultural setting. The creation of the euro as a thing of widely recognized, if fluctuating, value is the story of a social fact, a collectively held belief so robust that it takes on the characteristic of objective reality. It is the cultural setting that gives the euro meaning, but the everyday use of that piece of paper carried in pockets and wallets also reverberates back onto that culture. These social processes link the euro, however tenuously and conflict-ridden, to the broader project of making European governance seem natural and legitimate.

Currency is not the only economic site of everyday cultural interaction in Europe, however. The EU is first and foremost a project of market integration, centered on a robust common European space for economic transactions of all kinds. The single market, a vast multi-year program to integrate European markets for goods, services, capital, and labor, has fundamentally changed the experiences of consumers, businesses, and investors. When people transact, choose, or use products, the single market is a powerful generator of a myriad of symbols and experiences that create a sense of a territoriality and boundedness. Standardized rules and practices reinforce similarities of experience for those "internal" to the EU while setting up distinctions for those outside its borders. From the Italian hair stylist who cuts hair in Amsterdam without having to get a Dutch license to do so, to the German families that buy their children toys with the CE symbol on them knowing they adhere to high safety standards wherever produced, to the German bankers who (over) invested in Greek banks in Europe's unified financial market, the single market has redrawn national economies into a common European space. What is often missed, however, is how much market integration is built on and builds social interactions. Just as with the social construction of money, the symbols and practices of markets constitute a particular cultural infrastructure for governance. Markets provide powerful vehicles for shaping perceptions and the "taken-for-granted" everyday reality of citizens. Looking more closely at the development of this European economic space can help us to see the underlying dynamics of both cooperation and contestation that bind some within the EU, while pushing others apart. Just as in the historical formation of the modern nation state, markets are a potent source of political development whether they produce positive or negative outcomes alike (Berman 2006).

This chapter first takes up the question of why we should consider markets as cultural sites. It considers the EU's Economic and Monetary Union (EMU) and its centerpiece, the euro, and then the single market project. For each, I sketch out the basic historical outlines of their development, and then highlight various symbols and practices intrinsic to these projects. I describe how they create an imaginary Europe for citizens through specific processes of labeling, mapping, and narrating. As with the historical experience of nation states, these processes work to legitimate the contentious transfer of sovereignty. Unlike new emergent polities in the past, however, we will see the EU using strategies of localizing Europe in national settings and of deracinating potentially highly contested policies to make this transfer more palatable. Whether the cultural infrastructure built through this strategy is sustainable in the longer run, however, is very much open to question.

Why Are Markets Cultural?

It is self-evident to those of us living in the contemporary Western world that markets are underpinned by economic logics. Built on the foundation of Scottish Enlightenment theorists such as Adam Smith, modern economic theory has created a law-like, abstracted model of the workings of the price mechanism and the quest for profit that seems more akin to a natural science than one made up of social beings. But this orthodox view offers only a partial view of how markets actually work. Markets cannot be durable or stable without a broader framework of rules to govern market interactions. Those rules do not arise spontaneously through economic interests, but rather are the product of politics, mediated through social interactions. To fully understand outcomes in the economy, markets therefore should be recognized as embedded in social and political logics, as well as economic interests (Polanyi 1944; Fligstein and Dauter 2007; Woll 2008). The logics of supply and demand taught in Economics 101 are powerful drivers of action, but they are always and everywhere embedded within these larger structures of power and authority, which privilege some actors while disadvantaging others. Larger structures of meaning likewise locate and connect market actors and shape the way that self-interest is calculated. These broader cultures of meaning make possible the stuff of markets, from money itself to corporate mergers, to labor union contracts, to patents for new category-busting technologies. Culture, in the sense of systems of meaning and practice that make the world intelligible to some subgroup of peoples, helps to bring order to action and make market transactions possible.

The embedded nature of markets means that they have played a critical role in shaping the historical process of state building. A recursive causality enables markets to promote the building of state power, just as state power can build markets (Fligstein and Mara-Drita 1996). Of course, the opposite is true as well: failed states can lead to failed markets, and vice versa. This broader view of markets as cultural and deeply intertwined with state building is common in the field of economic sociology, but sometimes challenging to those who are implicitly taught that markets, and the firms that constitute them, reflect universal economic laws rather than social customs and political rules rooted in particular times and places (Fourcade 2009). Scholars have convincingly demonstrated the working of culture in market decisions and outcomes, and have linked market building to state building across a range of empirical examples (Fligstein 1990; Dobbin 1994; Roy 1997; MacKenzie 2006). Seeing markets in these broader ways and appreciating their cultural foundations allows us to analyze how the single European market and the euro and monetary union have invoked symbols and prompted practices that provide the raw materials for a particular type of imagined community of Europeans.

Yet as in our other examples of the social construction of Europe, the imagined community constructed by the single market and the euro is not unproblematic. The development of a market-based, integrated EU has been simultaneously viewed as a disastrous neoliberal project that is a betrayal of the foundational beliefs of social democracy and, from the opposite side of the partisan spectrum, as "Fortress Europe" that has evaded economic reform and protected the welfare state and labor at the expense of market efficiency.

115

These clashing narratives persist, even as a larger process of recategorization from national to European has proceeded apace with the single market program and the euro, just as the consolidation of single national markets and the development of single national currencies promoted earlier episodes of state building (Skowronek 1982; Spruyt 1996). It is to the euro that we first turn to see how the EU is naturalized through symbols and practices, even when its material policies may have disastrous effects on some EU citizens.

The Euro and European Monetary Union

The euro can both be seen as a breathtakingly bold innovation, and stupendously foolhardy, depending on your perspective. The European Monetary Union (EMU) is a historical anomaly, as never before in modern history has a single currency existed absent a single nation state. A few efforts to create monetary unions of sovereign states failed miserably, but those tightly connected to larger state-building projects in the second half of the nineteenth century all succeeded in accruing power and political authority to the state (Helleiner 1998, 2002; McNamara 2013, 2015). But there are also important symbolic elements in the standardization of money: as euros replace francs, Deutschmarks, pesetas, and so on, symbolic forms shift and become universalized and recategorized as European. The new currency, aside from presenting a host of policy challenges, is reliant on a complex system of intersubjective understandings. These understandings are both rooted in local interactions, as euros pass from hand to hand at the greengrocer or newsstand kiosk, and on pan-European and transnational interactions, as mortgages and credit-card bills are paid and euro-denominated financial instruments sold across borders. The creation of EMU, with the euro and the European Central Bank (ECB) at its center, brought the EU both a powerful economic policy tool and a way to symbolically represent Europe as a bounded political entity (Risse 2003; Kaelberer 2004; Fishman and Messina 2006; Manners 2011). The ECB, which sets and executes the monetary policies that govern the euro, represents a massive transfer of political authority, even as it also creates a new category of European actor, a set of new practices of governance, and physically represents the EU in its new gleaming glass towers on the banks of Main River in Frankfurt. The national central banks continue to exist as members of the European System of Central Banks (ESCB), however, carrying out the policies of the ECB, somewhat like the US regional Federal Reserve banks, and reinforcing the notion of a "localized" Europe, embedded in national settings.

A European currency therefore forms part of the cultural infrastructure of the EU, contributing to the process by which the EU has become a taken-for-granted political entity, even as the Eurozone's governance may be vehemently criticized. The opaque and complex area of monetary policy presents an opportunity for the type of deracination that I argue is a key part of the EU's strategy for constructing an acceptable "imagined community" of Europeans. This legitimation process is ongoing as the circumstances and interpretations of the euro change over time, extending even to the dramatic contestation over the merits of the European currency after the eruption of the Eurozone crisis in late 2009. Placards displaying a euro in flames at a demonstration in Portugal show the power of symbols as political vehicles for expression and meaning. Yet they also challenge the status quo of European governance and push back on the efforts to naturalize that governance, bursting the bubble of protection that the original narrative of a technocratic, deracinated monetary union and the euro had created. The story of the euro is one of immense accrual of power and a legitimacy generated through the daily symbols and practices of EMU. The thin foundation of Europe's imagined community and collective identity that was created through the euro and the other policy areas catalogued in this book are now being tested by the stresses and strains of this deep transformation in governance.

The Curious Case of EMU

European political leaders viewed a unified single currency as a particularly potent way to bind together the states of Europe, and spent decades preparing for it, in fits and starts, with two steps forward and three steps back. Indeed, monetary union has been on the agenda of the EU states since at least 1970, with passing mentions in official documents even before that (Tsoukalis 1977). In 1970 an official EU study, the Werner Plan, proposed that the member states of the European Community move in three separate stages to an integrated monetary area by 1980. The first and only stage of this plan to be implemented was a short-lived exchange rate agreement created in 1972. But by the second half of the 1980s, new European leaders began to warm to the revival of the monetary union project. At the June 1988 European summit in Hanover, the heads of state and government of the EU charged the then commission president, Jacques Delors, with developing a plan for EMU. The committee formed to address this goal delivered its Delors Report to the European leaders at a summit in Madrid in 1989, outlining a three-stage plan for achieving the single currency and monetary union (Gros and Thygesen 1999).

The Delors Report formed the basis for the subsequent Treaty on European Union, signed by the European leaders in Maastricht in December 1991, which locked in a timetable for the move to EMU (Moravcsik 1998). First, barriers to financial flows within Europe were removed and convergence in policies and economic indicators promoted, and the institutions built to govern

EMU, until finally the European Central Bank and a "virtual" euro of national currencies locked in a single rate together came into being on January 1, 1999 in eleven countries (Austria, France, Finland, Germany, Italy, Belgium, the Netherlands, Luxembourg, Spain, Portugal, and Ireland). Greece joined EMU on January 1, 2001, after a series of accounting efforts to meet the convergence criteria, later found to be dubious in nature. The physical currency was introduced at midnight on New Year's Day, January 2002 in 12 countries, and the national currencies were phased out of circulation entirely over a two-month period. Since then, Cyprus, Latvia, Malta, Estonia, Slovakia, Slovenia, and Lithuania have all joined as well, bringing the total to 19 euro states within the now 28-member EU. Britain, Sweden, and Denmark all "opted out" of the euro early on, as their publics viewed the single currency as undesirable for political reasons. Despite the ongoing euro crisis that began in 2010, countries from central and eastern Europe continue to queue up to join, with Estonia and Latvia joining after the euro crisis was in full swing, and Lithuania joining on January 1, 2015.

The basic tasks of the ECB and the ESCB (made up of the national central banks) are the formulation and implementation of monetary policy, most prominently through the setting of interest rates; the execution of exchange market operations; and the holding and management of official reserves (McNamara 2006). Although the formulation of monetary policy is located solely within the ECB, much of the execution and operation of monetary policy continues through the national central banks. The ECB is also responsible for the promotion of the "smooth operation of the payment system," which refers to the workings of TARGET, the intra-European large payments clearinghouse system, for which the ECB could be a lender of last resort in the event of a crisis.

Why the euro? What explains this radical act of merging of sovereign states into a monetary union with a single monetary policy and currency? One reason is the perception on the part of many of the EU governments, particularly those such as Italy that had a history of currency depreciation, that banding together would strengthen their economies. A consensus on the desirability of German-style monetary rigor, emphasizing low inflation, was also necessary for the euro's creation (McNamara 1998). But a deeper cause was the pursuit of peace and political unity. The series of wars that wreaked havoc and tragedy in Europe over the last century were a spur to political innovation and integration, as discussed in Chapter 1. With the fall of the Berlin Wall, the end of the Cold War, and the looming reunification of Germany, the leaders of Europe decided that a bold move was necessary, and the introduction of a single currency fit the bill (Sandholtz 1993).

Notably, the euro, while moving monetary authority to the European level, did not do the same with other linked policy areas, such as financial or bank regulation and supervision, and fiscal policy such as taxing, public borrowing, and government spending and redistribution policies. Unlike all the other single currencies in existence, the Maastricht Treaty set up a system where the ECB sits alone at the European level, with key levers of governance that normally accompany a single currency remaining at the national level. The Eurozone crisis of 2009 onward revealed the problems with this historical anomaly in a dramatic and wrenching fashion (Matthijs 2014a, 2014b; McNamara 2015; Matthijs and Blyth 2015).

Despite the shortcomings in its governance structure, the creation of the euro, particularly in its physical manifestation, has generated a chain of important symbolic representations and practices. The EU gained both a powerful economic policy tool and a way to symbolically represent Europe as a bounded political entity. It also provided an avenue for new sets of experiences that reshaped the logic of practice for those using the euro. Chris Shore's anthropological study of the launch of the euro documents the vast time and energy that the European Commission put into managing the social and symbolic consequences of the Euro (Shore 2000; see also European Commission 1998a, 1998b). In France, extensive education campaigns before the changeover to the euro were driven by national political elites sensitive to the shift in authority that the euro represented and the need to bolster confidence in the currency. Public campaigns framed the euro as a historic innovation, solidifying Europe together in peace and prosperity (Merriman 2006). The shift to an EU currency would involve emotional responses tied up in feelings of nationalism that would need to be carefully managed.

Yet those nationalist feelings also offered an opportunity to build a cultural infrastructure for EU governance if the transition could be strategized appropriately. The very fact of a physical object like the euro signals the presence of the EU and makes it real for citizens, while the value of the euro as an exchange rate traded on world markets and the economic data that groups countries together in a common category of the Eurozone represents Europe in subtle, everyday ways. Below, we consider the symbolic power of the iconography of the euro, the practice-based importance of the euro as material culture, the ways that the statistical reordering around the euro matter for the cultural foundations of governance, and, finally, the technocratic narrative of the euro.

Iconography of the Euro

We start with perhaps the most straightforward place for a discussion of the symbolic politics of money and the euro: iconography. The iconography of the euro is the most obvious way to represent the EU. When you hold a euro in your hand, the pictures and designs are inescapable, even as you get so used to seeing them that they stop consciously registering. The imagery on the euro is an ever-present backdrop to the lives of those who use it, even as the policies surrounding the euro itself may be contested and full of strife. The iconography of the euro, and the fights over it, reveal the type of imagined community being built in Europe. So what do we see when we look at the euro? And what messages are the EU trying to send with its designs? How do they differ from the national iconography that the euro has replaced?

Before the physical introduction of the euro in 2002, a Dutch person in the Netherlands would have used guilder inscribed with Van Gogh's sunflowers to pay for their morning *koffie*, while a Frenchwoman used francs bearing a representation of Marianne for her *café crème*. Today, across all 19 countries using the euro, over 330 million people in all, have the same set of symbols on the money they use to buy their morning meal. A new standardized monetary space and set of experiences has replaced the national variations that came before. These Europeans may be buying yogurt in Greece or *churros* in Spain, but the currency is the same. A single currency engages processes of symbolic standardization and replacement: at the most general level, as euros replace francs and so forth, symbolic forms shift and become universalized rather than localized, as the sunflowers, Marianne, and so on fall away to be replaced by the common depictions of bridges and windows.

The iconography of the euro can be broken down into at least three component parts: the euro symbol itself, the geographic mapping of Europe, and the particular set of images used on coins and paper. First, as an entirely new category of money was created with the euro, it demanded a new symbol to represent it across a variety of market settings. The € symbol has come to signal EU as a de facto logo, recognizable from afar and universally readable in any language. Note that very few currencies have their own widely recognized graphic symbol or currency sign. The British pound (£), Japanese yen (¥), and US dollar ($), and now the euro (€) are the world's most commonly used currency signs, and they represent the most widely circulated currencies in the world. Currencies such as the Swiss franc, the fifth most traded currency in the world, simply go by acronyms, CHF, or *Confoederatio Helvetica* franc. In contrast, as the second most traded currency, the euro's graphic representation is a shorthand that comes to signal Europe to the world. The € symbol appears on every price tag in the Eurozone, on shoppers' receipts, in currency exchange bureaus in airports or in foreign exchange markets, on computer keyboards, and whenever a euro transaction occurs. This is the political process of labeling, described in Chapter 3, taken very literally.

The value of the euro against other currencies has become another standardized, numerical focal point representing Europe, offering an external face of a consolidated Europe to the world. The euro's exchange rate has of course shifted and changed in the decade plus of its existence, and the political meaning of that rate has changed too. With the sustained rise in the value of the euro against the US dollar over its first decade of existence, and its relative stability even through the perilous economic stress of the Eurozone crisis, the European currency's appreciation may act as a source of symbolic strength. Appreciation has also allowed euro holders to go on spending sprees abroad, giving those travelers the experience of having a higher-status currency as they snap up Apple products in New York or Timberland boots in Los Angeles, reverberating positively on their experience as "Europeans" abroad. Prior to the recent crisis, extensive commentary in the press about the euro displacing the US dollar as the international reserve currency of choice constituted a status marker for Europeans as well (McNamara 2008). But from late 2008, as national level bonds denominated in euros have precipitously declined, those positive signifiers have been overshadowed by very negative associations in countries such as Greece, Portugal, Spain, Italy, and Ireland. The negative and positive both add up to symbolic representations of the EU. Even as they may have normatively different content, they both signify the EU's presence in EU citizens' lives and create it as a social fact, for good or for ill.

A second set of social processes generated by euro iconography involves mapping, another of the political technologies key to the creation of national identities and imagined communities as discussed in Chapter 3. The iconography of the euro locates Europe in a strikingly fluid and changing geographic space. It is so fluid that Europe's geography is represented differently between paper currency and coins. The paper currency denominations use a shaded map of Europe as a region, with no distinct states but rather a single, holistic geographic entity. The imagery suggests a community that is simultaneously inclusive and undefined as to its borders, one that is omnipresent and yet nowhere in particular (Hymans 2004). The symbols on the euro coins reinforce this fluidity, offering a rich, or confusing, array of geographic expressions of what Europe is. A unified image of a community of Europe with no borders appears on the most valuable coins (1 and 2 euros); a group of sovereign and distinct states appears on lower value coins (10, 20, and 50 cent coins); and the EU as a region in a global context is on the least valuable coins (on 1 and 5 cent coins). This "telescoping" out in scale in representations of Europe, from the most to least valuable coins, emphasizes the heart of Europe (although still with blurred boundaries), but with reference both to the sovereign states that make it up and to the broader world in which it is located. The representations in the maps of Europe on coins and paper vary slightly in terms of where the EU starts and stops. The paper currency is more inclusive and open to the gray boundary areas toward Russia and the hinterlands than the images found on the coins.

The mapping processes that historically have attempted to naturalize governance in new political entities are fiercely engaged in the iconography of the euro, even as the categorization of what "counts" as Europe varies across the different coins and paper currency. The consolidation of the euro and the replacement of national currencies implies a territorial reframing in imagined community terms, one that is quite literally represented in the symbols on the euro.

Maps are not the only prominently displayed imagery on the paper currency, however. The paper currency also features designs of European architecture, but in contrast to national currencies, the architecture is void of specificity, not anchored in any particular place or actual physical structure. The images feature bridges and windows, with the lowest denominations showing older, more historic designs such as Romanesque arches, moving through time up to drawings of modern architecture for the higher denominations. The feeling is vaguely European, without a clear sense of where in Europe the images resides—a feeling of pride, surely, for the artistic accomplishments of European culture, but a generic version of what that might mean. This is deracination, the uprooting and abstraction of political imagery that marks so much of the EU's particular political culture.

One scholarly study of currency imagery from the nineteenth century onward argues that, because the EU has chosen abstract themes, it actually maximizes its chances for political success (Hymans 2004, 2006). In this view, the EU's postmodern abstractions actually follow a more universal trajectory from the nineteenth century onward, one that starts with states using classical heroic and state-centered representations, moves to depicting social classes, then to focusing on individuals and, finally, to using abstracted images rather than "celebratory" images of specific actors or symbols. The very emptiness of the nonspecific EU images feed into a transformation more broadly toward universal symbols rather than those tied to specific referents.

As deracinated as these generic European architecture images seem, the process by which they were created was highly political and carefully considered, and signals what type of political entity the EU political elites are attempting to construct. The euro designs were chosen in a highly orchestrated design competition for both paper currency and coins (Shore 2000; Barker-Aguilar 2003). The design competition process underlines the EU's effort to be perceived as bottom-up and democratic, with open institutions, new forms of participation, and new practices of governance. This process matched, in a sense, the iconography of bridges, windows, and doors, which reflected the desire of European officials to highlight the openness and open-endedness of the integration project (Hymans 2004, 2006)

The iconography of the euro also engages what I have termed a strategy of "localization," one that also sets it apart from the historical consolidation of national currencies that occurred in the nineteenth century. In many instances, the euro's iconography contextualizes Europe explicitly within the extant nation states rather than attempting to displace national identities. This is most striking in the euro coins. Each participating Eurozone member state issues its own coins with standard European imagery on one side and national symbols and portraits on the other. All coin denominations display on one side a simple map of the EU with various indistinct blobs representing the major parts of Europe, along with the coin's numerical denomination, and the 12 stars as found on the EU flag. The coin's other side has different images depending on where it is issued among the 19 nations of the Eurozone. Mozart peers at you from the €1 coin issued in Austria, while Finland's has two stylized flying swans, France has a tree and the words *"Liberté, Egalité, Fraternité,"* Germany has its iconic eagle, and the Spanish €1 coin has a likeness of former King Juan Carlos (until his heir Felipe's likeness is minted).

As such, the implicit message is that the various member-state nationalities can be understood as embedded within, and complementary to, Europe. Situating the local within a broader European setting constructs a Europe that simultaneously coexists with national political entities, even those whose coins use traditional figurative symbols deeply rooted in national culture. That the euro coins have both a standardized EU side and a nationally specific design on the other side neatly reflects a "marble cake" identity of complementary and coexisting political allegiances, where the adoption of one can occur without the exclusion of the other but rather both simultaneously (Raento, Ikonen, and Mikkonen 2004; Risse 2010).

The Euro as Material Culture

Money is not only experienced as a series of images and symbols, but also as an object that is used in practice. Currency and coins are objects that sit in a pocket or on a dresser, that move from one hand to another, or that transfer virtually, in our minds and on computer screens, from one account to another. All money leaves traces and the euro is no exception (Callon 1998; Zelizer 1994, 1998). This creates an avenue for the euro to reshape the imaginary Europe through the physical circulation of coins and paper. They start out where minted by one member state, but they quickly disperse beyond their original borders and spread into the Eurozone. A euro initially introduced in Ireland, with the € symbol on one side, and a Gaelic harp on the other, begins its life in the pocket of a native of Galway, who then uses it in a grocery store, for example, to buy a bar of chocolate. The euro sits in the till, and then is put into the hands of a German tourist, who then takes it back to Germany where he or she uses it to pay for goods there. The Irish harp is welcome in Germany as it becomes part of the German marketplace, passed from hand to hand. The social fact of currency, which has value only because of shared agreement around that value, is manifested in practices that allow, in the example just given, the simultaneously Irish and European object to become accepted in Germany, equivalent to the locally produced euro that has a Brandenburg Gate on it. Cervantes, emblazoned on Spanish euro coins, becomes European as the coin circulates throughout the member states, mixing in pockets and purses with images of the Celtic harp, the Brandenburg Gate, and so on.

The physicality of the Eurozone has other manifestations beyond currency. The physical representation of governance extends to the ECB itself, sitting in Frankfurt at the virtual center of the ESCB, engaging symbolic representations that also seem to carefully balance between the European standardization and national localization of the euro. The creation of a physical location of authority provides a way to concretize and symbolize governance. The ECB's siting in Frankfurt was carefully thought out as part of an effort to reassure Germany and other Northern Europeans that the new bank would be as sober as the grey Frankfurt sky. At its founding, the ECB was housed in a downtown office building renamed the Eurotower, but, as detailed in Chapter 4, it constructed a new building, one that was chosen after an elaborate design competition, because it embodied the values of "transparency and unity," in the ECB's official words (Papademos 2005). The ECB buildings thus echo historical nation-building efforts at using architecture to represent and symbolize state power and national unity. Yet Frankfurt is of course not the EU's capital, and no other key EU institutions are housed in Frankfurt, while the national central banks are geographically woven throughout Europe. Finally, in addition to the bricks and mortar of the ECB, a more human focal point for governance has also been created with the appointment of a president of the ECB, who serves as the physical embodiment of both the euro and the EU. Testifying at the European Parliament, and appearing at summits, the president (currently "Super Mario" Draghi) gives the EU a face, albeit one of a neutral, purportedly apolitical central banker. All of these elements of the euro have reframed the social landscape of Europe for both the symbols and practices of governance—despite the contestation brought by the euro's role in the financial crisis dragging on in Europe.

The Technocratic Narrative of the Euro

A final set of representations consequential for the path of European integration is found in the particular narrative put forth by European officials, politicians, and supporters of the euro. The work done by this narrative is important, for it eased the transition to the euro by deemphasizing its political implications. The EU appropriates powerful, and tried and true national symbols of power such as currency, yet camouflages its actions by claiming that the euro is merely a *technical* and therefore apolitical solution to macroeconomic challenges. The key policy document setting out the case for the euro, *One Market, One Money* outlined the benefits and minimized the costs of the euro with reference to the idea that a single market *requires* a single currency in order to function effectively (Emerson, Gros, and Italianier 1992). This is a functionalist argument disputed both by academic economists and historical experience. Likewise, the Single European Act, signed in 1986, sparked a series of market integration initiatives the likes of which have never been seen in a non-national setting, yet was also marketed as simply a technical solution to the challenges of globalization and US and Japanese economic competition (Jabko 2006). Harkening back to our discussion of performativity in Chapter 2, the theories that underpinned these rationales were a perfect narrative to achieve deeper integration, because they framed European integration at the level of technocratic solutions, not dramatic stories of consolidation of power.

Not everyone bought into this narrative at the time of the euro's introduction, but the counterarguments came only from those on the margins of the political debate, thus reducing their effectiveness. Only extreme far right and far left politicians spoke out against the euro. Jean-Marie Le Pen stated in May 1998 that the euro was the money of occupation, as after all the ECB would be located in Germany. Far right Austrian politician Jörg Haider called it a "miscarriage" and the National Front warned of "social devastation" if adopted (Berezin 2006: 100). But there was surprisingly little mainstream political contestation over the euro, even in the midst of this gigantic shift in political authority to the EU (Messina 2006). The euro was not viewed as a politically salient issue, in part because political elites play a large role in shaping the views of the citizenry on monetary issues, and most elites were pro-euro (McNamara 1998). The lack of political contestation was in line with the tendency in recent decades for policymakers to depict macroeconomic policy, central banking, and exchange rates as technocratic, even banal exercises driven by purely economic reasoning (Berman and McNamara 1999; McNamara 2002).

Thus, the widespread public contestation around the Eurozone crisis has been unprecedented in EMU's history. When euro membership kept the so-called PIIGS countries from adjusting through their exchange rates and instead forced difficult austerity policies, the non-banal nature of the monetary union was starkly and painfully revealed. The euro crisis also has cast a negative pall on the very idea of Europe. As one French leader put it when asked about the turn to the far right among some French citizens, "With few jobs and weak unions," she said, "there is a very clear sense of abandonment—people find themselves alone." She added that people also feel victimized by "Europe" and immigration. For such economic distress "we need a European response, and that does not exist, and I think there is a bitterness about that" (Erlanger 2013).

The referencing of "Europe" in her statements indicates the robust construction of the EU as a social fact, a taken-for-granted governance system. But the comment also as indicates the creation of an everyday sense of Europe in symbols and practices has not meant the absence of contestation and political turmoil. The euro crisis in particular has opened up questions about the democratic legitimacy of the EU. This chapter catalogues how EU policies and programs subtly shift the backdrop of governance but the euro case also demonstrates how these processes have produced deep tensions in the face of the collective turmoil of economic crisis.

A Single European Market

Gloriously disruptive and with far-reaching effects unseen by its creators, the single market project is arguably the enduring centerpiece of European integration, one that has transformed the way that day-to-day life unfolds across the EU. The various treaties negotiated over the years, and the EU regulations that have flowed from them, have dramatically changed the nature of competition and market rules, product and service availability in Europe, and even prohibited national governments from favoring their own firms over other EU firms in public procurement projects (Majone 1994; Egan 2001). The project of market integration began within the six core founding states (France, Germany, Belgium, the Netherlands, Luxemburg, and Italy) and expanded along with the EU's membership. It is arguably the most durable and dramatic example of postwar evolution of European integration. Less well understood, however, is the way the single market has promoted a shift in European ways of life and subtly reshaped language, and thus the imaginary European landscape that politics unfolds within.

Market integration initially began with the signing in 1957 of the EU's so-called founding treaty, the Treaty of Rome. The treaty states in its preamble that it has as its goal the creation of "the foundations of an ever closer union among the peoples of Europe" to "ensure the economic and social progress of their countries by common action to eliminate the barriers which divide Europe" (European Communities 1987). The specific means for achieving these ambitious goals were found in the treaty's guiding framework, which called for the establishment of a common market, a customs union with the gradual elimination of duties for goods and services across the six states, and the common policies to support them. The previously nationally rooted basis for market action would be transformed into what the treaty named the new "European Economic Community" (EEC). In this EEC, the treaty emphasized the need for "four freedoms," that is, the free movement of goods, services, money, and people. The vision contained within the treaty and its four freedoms was of a single, seamless market for the free flow of all the factors of production. This demanded the erasing of national borders and barriers to commercial products manufactured or created within the participating European member states. Whereas previously, each European state could and did have customs duties on the importing of German cars, for example, the Treaty of Rome ushered in the process of the dismantling of the entire concept of "imports" within Europe. Instead, it created a single, competitive market for European goods, be they Italian Fiats, German Audis, or French Renaults. The creators of the single market explicitly looked to a domestic model of governance rather than an international trade regime for guidance. The goal was to emulate the big, open market of the US federal system, which had to undertake its own historical efforts to break down the initial barriers to trade across the US states (Egan 2001: 40).

The Treaty of Rome ushered in the eventual removal of customs duties within the six core states of the EEC, the establishment of a common EEC external customs negotiating position in the fledging international trade rounds of the General Agreement on Tariffs and Trade (GATT) system, and the development of rules to promote open and fair competition between firms for national markets, regardless of the origin of goods. However, multiple national-level regulations, procedures, and practices meant that the so-called four freedoms were far from being achieved. Services remained subject to local strictures that made it hard for external actors to compete for construction contracts or sell insurance. Labor mobility had begun, but financial integration lagged far behind goods market integration.

The global economic downturn and OPEC oil crisis of the 1970s hit Europe hard, and fears of being left behind in the midst of an American recovery and Japanese export juggernaut were gathering amongst European policy and business elite, even as the workers of Europe saw their wages stagnate and prices rise. The unease in Europe presented savvy political entrepreneur Jacques Delors, the new head of the European Commission, with the right political conditions for a "*relance*" or relaunching of the single market project (Green Cowles 2012). This relaunching occurred with the Single European Act (SEA) of 1985, an addition to the Treaty of Rome that specified a series of reforms to allow for the deepening and extension of the common market originally begun in the 1950s. The SEA put in place a host of regulatory changes meant to be enacted by the putative deadline of 1992, and established principles that could then be used through the European Court of Justice (ECJ) to push forward a very wide range of activities and principles (Fligstein and Stone Sweet 2002).

The ECJ facilitated market integration through two key rulings (Stone Sweet and Caporaso 1998; Fligstein and Stone Sweet 2001). First, the court's rulings on "direct effect" meant that individuals and firms could bring cases for adjudication against national entities for violating the treaties. Rather than states suing other states for noncompliance with the principles of the single market, the people of Europe could protest discrimination directly. The court also established early on the principle of "supremacy," that the EU's laws would trump national-level law in the event of a clash between them. This meant that rules across a wide swath of issues would be set at the European level, and national laws would have to become Europeanized and harmonized across the member states. A further legal development, the establishment of "mutual recognition" as the guiding principle for dealing with different levels and types of national regulations, was also critical to the single market (Alter and Meunier-Aitsahalia 1994). In the Cassis de Dijon case, German liqueur manufacturers had sought to bar French cassis from being sold in Germany, arguing it had not been produced in accordance with strict German phyllo-sanitary rules. The ECJ ruled against the German liqueur producers, stating that in the Common Market states must recognize other states' regulatory regimes as equal to their own and cannot bar entry to goods. "Mutual recognition" of each others' regulatory regimes rendered a host of potential barriers to market integration moot. In many ways, this has resulted in cross-border economic activities that actually surpass that found in standard federal systems, such that, for example, hairdressers in the EU may practice their trade throughout the member states because of mutual recognition, whereas in the US they must pass state certification tests when changing venues (Hoffmann 2011: 202).

As the Treaty of Rome and the Single European Act dismantled barriers and set common external policies, they also simultaneously engaged a process of symbolic representation and cultural practice and, in so doing, helped to constitute Europe as a singular space—bounded, located, and named. The EU has standardized and flattened the regulations regarding all manner of economic activities, from elevator design to cell-phone roaming charges, within the borders of the 28 states that make up the EU. Less appreciated is how these changes have generated symbols and practices that change the cultural landscape of the market as well. The comprehensiveness of the market and its penetration into all aspects of modern life meant that the EU would be much more readily accepted as a social fact as consumers, firms, and governing officials all participated daily in its various activities and dimensions. The words used to describe market integration tell the story: from the "Common Market" of the 1960s to the "single market" of the 1980s to the "internal market" of today, a trajectory of transformation is encoded in the labels that move from cooperation among sovereign states to a single internal political space.

The reclassification and standardization of previously national phenomena into "European" is at the heart of the redrawing of the political boundaries that, I argue, underlie the creation of a new cultural infrastructure for Europe. However, these market-making dynamics do not call attention to themselves but rather occur in a banal way, deracinated and under the radar of the more fervent politics we associate with nation building. The single market helps to accrue symbolic and cultural power to the EU and naturalize its authority, but it does so in ways that seem purely technical and administrative, masking these deeper dynamics. The examples of Societas Europea, the CE mark (€) the potential impact of consumption practices and material culture, and EU public procurement policies illustrate these dynamics more precisely.

Labeling Europe: Societas Europea (SE) and €

The dynamics of the single market have included some very potent examples of taking national-level activities and rebranding them, with logos and acronyms, into a common category of "European." In the corporate governance sphere, a stark example of the recategorizing that the single market has prompted is in the development of a new European-level option for legal incorporation, the European Company Statute (ECS). Beginning in 2001, the Council Regulation on the Statute for a European Company created a new legal category for public limited liability businesses operating in more than one member state. It would be the choice for those wishing to be subject to a European-wide governance instrument, rather than incorporating only within a specific national context. This Societas Europea (SE) legal identity is notable for being the only supranational or transnational corporate incorporation instrument in the world. As with public procurement, control over the rules about incorporation, board structures, and reporting by corporations have usually been guarded as part of the national instruments of policymaking, despite globalization and market integration (Gourevitch and Shinn 2005).

The European Company Statute offers EU member states the ability to standardize their organizational and legal structures so that rather than being subject to different national laws in each member state where a subsidiary is located, a company can choose to operate under one set of EU rules with unified management and reporting systems throughout the entire single market (Fioretos 2007). This represents a clear benefit to the company in terms of the simplicity and standardization it offers, yet despite the longstanding interest in implementing such a code dating back to the Treaty of Rome, it took decades for a European Company Statute to be enacted. Wide differences in the delicately negotiated laws around business–labor relations, much more complex and protective of workers than in the US, made it hard to reach a consensus at the EU level. The final statute was achieved in part because some of the key provisions around labor relations were left aside and many of the diverse national rules on employee representation were kept intact. For this reason, the European Company Statute is viewed as a less than optimal effort at Europeanization of corporate governance. Nonetheless, the symbolic importance of the SE moniker, and the new practices that it engenders across firms registered as SE, are worth noting. Companies opting to incorporate under the ECS have the letters SE preceding or following their name (for Societas Europaea, Latin for "European company"). As of 2014, about 1800 companies had incorporated as European companies, concentrated in Northern Europe, particularly Germany (European Commission 2014b). Allianz SE, a diversified insurance corporation ranked number one worldwide by *Forbes* magazine, has the SE registration and uses the moniker on its websites and management information. BASF SE, the largest chemical company in the world, is also incorporated as a Societas Europaea, as is Bertelsmann, Europe's largest media company. If language has the latent ability to call into being that which it appears to merely represent, then the creation of the legal category of Societas Europaea and its acronym SE is an example of the work that seemingly technical and arcane regulatory changes might have on the imagined landscape of Europe, as national companies are rebranded as European.

Graphic symbols convey information nonverbally through visual design. In the realm of the single market, another such symbol is the $ or "CE" mark. This particular symbol was developed as a conformity marking for all products sold in the EU, whether produced by a European or foreign company, which meet specific EU rules, usually protecting health or safety, regulating environmental impacts, or regarding measurement and standardization. To adopt this symbol for their products, producers must go through a multistep documentation and testing process, often involving the assessment by an outside, third-party standardization body. The CE mark is present not only in the EU's internal market but, once on a product, travels with it wherever it goes to be sold around the world. For example, a plush Steiff teddy bear sold in New York displays the CE mark on a small white label sewn into its fur, just as it does in Prague. The CE certification mark gives the imprimatur of the EU's regulatory authority to an item, be it a cell phone or a lawn mower, and is one of the myriad ways in which the background for the single market is imprinted, literally and figuratively, with the EU's political authority. While most consumers and users of products have no idea what the process is for CE certification, the logo with the distinctive typography brands the reach of the EU and makes it part of the daily backdrop of life for consumers, and part of the process of manufacturing for producers.

I Shop, Therefore I Am

As markets integrate, they create new fields and forms of interactions through sustained exchanges among actors. Rules are created at the European level, creating new practices across previously nationally oriented regulators who must now continually interact with one another in creating a European regulatory network. Producers and firms as well must now transact with each other in new ways across national borders, developing ties both formal and informal, forging strategic alliances, investing, merging, or creating supply chain and marketing relationships. While much scholarly attention has been paid to the ways in which market integration has deepened and transformed these relationships across the national regulators of Europe, and to how producers of goods and services have reacted to changing opportunities, we understand much less how market integration has impacted consumers within the EU. This is odd, as the creation of a single European market has surely prompted consumers to change their shopping habits, and to buy goods and services previously "foreign" but localized as "European" in their grocery stores and elsewhere. Cars, cheese, life insurance, or cell phones, those items national consumers once purchased from their national companies or local firms, now are produced across the EU 28 and are integrated, even if not seamlessly, into the daily shopping habits of all Europeans.

Some anthropologists of the economy have suggested that we should think more carefully about these dynamics. In this view, consumption is a social process where goods are "coded for communication," but we need to dig into particular cultural settings in order to understand their meaning to those using them (Douglas and Isherwood 1996: xxiii). Goods can be thought of as both bridges and fences, drawing some closer while keeping others out, as "Social life is a matter of alignments, for and against, and for signaling alignments goods are like flags" (Douglas and Isherwood 1996: xxiv). In the EU case, what might this mean in the context of the new availability of products across the EU, and the new shopping experiences generated by various chain stores such as Zara, the omnipresent Spanish clothing store, or Aldi, the multinational grocery chain headquartered in Germany? The alignments of wealth and poverty signaled by material goods may well be crossing borders along with fashionable skirts or *crème fraîche*. Shopping is a daily practice for many. As boundaries are lessened, and products and experiences become more uniform and available across a territorial space, it shapes the cultural setting for governance in Europe.

Beyond goods, Europeans have seen a dramatic change in opportunities for consuming common services in the single market, especially in areas of intimate, personal care. A series of ECJ rulings have given EU citizens the right to be reimbursed for medical treatment anywhere in the single market, should the need arise (Anderson 2015). Others have engaged in dental tourism to get cavities filled in Prague or Budapest, for example. Polish home-care workers from lower-wage countries are brokered with families needing help caring for aging parents in Germany, while in Italy, these services are provided by Romanian *badanti*. The single market's freedom of movement is the facilitating factor, while wage differentials are the stimulus. How do these various examples of market exchange in services change the everyday experiences of both employers and employed? These last questions about the exchange of goods and services under the single market's erasure of formal boundaries have not yet been fully analyzed by scholars, but are worthy of future study and reflection.

Mapping Europe: What Once Was "Them" is Now "Us"?

The arena of public procurement policies is a final example of how the single market has recategorized European space with labels and classifications that reinforce a new vision of what constitutes Europe's political community. The label "internal market," which is used by the European Commission to describe the single market, itself reinforces the notion of a new set of borders that is inclusive of the members of the EU, and portrays everyone else as outsiders. This language is reflected in the EU's laws regarding previously jealously guarded sovereign practices of public procurement. Modern nation states spend huge amounts of government money on various goods and services, and this spending can often comprise up to one-quarter of the overall GDP, or economic activity, of any modern national economy. These public sector activities, such as building airports, providing disaster relief after hurricanes, and procuring goods such as F-22 high-tech fighter jets, have long been used to provide essential public goods that make a society function. But they have also been used to direct the economy toward specific sets of ideological and partisan views about what and whom to invest in and spend tax dollars on. Thus, national public procurement programs reflect deeply political decisions about how to deploy the key resources of the modern state. As the single market evolved, EU Commission officials, well-placed firms, and European national leaders began to advocate for common rules regarding public procurement across the entirety of the internal market. Eventually, a view gained traction that a level playing field for European firms across borders had to include rules opening up the bidding for such contracts to all European firms, not just national corporations. In essence, governments could not discriminate against firms outside their national borders when awarding the prized government contracts (Kelemen 2010: 143–95).

The result has been an EU-wide public procurement regime purportedly based on principles of non-discrimination, transparency, and economic efficiency. Although imperfectly applied in the EU and often passionately contested, this program represents a startling departure from the traditional model of sovereign state cooperation, and even goes beyond some federal nation state practices. For example, in the United States, particular states still freely discriminate against out-of-state bidders in public procurement. As one scholar has written, even the "US Supreme Court, in the absence of Congressional preemption, has repeatedly validated the right of states to discriminate when acting in their roles of proprietor of their respective public domains or as employer leading to pervasive preferential treatment for in-state products and companies, including openly exclusionary preferences in various states" (Hoffmann 2011: 8). While the EU obviously has many fewer elements of a common political identity and federal institutions than the US today, the EU public procurement practices create a deeper commitment to shared political community in Europe than that of the US.

These examples of legal incorporation of European firms, European product safety symbols, the flattening of consumer practices, and a European-wide competition policy may seem like only economic things, politically inconsequential. Yet they rest on something much more profound—a sense of who is included as part of a political community, and who is outside that community. In effect, these symbols and practices of the single market create a living category of shared identity, a label of European that subtly shifts the felt boundaries of political authority even as it locates the reality of Europe as a political entity.

Conclusion

The creation of a robust single European market, the largest in the world, spanning over 500 million people and with a combined GDP of $16.5 trillion, has been a centerpiece of the EU's integration project. The euro still reigns, despite its bruises, as the second most widely used international currency, holding its value against the US dollar on currency markets, and defended by the ECB and national political leaders despite significant political costs. These are extraordinary examples of the political development of the EU, rivaling the historical state-building processes of the modern nation state. But the single market and the euro also matter for the creation of a broader European cultural infrastructure, or imagined community, to support the broader transformation of political authority that is occurring.

This chapter has specified the ways in which symbols and practices are generated by the single market, such as the creation of standardized rules regarding public procurement that encompasses the EU 28 in a single political space, or the legal category Societas Europaea and SE moniker that reframe corporations as European. The euro likewise has a series of symbolic repercussions arising from its iconography, as it inserts itself into the daily practice of citizens in the 19 countries that now use the coins and papers as legal tender. The chapter reminds us that the economy is deeply intertwined with culture and, as such, the EU's market and money both rest on a series of specific meanings and shared understandings about the locus of political authority, while also reshaping them. The historical role of markets and money in the development of political entities provides a template, but one with a twist, for understanding the development of the EU and its particular cultural foundation. The twist is that while the efforts to localize and deracinate the meanings generated by these symbols and practices allow for a certain banal acceptance, the repercussions of the EU's transfer of authority in the economic realm cannot be papered over with only a thin sense of community. We return to these challenges in Chapter 8, but first assess the cultural dynamics wrapped into the efforts at creating a European foreign policy in Chapter 7.

7

European Foreign Policy

Mention the phrase "EU foreign policy" in most American foreign policy circles and you are likely to be met with either a blank stare or a dismissive laugh. What foreign policy? The European Union (EU) simply cannot get its act together. The bloody wars that accompanied the break-up of Yugoslavia in the 1990s, despite being on Europe's doorstep, prompted little in the way of an effective response from the EU, even as the specter of civilian atrocities hung over Europe's conscience. In Washington, the persistent unwillingness of European publics to support higher levels of military spending galls those US officials who see the EU as freeriding on the US security umbrella. From internal disagreements over how to fashion a policy toward Putin's military incursions in Ukraine, to the lack of EU military response to ongoing violence in Syria, the conventional wisdom is that the EU is an inconsequential, unimportant actor in world politics.

Yet this dominant view seems puzzling given revelations made public by Edward Snowden in the summer of 2013. Official documents revealed that US intelligence agencies had been spending precious resources to spy on the leaders and institutions of this seemingly disorganized, motley arrangement of European states. The view that Europe has no role to play in the world would also likely be contested by the families of the members of EULEX police force shot dead under the blue and gold EU flag in Kosovo in September 2013 while supporting ongoing EU Rule of Law Mission stabilization operations. Indeed, while the EU has famously struggled to act in concert on issues of military conflict and high-level foreign policy, this did not stop the Nobel Committee from awarding the EU its prestigious Nobel Peace Prize in 2012. Media reports certainly discuss "European Foreign Policy" as if it were a tangible thing. Stories on Iran's nuclear program highlight "European Union foreign policy chief Catherine Ashton... leading negotiations with Iran on behalf of six world powers" seated at the exclusive negotiating table between US Secretary of State John Kerry and Iranian Foreign Minister Mohammad

Javad Zarif (Gearan 2014). Less visibly, American death-row inmates, and millions of US surgery patients, also face the impact of the EU's foreign policy. In October 2013 Missouri's governor "halted what was to have been the first execution in the United States to use the anesthetic propofol, following threats from the European Union to limit export of the drug if it was used to carry out the death penalty" (*USA Today* 2013). The decision to call off the execution was driven by the fact that the European-produced drug is the leading anesthetic used in America's hospitals and clinics, and nearly 90 percent of the US supply of propofol is imported from Europe.

The debate will continue over how much these various episodes truly impact or shape world politics. But it is clear that important individuals, groups, and organizations are acting "as if" the EU is a legitimate, taken-for-granted actor in international politics. In the examples above, various actors implicitly characterize the EU as cohesive and important enough to spy on, to generate worrisome threats over the crashing of a global supply chain, to award a prize to for its contribution to peace, or to look to as a key negotiator in a tense nuclear standoff. Moreover, the EU is not discussed just as any actor, but one that is natural to mention in the same breath as the world's most powerful, sovereign nation states. From this perspective, US diplomatic or military officials who scoff at the EU's inability to match the US in its geopolitical importance are unexpectedly paying a backhand compliment to the EU, even as they rightly find Europe lacking in the ability and willingness to project power abroad *à l'Américaine*.

What social and political mechanisms have produced this strange outcome? One key dynamic rests in the cultural processes constructing social facts and in classification, discussed in Chapters 2 and 3. Classification does important work in making sense of the world around us and stabilizing our shared expectations (Bourdieu 1984, 1999; Zerubavel 1999). Lumping the EU into the same category as the US helps to reframe Europe as a sovereign actor, despite its novelty. This process of meaning construction is reinforced, as we will see, through the slow build-up of an array of symbols and practices that label, map, and narrate the EU across a range of foreign policy arenas. In turn, this naturalizes and makes palatable the EU's new political authority even as it does not inoculate it from criticism.

As in the previous policy areas surveyed in earlier chapters, the particular symbols and practices generated by the EU are often quite banal in nature, as they must finesse national prerogatives and shy away from the most contested issues of foreign policy. Europe is far better at saying things than doing things, and what it says is often facile or irrelevant when international events move quickly. Still, the EU is simultaneously deepening its governance while also navigating around the political identities and powers of its member states. In the foreign policy area, the task is much more difficult. Foreign policy cuts right to the heart of state sovereignty, directly challenging the EU's legitimacy. It therefore presents the hardest case for my argument that we should understand the EU as a case of comparative political development in ways similar to the rise of the nation state. While earlier chapters analyzed areas such as "buildings, spectacles, and songs" (Chapter 4) that are not overtly challenging to core state powers, subsequent chapters on citizenship and mobility (Chapter 5), and the euro and single market (Chapter 6), move along a continuum towards policy areas much more linked to the historical centralization of power and authority of the nation state. This final empirical chapter takes up foreign policy as the core state power that would seem difficult to naturalize as "European" using only symbols and practices. Yet the EU has in fact done so, to a surprising extent.

We will see in this chapter that the EU has gone about its foreign policy in ways that construct itself as a sovereign actor, but one that is notably defanged, easing the transfer of foreign policy capacity toward Europe. The EU borrows nation state forms and labels, but makes them banal by design, with a welter of confusing acronyms and multiple, overlapping institutions. Key foreign policy leadership positions are given opaque names and are often filled by uncharismatic individuals. The actual substance of EU foreign policy departs sharply from traditional national security by focusing on overwhelmingly deracinated, "post-national" human security concerns, rather than defense of territory or the projection of force abroad. In addition, just as in other policy realms such as citizenship or the economy, the symbols and practices of EU foreign policy are always "localized," in an effort to legitimize this highly sensitive shift in authority. EU foreign policy actions are nested upward within political institutions such as NATO and the United Nations, or nested downward in networked groups of member-state military forces. Deracinating security issues and localizing EU security efforts in multilateral and member-state institutions in this way builds an important cultural foundation for the shifts that are occurring, albeit haltingly, in the foreign policy arena.

This chapter begins with a brief discussion of the role of cultural dynamics in foreign policy, reminding us of the importance of social logics, as well as material motivations, in producing outcomes in international relations. I then briefly review the surprising historical evolution of European foreign policy, highlighting the slow institutionalization of EU diplomatic capacity and increasing security coordination. I then empirically catalog some of the symbols and practices that label, map, and narrate European foreign policy. The legal construction of the EU as a sovereign actor, the creation of European diplomats, the development of a European grand strategy, and the networking of European security forces are examined in turn. The conclusion returns to my argument that the naturalization of the EU as a social fact in the world of foreign affairs is occurring even in this most unlikely of arenas for the EU to legitimate its authority. The meanings generated from European foreign policy form a key part of the creation of a broader imagined community of Europe, but they also demonstrate that this community is one with substantial built-in limits and weaknesses.

What Does Culture Have to Do with Foreign Policy?

We normally think of foreign policy as the realm of high politics—the stuff of missile silos, shuttle diplomacy, and geopolitical crises. What does culture have to do with such things? But just as with the other policy areas examined in earlier chapters, when culture is defined as a dynamic process of meaning making shared across some particular group of people, it is evident that culture plays a central role in foreign policy. The seminal work of Alexander Wendt emphasizes how broad, historically contingent cultures shape the basic assumptions guiding state-to-state relations (Wendt 1999). Social structures and actors' identities vary importantly in Wendt's account, constituting the basic assumptions and dynamics of international politics. Peter Katzenstein and colleagues demonstrated the role of culture in the generation of specific national security strategies and in the regimes that developed across a wide range of issues, including the use of chemical weapons (Katzenstein 1996). For example, we can see how a transformation in the broader cultural views about universal human rights shifted policy assumptions about humanitarian intervention and enabled the campaign for R2P, the UN's "Responsibility to Protect" initiative starting in the mid-2000s. Likewise, the liberalization of world trade and investment has been understood to be partly a function of the rise of the culture of neoliberalism that informed foreign economic policy decisions (Meyer et al. 1997).

Scholars have more recently examined how the symbolic representations and practices that frame policymakers' and leaders' understandings of each other and the environment they work within are critical to the stabilization of their interactions, be they NATO negotiations, the meaning of the 9/11 attacks, or Chinese foreign policy (Johnston 1995; Krebs and Lobasz 2007; Pouliot 2010). While culture stabilizes interactions by fixing expectations, those interactions are not necessarily positive or welfare enhancing, as social structures and identities may produce the deadlock of cold war or the horrors of genocide. In the EU, however, the social structures generated through integration have produced "a pacific security community" with "an extremely dense institutional and symbolic environment where common understandings and practices are produced and reproduced (Mérand, Foucault, and Irondelle 2011: 15). Viewed this way, the security side of foreign policy is a "structured and hierarchical social space" where social representations, even if contested, shape policy outcomes (Mérand 2008: 13). These cultures of meaning making become institutionalized self-sustaining systems, out of any one actor's control even if initially promulgated by particular self-serving interests.

Situating foreign policy in terms of this understanding of culture allows us to see more clearly the EU's challenge to the accepted, "taken-for-granted" meaning making that infuses international politics. Despite the talk of new global governance forms in the twenty-first century, the nation state remains the *ne plus ultra* of a legitimated, standardized, and accepted political form in the international system (Krasner 1999). Foreign policy is the area where status as a sovereign state is the most consequential, determining who can act, how other states treat you, and legitimating or undermining your claims. Foreign policy also seems to demand a single, authorized political agent to negotiate, bargain, and act within an international system made up of unified, territorial, hierarchical nation states. While the EU can adopt national symbols and practices of diplomacy, those actions can easily be a lightning rod for political pushback if the EU is too obviously isomorphic in copying nation states. "National" security is hard to make banal and, by definition, hard to denationalize. Any cultural symbols and practices constructing the EU as a foreign policy actor do so in a minefield of strongly nationalist sentiments (Meyer and Jepperson 2000). So the puzzle remains: how can the EU legitimate itself and be an accepted actor given this uneasy relationship with nationness?

The EU's Foreign Policy Evolution

As the introduction of this chapter indicated, European foreign policy has been less of a policy than the butt of jokes and derision over the course of decades, especially on the American side of the Atlantic. Frustrations with the EU's lack of centralized decision making on foreign policy is encapsulated in a quote attributed to (but later disavowed by) former US national security advisor Henry Kissinger: "When I want to speak to Europe, who do I call?" Into the 2000s, most textbooks and scholarly encyclopedias about the EU did not even include Europe's foreign policy as a topic (Carlsnaes 2006: 545). Scholars have debated for years to figure out how to conceptualize Europe's role as, among others, a civilian power (Duchêne 1972, 1973) or a normative power projecting its values into the world (Manners 2002). A widely read essay compared the EU (and not positively) as Venus to America's Mars, arguing that while the US was a forceful global presence projecting its power and stabilizing the world, the EU could do little but tidy up around the edges (Kagan

2002). Christopher Hill's influential work framed the issue of European foreign policy as one of a "capabilities-expectation" gap, where the progress in European integration across other policy realms had created an expectation that the very real material and political power that rests in the individual nations of the EU should translate more forcefully into a single foreign policy (Hill 1993). More recently, Toje (2010) has characterized the EU as a "small power," while Damro (2012) has presented it as a "market power" which becomes less and less powerful the more it tries to move beyond the realms of low politics (see also Newman and Bache 2007).

For some observers, arguably the most important foreign policy of the EU lies in its unique ability to promote regime change abroad through the incentive of EU membership. The EU fundamentally shaped the paths of Greece, Spain, and Portugal, and more recently, a dozen countries in Central and Eastern Europe, through membership. Establishing a series of criteria for the transition to democracy and liberalization of markets, and providing the legal, bureaucratic, and financial support to help with those transitions, has been a powerful source for change. The EU's decision to tamper down the prospect of membership to other states, such as Turkey, has been equally consequential (see Smith 2008). This type of external leverage is unique to the EU, however, and does not fit easily into traditional understandings of foreign policy.

The EU is not a superpower in conventional terms. While its combined gross domestic product (GDP) and military strength puts it, in material terms, at the top of the list of powerful states (Moravcsik 2010), its ability to project that power internationally lags far behind the United States. But if the EU does not have a robust, unified, single foreign policy, it does have a significant common foreign policy (Smith 2003; Smith and Ginsberg 2007; Hill and Smith 2011). The EU is formulating highly coordinated external policies, institutionalizing relationships across its own national foreign policy elites, creating ongoing bureaucracies to support these policies, and growing a generation of European diplomats who cannot remember a time when their policymaking did not involve consultation and coordination across their EU partners (Cross 2007; Adler-Nissen 2014). These processes do not simply replicate traditional nation state foreign policies, making it harder to see them as such. But if we step back and look across the EU's security, economic, environmental, and cultural policies, we can get a sense of the overall weight of the EU in the world.

European foreign policy is first and foremost institutionally centered on its formal Common Foreign and Security Policy (CFSP) and its military subset, the Common (formerly "European") Security and Defence Policy (CSDP). Beyond CFSP, however, the EU has an extensive list of activities that constitute what is often called its "external relations," encompassing peacekeeping;

democracy building; association agreements with a variety of countries; commercial, regulatory, and investment policies; trade policies in the World Trade Organization; the world's largest foreign aid program; a nuclear proliferation sanctions regime; joint European arms development and production; and episodes of strong geopolitical cooperation (Carlsnaes 2006; Hix and Hoyland 2011: 302–30; Lavenex and Peterson 2012; Peterson 2012b). Beyond the EU level, national foreign polices are coordinated and linked in a variety of ways that create a European profile and impact, even as they remain administratively sited within the member states (Lucarelli 2006: 9).

Most of these activities have been adopted relatively recently, but the entire European integration project itself arguably originated because of security concerns. As discussed in Chapter 1, after World War II, Europe's founding leaders were focused on the need to promote peace and stability across their previously warring states, particularly in the context of a new Soviet threat. Their innovative answer in the early 1950s was to bind those states together in the European Coal and Steel Community (ECSC), putting Franco-German war-making capability at the service of rebuilding the Continent instead of making war. In 1952, France, Germany, the Benelux states, and Italy agreed to a plan for a tightly integrated European Defence Community (EDC), which would have revolutionized European relations. The EDC appeared poised to become law until French elections unexpectedly shifted France's National Assembly against the plan and it failed in 1954.

Despite the demise of the joint European defense plan, the early 1950s saw forward movement on the creation of a European foreign policy in the economic realm. Signed in 1957, the Treaty of Rome, the key "constitution" of the EU, established Europe's Common Market at the core of the new European Economic Community (EEC). With a customs union came the need for common external European trade policy and the legal authority to conduct trade negotiations. Sovereign power in this area was granted to the EEC and Europe morphed into a much more highly integrated and institutionalized single European market (discussed in Chapter 6). As subsequent multilateral General Agreement on Tariffs and Trade (GATT) rounds slashed a host of high interwar barriers to trade, the EEC successfully took a seat at the negotiating table and undertook a common foreign policy in trade (Meunier 2000, 2005; Young and Peterson 2014: 48–70). By the late 1960s, the EU was well on its way to acting as a cohesive foreign policy presence in the economic realm.

Geopolitics did not completely take a back seat, however, as the EU's member states called in 1969 for enhanced European Political Cooperation (EPC), creating new, routinized interactions among foreign ministers and heads of government although outside the formal treaty structure. This loose intergovernmental framework was a way to leverage those specific, if rare, instances where national preferences converged. The EPC framework did produce some success in the 1970s and 1980s in forging collective diplomacy on key contentious issues such as the Arab–Israeli conflict and Europe's relationship with the Soviet Union (Smith 2004: 2). However, in the midst of the collapse of the Soviet Union and the revolutions across Central and Eastern Europe, the Gulf War, and notably, the instability and genocide in the war in Yugoslavia, it was clear that the EU was far from an effective foreign policy actor (Peterson 2012: 205).

The EU's foreign policy aspirations took a big institutional leap forward with the Treaty on European Union signed in Maastricht in 1992. Maastricht codified the existing disparate foreign policy activities, brought them under the EU's institutional framework, and gave the new CFSP treaty status, as well as establishing the Justice and Home Affairs policy area for internal security matters. Yet despite the creation of new institutions, national preferences for joint European action still lagged.

A key turning point was the 1998 Franco-British summit that produced the St Malo Declaration, promoting closer operational military cooperation in the face of ignominious failures to end the violence in the Balkans and Kosovo. Drawing on the so-called "Petersburg Tasks"—an already established list of European defense priorities of humanitarian operations, peacekeeping, military crisis management, and "peace making" (the last term was, revealingly, left undefined)—the EU codified its security priorities in the Treaty of Amsterdam, which came into force in 1999. The Nice Treaty of 2003 further deepened the institutionalization of CFSP with addition of a subset of policies, the European Security and Defence Policy, focused exclusively on military affairs. Rather than being a traditional defense alliance, it had an open-ended mandate, encompassing deeper political integration and subsidization of joint European defense industries (Mérand 2008: 2). The Nice Treaty also created the EU-level Political and Security Committee to support coordination among national foreign ministers, and even a Military Committee to coax operational cooperation from its members. These legal and institutional changes very gradually transformed national practices around the creation and conduct of foreign and security policy toward more intensive and routinized cooperation across national capitals, even as much of the basis for the security policies remained intergovernmental, rather than supranational (Smith 2004).

A seeming setback to the progress of European foreign policy occurred with the 2005 rejection by referendum voters in France and Holland of the European Constitution. As discussed more fully in Chapter 8, the constitution would have created a new single position coordinating all of the disparate external policies of the EU, the "Union Minister for Foreign Affairs," as well as a variety of institutional, voting, and semantic changes to make the EU conform more closely with nation state terminology and practices. Despite the constitution's failure, many of the initiatives were then repackaged without the offending symbols and language, and put into the Lisbon Treaty, which came into force in 2009. Lisbon moved the EU closer to a coherent, single foreign policy, as certain issues of internal security were no longer subject to the unanimity requirement but rather could be decided by qualified majority voting. The European Parliament also granted co-decision rights, broadening the democratic and supranational quality of at least one part of the EU's security policy. A new position, the High Representative of the Union for Foreign Affairs and Security Policy, was created to replace a less powerful foreign policy chief and the new European External Action Service (EEAS) was created as a dedicated EU diplomatic corps to support the EU's foreign policies (Adler-Nissen 2014). Lisbon also strengthened the European Defence Agency, which coordinates the objectives and operations of the EU's security policies.

The former European Security and Defence Policy was rebranded, with Lisbon, as the Common Security and Defence Policy (CSDP). A new "common European defence" section was inserted into the founding EU treaties, with a "solidarity clause" binding its signatories. Tasks now explicitly under the purview of the CSDP included the Petersburg Tasks of humanitarian and rescue missions, conflict prevention and peacekeeping, tasks of combat forces in situations of crisis management, disarmament operations, military advice and assistance, and post-conflict stabilization. These tasks are carried out using the assets of the member states, and can be delegated to specific states or groups of states, including multinational forces. Since its founding, there have been over two dozen small military operations carried out under the EU's CSDP. They have all, in some way, been executed in tandem with either NATO or the broader UN peacekeeping and rule-of-law organizations.

Yet longstanding and persistent differences remain across the national capitals of the EU on foreign policy, evidenced by the disagreement over how to deal with the 2003 US invasion of Iraq. Joint large-scale military action on the part of Europe is not ruled out, as evidenced by France's actions in Africa and elsewhere, or by the presence of 8,000 EU troops (in UN "blue helmets") in Lebanon since 2006. But the security tasks carried out under the EU flag are marked by low-intensity and small-scale operations, not the long-term, large-scale operations of NATO, or even of the UK or France acting alone. Moreover, the CSDP has "evolved from a concentration of military crisis management operations" to an almost exclusive focus on "long-term civilian stabilization operations and other security-related activities such as counterterrorism and combating the proliferation of weapons of mass destruction" (Bickerton, Irondelle, and Menon 2011: 4).

Big structural barriers to the development of a common foreign policy remain: insufficient funding, organizational complexity, barriers to interoperability across national militaries, a broader backlash against the European project, the inability to converge on policies, and the persistence of the national veto in the area of foreign policy (Krotz 2009: 563–8). Nonetheless, a visitor today to Berlaymont, the EU's headquarters in Brussels, would see military uniforms routinely, whereas there were none before 2000. And non-traditional security issues such as climate change, human rights, cybersecurity, and counterterrorism have certainly become fully coordinated and implemented through the EU institutions in partnership with the member states (Lavenex and Peterson 2012: 187).

This brief outline of the development of the EU's foreign policy demonstrates bumpy but continued progress toward a true foreign policy capacity: from the initial postwar fights over whether to create a "European Defence Community," to the building up of capacity in Brussels for external trade and other commercial policies, to highly visible failures of EU collective action in the wars in the former Yugoslavia, to the more recent development of a set of foreign policy actors and institutions. It points to the layering of institutions and policies in the EU foreign policy realm and the increasing tempo of those activities in the 2000s and beyond.

These various EU foreign policy activities are not only important in instrumental, material terms, but because of their cultural role in naturalizing the EU as a legitimate site of political authority. Processes of labeling, mapping, and narrating are at work in the realm of foreign policy, just as they are in the other areas we have examined in earlier chapters—but with a difference. The representations and practices around European foreign policy attempt simultaneously to mimic the traditional sovereign state while also creating an alternative basis for a post-national political authority at the European level. This task is much more difficult and requires political and symbolic finesse beyond the empirical areas surveyed in earlier chapters. The very real tensions in this project are evident as we survey some examples of the ways in which an imagined community of Europeans is being built, and the particular part played by the EU as a global actor. Below, I assess four specific examples of the EU's construction as a foreign policy actor: the symbols and practices around its international legal personality, the development of an EU diplomatic corps, the European Security Strategy (ESS), and the networked European military. The cultural construction occurring in these realms can tell us a lot about the particular type of emergent political entity the EU is, and thus what we can expect from it going forward.

Labeling the EU: International Law and Sovereign States

Diplomacy depends in part on the recognition, or not, of the legitimate representatives of political entities. While just a few centuries ago those actors might have included popes, monarchs, or emperors, in the modern era, international diplomacy has been an overwhelmingly state-to-state endeavor. When in 1994, our ailing planet's most important international treaty on climate change went into force, 194 of its signatories practiced their diplomatic prerogative within the standard sovereign nation state model. Only the 195th signature on the UN Framework Convention on Climate Change broke the mold, coming as it did from the EU. Europe is not, of course, a sovereign nation state, yet it appears in Annex I of the Treaty, alongside its own member states and a host of others (Baker 2006; Afionis 2009). Climate change is far from the only international diplomatic setting where the EU takes a place alongside sovereign states in negotiating and contracting international legal commitments. What was once the purview of the sovereign nation state is now partially and incompletely shared with the EU, as "virtually every country on earth is linked to the EU through a formal agreement" (Smith 2008: 55).

Placing the EU, even if tenuously, in a category built for sovereign states creates a set of expectations and understandings about what the EU is, even if the categorization is contested. Categories are powerful tools to divide the social world, and we rely on a shared sense of "this, and not that" to interpret the world, to bargain over its spoils, and to draw lines of affinity or conflict. The way we classify the world is both a product of the way we think, and a causal force that constitutes the social identities of those classified. As Bourdieu notes, the principles of "vision and division" of the social world that are bound up in classificatory schemes are a type of symbolic power that generates social order (Bourdieu 1998: 53). The labeling of the EU as a sovereign actor is important not only because of the specific policy achievements or failures that come with the EU's actions, but because these processes serve to naturalize the idea of the EU as a legitimate actor in international politics. Acceptance in multilateral regimes such as the United Nations climate change framework sends a signal about the power and capacity of the EU. Even in the more informal settings of the G8 or G20 global summits, the photos sent around the world of the first post-Lisbon Treaty EU president, the (deeply uncharismatic) Herman Van Rompuy, have symbolic weight. They signal EU sovereign actorness in a way that is concrete and imbued with the status that comes from appearing with the most powerful leaders in the world. This symbolic representation of the EU matters, even if the EU's ultimate decision-making capacity in fact lies elsewhere, with national leaders.

Yet the EU's official role in international legal settings varies widely, unlike the uniform sovereignty granted to nation states. Trade diplomacy is where the EU mimics nation states most closely and most effectively. Built into the foundation of the EU is its exclusive competence for international trade negotiations, whether bilateral, regional, or multilateral trade (Meunier and Nicolaïdes 1999,

2006). The World Trade Organization thus remains the place where the EU is the most legally and politically unified in foreign policy, speaking as a single voice, projecting its preferences as a single, global actor and using its massive economic weight as a power resource to achieve its goals. Even with the end of the big multilateral GATT trade rounds, the EU has continued to frame its trade positions in a unified way, using the Dispute Resolution Settlement system to project its power (Meunier and Nicolaïdes 1999). In the trade realm, the symbolic representation of EU negotiators hashing out anti-dumping rules for mobile telecom networks long into the night with their American and Chinese counterparts, and the routinized habits of referring to the "EU's position" on issues of foreign economic policy, have all contributed to the construction of the EU as a global actor. More recently, the EU has gained the power to take over negotiations over the liberalization and harmonization of rules regarding investment flows (Meunier 2014). As the EU is the world's largest inward receiver and outward sender of foreign direct investment, this creates the potential for big material impacts in the world (Niemann 2012). The EU's first effort under this new competence is a major symbolic coup: a new Bilateral Investment Treaty (BIT) negotiation with China.

The construction of the EU as a global actor has also gained weight with the more recent codification of its so-called "legal personality" in the Lisbon Treaty (Sieberson 2008: 17). Legal personality is the polite fiction of an organizational entity taking on the characteristics of personhood. Sovereign states have it, corporations have it, and various international organizations (including nongovernmental organizations like Amnesty International) have it. The very words used to describe this categorization link decisively to the image of a single voice, symbolizing the embodiment of the EU's political authority. In practice, however, and in contrast to nation states, the EU may have either exclusive, shared, or no competence in representing the EU in international settings, depending on the situation (Jørgensen, Oberthur, and Shahin 2011). Competence can range from providing policy content to member states (as with the International Monetary Fund), to signing treaties as an actor itself (the World Trade Organization or the Northwest Atlantic Fisheries Organization), to signing alongside the member states (UN Framework Convention on Climate Change and the Kyoto Protocol, the Convention on the Rights of Persons with Disabilities), or to needing to reestablish competence for each particular meeting (the Food and Agriculture Organization) (Wessels 2011: 624, 629). The EU is a de facto but not an official full member in the Organization for Economic Cooperation and Development, the postwar club for industrialized economies located in Paris. This wide variation in the extent of EU international legal sovereignty fits the notion of the EU as an emergent political entity whose authority is still ambiguous and contested in a world of sovereign states.

Arguably the most visible site of nationness in diplomacy in the modern era is the United Nations General Assembly. The EU is not recognized as a full member there. After foreign policy changes within the Lisbon Treaty, however, it now has "enhanced" observer status and can represent the EU on issues where there is a common position (Wessels 2011: 631). The lack of UN representation makes sense given the sensitivity of national sovereignty issues. The particularly circumscribed authority of the EU expresses itself more easily in the specific groupings of the UN over issues of fishing or corruption, where the symbols and practices of diplomacy can be made more banal and deracinated than in the General Assembly.

The modern state system is built on the notion of legal sovereignty, of a nation state acting as a unitary body with its own rights and obligations. Recognition of that status is key to being able to participate in international diplomacy, to sign treaties, or to sit at the table when intergovernmental negotiations are held. Think of the difficulties faced by actors not recognized as the sole representative of their territorially exclusive area, such as opposition forces in Assad's Syria. The efforts to construct the EU as a social fact to the outside world matter perhaps the most for diplomats. Can political authority adhere to the EU as a new actor without decisively shifting away from the member states? The next section looks more closely at the embodiment of international sovereign actorness through the creation of an EU diplomatic service.

The Mouse That Squeaked? Embodying a "European" Foreign Policy

Diplomacy—negotiations, the signing of treaties—requires diplomats. In the EU, a new cadre of diplomats has been created to embody Europe's foreign policy, to "practice the EU" in their diplomatic actions, and to construct Europe as an actor in the international system. The Lisbon Treaty ushered in these new diplomats, but under titles and labels that are slightly out of focus and that seem to downplay their powers. Consider the most visible European diplomat created with Lisbon, the new "High Representative of the Union for Foreign Affairs and Security Policy." British politician Baroness Catherine Ashton was appointed at the end of 2009 to hold the new post. For the first time in the EU's history, there is one single foreign policy chief to preside over the complex series of policies and programs that make up the EU's external relations, and to chair the meetings of the national foreign ministers with an eye toward building consensus. Finally, the complaint purportedly made by Kissinger that "there is no one to call when you need to speak to Europe" would be put to rest. The squabbling of the member states over divisive issues such as supporting the US invasion of Iraq, or how to deal with Russia, would be worked out and a strong, unified position now could be projected in diplomatic affairs. Or would it?

Critics immediately complained that Ashton was a person with little international political standing and minimal foreign policy experience. Although of rising importance in the British Labour Party, she was not viewed as having the necessary "gravitas," particularly in comparison with the pre-Lisbon EU foreign policy head, the charismatic and forceful Javier Solana. A British foreign office source was quoted as saying: "The appointment of her and Herman Van Rompuy [as European Council president] were a complete disgrace. They are no more than garden gnomes" (Watt 2009). The *Wall Street Journal* opined that far from putting the EU on the map, the appointment of Ashton (and Van Rompuy) seemed to say "Nothing to See Here" (*Wall Street Journal* 2009). *The Economist* magazine ran a story entitled "Behold, two mediocre mice," referring to Ashton and Van Rompuy (*The Economist* 2009).

But the appointment of the low-profile Ashton may be a case of banality by design, in keeping with the particular construction of the EU's political authority. Ashton was chosen after intensive horse-trading over the two new EU positions among leaders, including French president Nicolas Sarkozy, German chancellor Angela Merkel, and UK prime minister Gordon Brown. They ended up initially filling these revolutionary new positions with people who would temper the potential for an overt contestation with the prerogatives of the nation state. Such navigation of the national symbols and practices of diplomacy on the part of the EU is clear not only by the choice of the self-styled "grey mouse" Ashton, but also when we notice that the new position is not called the EU Foreign Secretary, as it would be in the UK, or Minister for Foreign Affairs as in Germany or France. Instead, it is called the High Representative of the Union for Foreign Affairs and Security Policy. The long and confusing name, which few can remember, is often shortened to "High Rep." Originally called the "Minister for Foreign Affairs" in the European Constitution, after the failure of the national ratification process in 2005 the name was amended in the subsequent Lisbon Treaty. A "Minister for Foreign Affairs" sounds much more federal, state-like, and therefore important, after all, than a High Representative, which could mean almost anything.

The high representative is also head of the reorganized, strengthened, and renamed body of EU diplomats, the European External Action Service (EEAS), a second innovation of the Lisbon Treaty (David 2012; Bátora 2013; Adler-Nissen 2014). The EEAS establishes an expanded, permanent, and institutionalized European diplomatic corps, but one that is called by the obscure label of "External Action Service" rather than a Foreign Service or Diplomatic Service. Prior to 2009, EU diplomatic activities of a more limited scope and size had previously been carried out under the system of Delegations of the

European Commission, made up of civil servants rather than professional diplomats (Bruter 1999; Cross 2007). Now placed under the high representa- tive, the EEAS diplomats signal representation not of one bureaucratic part of Europe (the European Commission), but of the whole of Europe. While rec- ognized as traditional embassies under international law, as per the Vienna Convention of 1961, the offices of the EEAS are still not called EU embas- sies, but rather "Delegations of the EU." Nonetheless, the head of the del- egation goes by the title of EU Ambassador, and is received as such when presenting credentials to their host country, as EU Ambassador to the US João Vale de Almeida did to US president Barack Obama at the White House in August 2010.

Why should any of these labels and positions matter for the EU's political authority? As discussed in Chapter 2, the names we use for things have causal force, as they categorize and constitute the world in ways that may be implicit but still do social and political work as "speech acts" (Austin 1962; Searle 1969; Butler 1993). Diplomacy is a game of power, but is also a game of recog- nition, negotiation, and status. Yet the new, post-Lisbon Treaty foreign policy apparatus seems designed to place the EU on the board game of diplomacy in ways that both strengthen its presence while also tempering its power and legitimacy. In the diplomatic world, as in other social realms, status is in part conferred through the official title you hold, and the mimicry of the trap- pings of modern, sovereign states would suggest that the EU should aggres- sively try to mold itself on the legitimated titles already in existence. After the failure of the European Constitution and its EU Minister of Foreign Affairs, the EU instead returned to titles that sound vaguely familiar but seem to navigate around the nation state. While this has allowed for the slow march of EU foreign policy to proceed, it reveals the limits of the projection of the EU's foreign policy power to Washington, Moscow, or Beijing.

In practice, most media accounts use "EU foreign minister" or "foreign policy chief" to describe Ashton, unconsciously subverting the careful cho- reography of labels and placing the EU squarely back in the same category as sovereign states. This common usage creates a challenge to the efforts of the national leaders, particularly the British, to downplay the diplomatic weight of the high representative position. Some of Ashton's most high-profile efforts have been in international negotiations with Iran over its nuclear plans. In the so-called "P5 +1" talks, the EU has played a prominent role along- side the UN Security Council's P5 states (the US, China, Russia, the UK, and France), aligning itself with the widely viewed "world powers" in the practice of high-stakes diplomacy. This categorization of the EU in the same breath as the most powerful states in the international system is surprising, and reverberates back on the EU despite being "under the radar," and despite the putatively banal nature of the high representative's position and reputation.

Meanwhile, the day-to-day work of the EEAS in the trenches of diplomacy around the world is likely to also consolidate the EU as an actor in terms of the general public (Bruter 1999).

Narrating European Foreign Policy: A Grand Strategy for Venus?

What is the particular narrative generated by the EU's foreign policy symbols and practices? How might that narrative shape the content of the EU's imagined community and, ultimately, its legitimacy as a political authority? A series of key EU texts and declarations portray a European foreign policy that is congruent with, and unthreatening to, national sovereignty. The narrative has two main lines of argument: first, European security is sharply delinked from its traditional relationship to defense of national territory, and geared instead toward "human security" objectives. Instead of being concerned with balance of power issues, the EU's foreign policy is directed toward threats to humanity such as climate change, genocide, peacekeeping, or cyberterrorism. Second, in the EU narrative, these goals are further distanced from national interests by being nested inside NATO and the United Nations, transnational international organizations whose actions presumably reflect collective ideals and goals, not national interests. The Maastricht Treaty language establishing Europe's initial foreign policy capacity, the subsequent St Malo and Laeken Declarations, and the official European Security Strategy document all project a vision of the EU's rightful role in the world. This vision rests on these two precepts (human security and legitimation through NATO and the UN), allowing the EU to take a position alongside nation states yet also to pacify internal critics wary of the shift of sovereignty to Brussels.

The Maastricht Treaty first established the institutional framework for the EU's Common Foreign and Security Policy (CFSP) in 1992, and its five key objectives set the tone for what was to come. Maastricht outlined the goals of CFSP as strengthening the security of the EU in accordance with the UN Charter; preserving peace; promoting international cooperation; and developing and consolidating democracy and the rule of law, including human rights. A series of statements continued to refine the foreign policy objectives of the EU, and frame the narrative around it while projecting a subtly ambitious view of the EU's potential place in the world. One such text was the 2001 Laeken Declaration, a statement from a European Summit, which calls for Europe to play a "leading role" in the "new world order," both stabilizing the world and able "to point the way ahead for many countries and peoples." This leading role is appropriate, according to this declaration, because Europe is no less than the "continent of human values, the Magna Carta, the Bill of Rights, the French Revolution and the fall of the Berlin Wall, the continent of liberty, solidarity and above all diversity, meaning respect for other's languages, cultures and traditions" (European Council 2001). The Laeken Declaration notably frames Europe as a "power" doing battle against the ills of the world, rather than against the states of the world (Biscop 2001: 132; European Council 2001).

While these texts portray the pursuit of European foreign policy as a natural and laudable activity, the actual reality of the EU's foreign policy differed sharply. The early years of the CSDP saw leaders making use of the constructive ambiguity of these various official statements to fashion a loose narrative about the purpose and methods of the EU's security policy. But they continued to struggle to keep the diverse and conflicting foreign policy traditions of French Europeanism, British Atlanticism, and German federalism under one fold (Norheim-Martinsen 2013). The limits of such a posture became clear in the wake of the profound split that opened up between EU member states that supported and those that opposed US president George W. Bush's invasion of Iraq in 2003.

Partly in response to this split over post-9/11 US strategy, EU member states supported the drafting and adoption of a formal document, the European Security Strategy (ESS), at the Brussels European Council on December 12, 2003. Titled "A Secure Europe in a Better World: European Security Strategy," the document attempted to create a coherent overall framework or grand strategy for European foreign policy. It was drawn up astonishingly quickly: seven months from creation to adoption. EU foreign policy chief Javier Solana and his staff exploited the reservoir of anger about US unilateralism under George W. Bush to come up with a consolidated European position (Norheim-Martinsen 2013: 41). The 2003 document, with some updating, is today used as a point of reference for the ongoing external affairs activities of the EU.

The ESS, as a public policy document, is not an original innovation but rather directly mimics the template pioneered by the most powerful sovereign nation state in the international system, the United States. US presidents are required by law to periodically draft an official National Security Strategy document. This important focal point for foreign policy has been viewed as a mechanism for developing consensus across the US government, setting priorities for budgeting, and legitimating US security policies. The symbols and practices of US grand strategy constitute a cultural resource for EU officials seeing to legitimate Europe as an actor in the international system. This European mimicry was done very consciously by national leaders and policymakers in Brussels who wanted to set Europe on a similar footing with the US in international politics, while projecting a very different European foreign policy rooted in multilateralism and obedience to international law (Toje 2005: 120; Dannreuther and Peterson 2006; Norheim-Martinsen 2013: 42).

The ESS conveys important information about the aspirational direction and meaning of European foreign policy. The title itself suggests a clear break with traditional national security: "A Secure Europe in a Better World" deftly shifts the unit of analysis and the focus of concern from the member states themselves to Europe, and then beyond to a collective humanity, without borders. While US national security documents start with a straightforward assessment of perceived foreign threats to US interests, the ESS starts not with pragmatics, but with principle: a rationale and defense of the very idea of a common European foreign policy as informing a more evolved paradigm of international cooperation. While the US documents have framed their grand strategies in terms of specific adversaries (Islamic jihadists, or a rising China), the EU has issues, not adversaries (so climate change becomes a security threat). Where the National Security Strategy talks about US values of freedom and liberalism, the ESS leverages what has been called the "founding myth" of the EU to frame its security narrative (Schimmelfennig 2003; Gilbert 2008). The ESS text proclaims:

> Europe has never been so prosperous, so secure nor so free. The violence of the first half of the 20th Century has given way to a period of peace and stability unprecedented in European history.
>
> The creation of the European Union has been central to this development. It has transformed the relations between our states, and the lives of our citizens. European countries are committed to dealing peacefully with disputes and to co-operating through common institutions. Over this period, the progressive spread of the rule of law and democracy has seen authoritarian regimes change into secure, stable and dynamic democracies. Successive enlargements are making a reality of the vision of a united and peaceful continent. (ESS 2003: 1)

The message is clear: institution building, rule of law, and democracy under the EU's particular form of political union are the keys to peace, wealth, and freedom. This vision of utopian cosmopolitanism and Kantian peace rests not on the exercise of power, but institution building—on carrots, not sticks (Cooper 2003). Although the ESS admits the importance of the US in providing for the world's military security, it rejects the notion of unilateral power as the answer to future security challenges, stating:

> The US has played a critical role in European integration and European security, in particular through NATO. The end of the Cold War has left the US in a dominant position as a military actor. However, no single country is able to tackle today's complex problems on its own. (ESS 2003: 1)

The ESS elaborates by stating categorically that "Large-scale aggression against any Member State is now improbable. Instead, Europe faces new threats which are more diverse, less visible and less predictable" including terrorism, the spread of weapons of mass destruction, regional conflict, state failure, and organized crime. To deal with these challenges requires international law and effective multilateralism, as "The fundamental framework for international relations is the United Nations Charter" in a "rule-based international order" (ESS 2003: 9). But those countries that "have placed themselves outside the bounds of international society" and "persistently violate international norms... should understand that there is a price to be paid, including in their relationship with the European Union," although the EU also stands ready to offer assistance to those that are willing to come back into the fold of civilized nations.

What is the precise role of force and military action in dealing with these pariah states outside the pacific order? The ESS talks of preemptive engagement, not preemptive military action—of cooperation, dialogue, and partnership. The last section of the ESS gingerly takes up the question of use of force, stating that "We need to develop a strategic culture that fosters early, rapid, and when necessary, robust intervention" working with its partners and creating institutional capacity for action that leads to a "safer and more united world" (ESS 2003: 11, 14). This potential can only be achieved, in this telling, by integrating across all the various parts of the EU's foreign policy, including aid, trade, diplomacy, as well as military actions (Norheim-Martinsen 2013: 48). Any EU military action should always support the principles elucidated in the so-called Petersburg Tasks: "joint disarmament operations, humanitarian and rescue tasks, military advice and assistance tasks, tasks of combat forces in crisis management, including peace-making and post-conflict stabilization."

The overall narrative of the EU's foreign policy reinforces EU public values that depart from those expressed in polling data in the US and China (Manners 2006). Europeans are concerned about genetically modified organisms (GMOs) and technology policy, privacy policies and internet security, foreign debt forgiveness, foreign development aid, landmine bans, human rights and election assistance, climate change, and the International Criminal Court (Lucarelli 2006; Welsh 2006; Newman 2008). The EU's efforts at narrating this human security foreign policy framework have been assisted also by a redefinition of security occurring across many non-European settings as well (Moskos, Williams, and Segal 2000).

A shift of foreign policy power to Brussels should imply a zero-sum shift away from power in the national capitals, making European foreign policy a highly contentious political issue. And indeed, foreign policy is the least developed policy area for which the EU is responsible. But the storyline embodied in the ESS and other foreign policy pronouncements is one that narrates EU foreign policy as congruent with, and unthreatening to, member-state sovereignty. The delinking of security from the defense of territory and the pivot toward human security objectives serves to deracinate, or temper, the traditional real-politik prerogatives of the nation state. This securitization of issues tradition-ally outside of the geopolitical world of Hobbes, Machiavelli, or Thucydides is representative of a broader global trend that places individuals, not states, as the focus of security policy (Buzan and Waever 2003). Conveniently for the construction of the EU as a legitimate foreign policy actor, this means that the EU can find things to do that can be seen as complementary to, but not directly competing with the member states (Bruter 1999: 194). While the EU's particular emphasis on human security and meshing its policies tightly with NATO and the UN have not magically transformed the EU into a super-power, it has allowed for balancing across different levels of governance, and conflicting interests within and across states. The symbols and practices that have been engaged in this particular narrative of human security have pro-vided an effective cultural foundation for the EU's governance.

Practicing Security? A Networked and Localized European Army

International law, diplomacy, and grand strategy aside, what happens when the EU faces the possibility of actual military conflict? When the EU moves beyond its high-minded foreign policy narratives and symbols and gets to work, what are its actual security practices? What sort of political authority, if any, do those practices help to construct? It is not widely known that the EU does have a substantial military remit. Specific tasks now explicitly under the purview of the European Security and Defence Policy include humanitarian and rescue missions, conflict prevention and peacekeeping, the organization of combat forces in crisis management situations, disarmament operations, military advice and assistance, and post-conflict stabilization. Yet rather than building a new European-level defense capacity to carry out these tasks, these activities are implemented using the existing assets of the member states, and delegated to a changing roster of varying groups of states. The opera-tions are also carried out in concert with NATO's multinational forces, as was done with the 2011 humanitarian intervention in Libya and the rest of the more than 20 operations that have been carried out under the Common Security and Defence Policy. While the on-the-ground follow-up after the shooting stops has mostly been done through the EU's own peacekeepers and rule-of-law operatives, the EU also remains a part of the extensive United Nations peacekeeping operations (Mérand 2008: 53). The symbols and prac-tices reflecting the particular nature of EU security strategies anchor EU military efforts firmly within the national armies while framing these efforts as European, what I call "localizing" the EU. The "European army" that has emerged looks nothing like the centralized, national hierarchy of Napoléon's or Hitler's militaries, and the label is never used in a European setting, partly because of its inflammatory potential, but also because it is a poor description. The EU's military capacity is networked and localized, bound together by a set of loosely joined institutions that attempt to symbolically and practically balance European and national power while firmly anchoring its activities in multinational organizations.

It would therefore be a mistake to simply dismiss, as many outside observers do, the notion of the EU as having any military integration at all. But trying to make sense of European security practices is not for the faint-hearted. It is readily apparent to even the most casual observer that the institutional foundation for EU security is a spaghetti bowl of acronyms, of overlapping, confusing, and constantly changing names and responsibilities. Where to start? The European Union Military Committee (EUMC) is the highest EU military body, set up within the European Council (the member-state executive body that sets overall strategy for the EU). The EUMC directs all EU military activities and provides the Political and Security Committee (PSC) with advice and recommendations on military matters. The EUMC is composed of the chiefs of defence (CHOD) of the member states, who are regularly represented by their permanent military representatives (MilReps). The EUMC has a permanent chairman, selected by the chiefs of defence and appointed by the council. The EUMC is responsible for commanding the overarching European Union Force (EUFOR), and the key elements of EU security forces: the Eurocorps, the European Gendarmerie Force, the European Maritime Force, and EU Battlegroups, all of which operate under the CSDP.

As evidenced by the above paragraph, the EU security structure seems to be collapsing under the weight of its various acronyms alone. You will look in vain for a straightforward European security organizational chart with a hierarchy of military command, as you might find with the US Joint Chiefs of Staff. Instead, a networked National/European structure produces a host of different configurations of military forces depending on the security challenge at hand. Rather than mimicking a typical static national security apparatus, European defense resembles instead an ever shifting and opaque network, with key actors emerging and acting together to address a particular security concern, and then fading into the background until reconstituted in a different configuration for the next series of operations. This network includes the EU Naval Force (EU NAVFOR), whose Operation Atalanta attempts to prevent piracy and armed robbery of international aid organizations off the coast of Somalia. EUFOR's European Rapid Operational Force, in turn, is made up of the land forces of Spain, France, Italy, and Portugal. Four EUFOR missions have been carried out as of this writing: in the Republic of Macedonia (2003), in Bosnia (2004), in the Democratic Republic of the Congo (2006), and in Chad and the Central African Republic (ongoing since 2007). The Eurocorps is made up of land forces from Germany, Belgium, Spain, France, and Luxembourg, while the European Maritime Force (EUROMARFOR) is made up of naval personnel and equipment from Italy, Portugal, France, and Spain, and finally, the European Air Group encompasses the core countries of France and the UK, plus five other air forces.

The EU's high-profile Battlegroup program, introduced in 2004 and operational since 2007, is targeted at creating a more permanent, standing "Rapid Reaction Force" that can meet the demands for flexible real-time response. It has evolved to have at the ready 18 arms battalions of 1,500 troops, capable of rapid deployment and with the capacity to stay in the field up to 120 days with appropriate logistical, naval, and air support. The Battlegroups are made up of various combinations of national armed forces, under the command of the European Council (the heads of state and government). The Nordic Battlegroup is praised for interoperability and integration across the military forces of Sweden, Finland, Norway, Estonia, and Ireland. The Eindhoven-based European Air Transport Command, which controls aerial refueling and military transport, is run jointly by Belgium, France, Germany, Luxembourg, and the Netherlands. It includes the European Airlift Centre (in High Wycombe, UK), assembling European assets together in integrated package that is always on standby. The striking and elegant website of the multi-European member state Eurocorps, one of the earliest EU military groups geared toward the Petersburg Tasks, declares that it is: "A Force for NATO and the European Union." The words are superimposed over a photo of a camouflaged jeep burdened with strapped-on supplies and a battleship steaming in the background. Yet the efforts at military integration have yet to be seriously tested because the Battlegroups have not yet officially been put into battle.

How might all these preliminary efforts matter for the EU's emergence as a political entity? Can we link these efforts to broader processes of political development that have occurred throughout history, most lately in the case of state-building? Frédéric Mérand's close study of the evolution of a European defense finds important social processes at work that are reshaping the nature of European politics (Mérand 2006, 2008). He notes that within the operations of NATO's Supreme Headquarters Allied Powers Europe (SHAPE), the European officers share one command structure, where "a British general can give orders to a German Colonel, who will in turn have a Dutch lieutenant as his aide de camp" (Mérand 2008: 56). Service personnel likewise are being integrated in the EU context, for example in the European Rapid Operational Force based in Florence, Italy where: "Infantrymen and support staff from different EU countries will regularly train together and deploy under the same rules of engagement and the same command structure" (Mérand 2008: 37). Other researchers have noted how British, French, and Dutch soldiers, among others, have been brought together to support peacekeeping and post-conflict goals, while at the highest levels, member-state military leaders regularized intergovernmental security interactions that shape national strategies and interests (Krotz 2010, 2011; Cross 2011).

These practices seem to subvert the notion of the military as a separate sphere that will never be subject to penetration by European governance processes. Operation Artemis, carried out in the Democratic Republic of Congo in 2003, is an example of how the symbols and practices of military operations might matter for the naturalization of European political authority. After a call from the UN secretary general for help with stability operations, the EU launched an operation that lasted four months, with 1,400 troops engaged. Viewed as successful in stabilizing a turbulent situation involving many civilian casualties, the EU troops secured the city of Bunia, the airport, and refugee camps. While its success would not have been possible without robust and experienced French forces and French commanders, nonetheless, under the EU banner, soldiers would "wear an EU badge and risk their lives for EU foreign policy objectives" (Mérand 2008: 37). The name Artemis, the Greek goddess of the hunt, symbolically gestured to Europe, but the operation was firmly nested within the UN, as befitting the EU's continual legitimation of its military activities through international organizations. Ad hoc arrangements such as the supposedly temporary "framework nation command" structure used for Artemis have ultimately been formalized and institutionalized, moving European practices toward more autonomy and away from UN and NATO control (Norheim-Martinsen 2013: 21). This is despite objections across many national capitals, particularly London, to the shift of responsibility for military action to the European level.

EU security and defense symbols and practices are slowly shaping the EU as a new emergent political authority. But it is clear that the EU's activities are only a very blurred copy of the nineteenth- and early twentieth-century efforts at nation building, when armies were the locus of intensive symbolic work intended to create nationalism sentiments and legitimate the use of force. National armies have been considered the historic "school of the fatherland" for state-building projects across Europe, albeit with some caveats (Weber 1976: 298; Krebs 2004). In late nineteenth-century France, national military service made soldiers literate and standardized their patois into a nationalized French, while regimental festivals and rituals around the presentation of the tricolor flag "prepared the way for national allegiance" (Weber 1976: 298). Military uniforms symbolize conformity to a larger collective and to patriotic values, but the EU Rapid Reaction Forces wear uniforms of their own national services, with only EU badges classifying them as

European armies. Military service academies have long played a central role in the formation of the nation's elite officers, who are fertile ground for the legitimation of state power: England's Royal Military College at Sandhurst, the West Point Military Academy in the US, or Ecole Spéciale Militaire de Saint Cyr, created by Napoléon Bonaparte in France. The contrast is extreme with the European Security and Defence College (ESDC), which exists only virtually, as it is made up of a network of national universities, academies, colleges, and institutes across Europe, linked together to provide resources and "training to civilian and military personnel in the field of European Security and Defence Policy (ESDP), promoting a common understanding of that policy and disseminating best practice in this area" as timidly stated on the central EU website.[1]

But it would be unwise to dismiss the importance of the EU's security activities for the evolution of European political authority just because the EU's security apparatus and processes do not mirror those of the nation state. The design, the setting, and the conduct of European security policy are fragmented and opaque, yet there is an underlying coherence that constructs the EU as a security actor. The practices that come out of this design contribute to a cultural construction of Europe as a new emergent political form that must uneasily navigate the preferences of its member states while also attempting to carry out a truly European set of missions. It is no accident, in short, that the practice of European security is a confusing morass of overlapping acronyms that focus squarely on human security, and is firmly located both upward in international organizations and anchored downward in the member states themselves. Instead, it is all representative of the particular mode of political development that the EU is engaged in. While it does not look exactly like the path of the nation state, it does signal a critical shift in political authority in Europe.

Conclusion

What explains the EU's ability to be taken as a legitimate actor in the international system, despite not being a traditional sovereign nation state? The answer lies in part in the particular cultural construction that is occurring around the EU's foreign policy activities. The EU has adopted certain characteristics and capacities of nation states but masks them with new labels, and maps and narrates them in ways that temper the shifts in political authority that are occurring and make it acceptable to audiences within and outside

[1] <http://europa.eu/legislation_summaries/foreign_and_security_policy/cfsp_and_esdp_implementation/r00003_en.htm>.

the EU. Day in and day out, strategies are being put to use to simultaneously borrow legitimate authority from national tropes while carving out the EU as complementary to, not in contestation with, the nation state. This repetitive cultural construction helps to naturalize the EU as a site of legitimate authority.

In the contentious field of foreign and security policy, these processes of cultural construction are critically aided by the intersection of the EU's strategies with more universal trends away from purely geopolitical notions of security to broader goals of human security (Paris 2001). A narrative about the additive nature of security, where national security is not isolated and set apart, but rather linked to overarching humanitarian, environmental, and welfare concerns, has become accepted as a legitimate discourse among foreign policy elites, NGOs, and the United Nations community, even if not always embraced in practice. In foreign policy and security, the EU is therefore able to culturally resituate and defuse sensitive "sovereign" activities by portraying itself as a legitimate analog, but not replica, of nation states. These efforts parallel the strategies of deracinating found in the other cases considered in this book, such as the move to make the euro simply about "completing" the single market rather than a profound shift in monetary policy, considered in Chapter 6.

A second important strategy pursued by the EU is the "localizing" of the EU's security activities both upward in international multilateral organizations, and downward into national settings. The dilemmas around a European foreign and security policy are again helped by the broader historical trajectory of increasing multilateralism, of nation states working through international regimes and organizations. This post-national security infrastructure nests national policies upward inside transnational security structures such as the peacekeeping operations of the United Nations or in joint strategic planning and execution in NATO (Moskos, Williams, and Segal 2000). These strategies of nesting upward into multilateral institutions are pragmatic answers to the high political resistance to a true "European Army" consolidated at the EU level.

In addition, the EU's localizing strategies also move downward, as the most sensitive EU activities are firmly nested within networks of member-state militaries, rather than being fixed at the European level. So the long-term EUFOR Althea operations in Bosnia-Herzegovina, overseeing the implementation of the Dayton Agreement, pulls troops from 21 of the EU's 28 members, while the 2014 EUFOR RCA peacekeeping mission in the Central African Republic is centered on French troops with assistance from Estonia, with more troops from other European states expected to join. The EU's drive to nest policies upward and downward helps to legitimize its foreign policy activities while also leaving military capacity in member states' hands. This neatly parallels strategies such as physically locating European regulatory agencies in a wide variety of regions throughout the EU, geographically nesting them in the member-state communities, as described in Chapter 4. It also reflects how European citizenship is anchored within the legal framework of each individual member state, such that to be European is first to be legally recognized as Czech or Italian, for example, as described in Chapter 5.

The EU's development as an international legal personality, its new diplomatic profile, its European Security Strategy (ESS), and its security and defense operations demonstrate the tensions of being a new political entity playing the high politics of foreign policy among sovereign states. Most notably, when use of force is required or deep divisions in national interest occur, the legitimation strategies break down and political support wanes. Even in the postmodern era, force is the *ultimo ratio* in international politics, and the cultural foundation for EU legitimacy remains attenuated and of a different nature than the patriotic nationalism that supports war. A strongly united EU position on how to deal with Putin's Russia has been difficult to achieve, because Putin implicates the traditional hard politics of security policy rather than diffuse human security issues. Despite the bloodshed and turmoil around Ukraine's turn to the EU, it was only with the dramatic downing of a commercial airplane over Ukrainian airspace that the EU finally responded to Russian aggression with strong sanctions. The entire symbolic and practical apparatus of European foreign policy is not built to address such issues, and severely strains the cultural foundation of the EU's particularly banal imagined community.

At the same time, however, the reach of European foreign policy is wide and far. The potential for the EU to become a more forceful foreign policy actor causes outrage and shores up nationalist movements such as the UK Independence Party (UKIP), who see the EU as unacceptably upstaging the historical roles of member states. Both the progress of EU foreign policy and its particular shortcomings—the scoffing from certain quarters about its irrelevance, on the one hand, and the vehement resistance in the same quarters to discussions about a "European Army," on the other—become more intelligible when we understand the underlying cultural construction of Europe.

8

Conclusion

This book argues that the reconfiguration of daily life in the European Union (EU) has generated new cultural symbols and practices that work to make more natural the emergence of the EU as a legitimate political authority. The EU has become a very potent, but relatively unappreciated, source of rules in Europe, from capital requirements for banks from London to Prague, to the granting of asylum status for immigrants entering the EU from Syria, to the terms under which businesses can sell products from cellphones to airline tickets, to the structure of university degrees from Porto to Glasgow and beyond. While self-interest and material capacities can explain much about the evolution of the EU, I argue that we need also to consider a host of underlying social processes at work in creating a foundation for the EU's powers.

The EU, like all new emergent governance forms, must solidify its legitimacy by reframing people's assumptions about the appropriate locus of political authority. EU officials and agencies have done this quite intentionally through carefully crafted symbols and practices, using their cultural power to shore up the transfer of sovereignty to the European level. But the extension of EU activities into so many areas of everyday life also has shifted the cultural setting in ways not intended by, nor under the direct control of, the EU. The side effects, for example, of policies increasing people's travel for work, study or pleasure, of rules unifying the European market, or of the projection of European foreign policy into the world, all shape the environment in which meanings about the EU are fixed. Other actors beyond the EU also have constructed Europe as a category of lived experience and symbolic activity, from civil society groups promoting increased participation in European elections, to the producers of the Eurovision Song Contest, who promote Europe in their carefully choreographed and often over-the-top spectacles.

I argue that this "imaginary Europe," the symbols and practices of daily life, provides part of the necessary raw material for the EU's political authority and the emergence of European citizens. Europe's authority construction shares much in common with earlier historical episodes of political development, particularly the invention and rise of the nation state. But whereas emergent political authorities traditionally have displaced previous rulers, the EU must layer itself on top of its members, and carefully navigate the symbols and practices of those states, be it France, Spain, the Czech Republic, or any of the 28 member states that make up its political community. Because the EU is a historical innovation in governance that continues to coexist with its political predecessors, the EU must not only tolerate but instead celebrate national traditions and political authority, both symbolic and material.

Clever strategies have been used by EU officials to try to navigate these dilemmas, yet the resulting cultural infrastructure for integration remains fragile. Most centrally, while the nation state's cultural infrastructure of nationalism has been constructed to elicit emotional loyalties and fierce sentiments of belonging, the EU has largely depicted itself in deracinated, abstracted ways without strong roots or passionate politics. The EU is a banal political authority, tolerated but not loved. The EU's imagined community is also tempered by its depiction in ways that "localize" the EU by nesting national symbols and practices inside an EU shell. There have been moments when the EU has set aside these cultural strategies and seemed to overstep its boundaries. Most notably, the pattern of deracinating and localizing the EU to make it seem complementary to the nation state was broken by the European Constitution. Drafted in the early 2000s and eventually abandoned after Dutch and French voters rejected it in referenda in 2005, the experience of the European Constitution suggests the constraints of the EU's banal authority, and the consequences that arise when the facade of banal authority cracks open. The failure of the constitution, seen through the lens of my argument about the importance of a legitimating cultural infrastructure for governance, has important lessons for the current conflicts and disillusionment with the European project in the wake of the Eurozone crisis.

A Constitutional Convention for Europe?

The European Constitution was initially motivated in part by the goal of creating a single document that would become an official constitution, rather than continuing to rest EU law on the series of intergovernmental treaties that formed what many argued was already a de facto constitution. It was hoped in some quarters that this document would make the EU more capable of action by streamlining its institutional structure while also making it more transparent and bringing it closer to the people of Europe (Sternberg 2013: 173). Yet the trappings of the constitution, the labels chosen, and the narrative around the process pointed to much more grandiose ambitions for the EU. The drafting of the European Constitution was explicitly modeled on the Constitutional Convention held in 1787 in Philadelphia. That meeting drew up the 20-page document that formed the foundation for the new United States of America. Drawing a direct parallel with such an iconic historic moment framed the European effort as something far beyond the usual tedious EU administrative and bureaucratic activities. Focusing popular attention on the expansion of EU governance, it put the EU in the public eye in new ways, and drew widespread debate.

Under the leadership of former French president and EU champion Valéry Giscard d'Estaing, a series of open forums, discussions, and formal meetings with national delegates were assembled in what some hoped would be a true "European public sphere" legitimating of the EU itself (Habermas 2001). The Convention on the Future of Europe eventually produced a document of over 300 pages, the *Draft Treaty establishing a Constitution for Europe*, much of it alas written in a convoluted manner accessible only to those trained in European law (European Union 2004). The first part of the constitution outlined a series of institutional changes targeted toward more efficient decision making in the ever-enlarging union. Specific reforms included revisions in the way that voting occurs in the European Council and co-decision-making procedures for the European Parliament. This part of the constitution also created two new high-profile positions, namely a permanent president of the council and a foreign policy chief, in an effort to address what many saw as the opaque and hydra-headed complexity of the EU's governance system. The constitution also included, for the first time, a formalized process for exit from the union. The second part of the constitution codified an EU charter of fundamental rights, which delineated a series of citizen protections such as the right to a fair trial, the prohibition of torture, the protection of personal data, and various workers' rights. Much of this part of the text echoed existing agreements in the non-EU European Convention on Human Rights as well as existing EU case law. The third section simply combined and organized all previous treaties into the new constitutional document. Although signed by the heads of state in October 2004 and agreed to by all EU member legislatures, the promise to bring the constitution to a direct vote in public referenda in certain states soon proved problematic. Ultimately, when voters in the Netherlands and France turned down the constitution in late spring 2005, the decision was made to abandon it.

Most of the new additions to EU law embodied in the constitution ended up being revived, however, and cut and pasted directly into the subsequent Lisbon Treaty adopted at the end of 2007. Coming into force on December 1, 2009, Lisbon put into place institutional changes such as more qualified majority voting and a bigger role for the European Parliament. The two new leadership positions and a new EU diplomatic corps, the European External Action Service (discussed in Chapter 7), soon were up and running. The Lisbon Treaty did drop one part of the constitution: all of the labels and symbols that framed the European polity in the same terminology as a nation state. In addition to switching the name of the agreement from the European Constitution to the Lisbon Treaty, certain of the innovations were either dropped or reframed back into the traditional deracinated and localized symbols that have traditionally underpinned the emergence of European political authority.

In a section aptly named "The Symbols of the Union," (Article I-8), the European Constitution had proposed to make official the adoption of an anthem, a flag, the EU motto, an official Europe Day, and the euro as symbols of the union (European Union 2004):

Article I-8: The Symbols of the Union
The flag of the Union shall be a circle of twelve golden stars on a blue background.

The anthem of the Union shall be based on the "Ode to Joy" from the Ninth Symphony by Ludwig van Beethoven.

The motto of the Union shall be: "United in diversity".

The currency of the Union shall be the euro.

Europe day shall be celebrated on 9 May throughout the Union.

While all of these symbols are used in practice every day throughout the EU and worldwide (for example, the EU flag flies in every embassy around the world alongside the member-state flag), they do not have legal status in any of the EU treaties. The EU's effort to leverage these symbols was abruptly set aside for the status quo, as the entire section was stripped out of the Lisbon Treaty (albeit without impacting the euro's status as the currency of the Eurozone countries). A subset of 16 countries signed on to a declaration attached to Lisbon that stated that the symbols will continue to be used by those signatory states "as symbols to express the sense of community of the people in the European Union and their allegiance to it" (European Union 2008). In a sign of support for the symbolic project, the European Parliament, after the constitution's demise, collectively agreed to increase the frequency and visibility of their use of the symbols.

The language in Article I-8 was of course at the center of the long history of initiatives to "bring Europe closer to the people" by surrounding them with symbolic representations as advocated by the Adonnino Committee in the mid-1980s (Sternberg 2013: 90, discussed in Chapter 4). But the failure of the European Constitution's effort to directly mimic national symbols, upending the tradition of deracination and localization, should not be surprising given my argument about the logic of the particular banal authority constructed by and around the EU.

In addition to the removal of the highly visible symbols of the nation state from the text of the Lisbon Treaty, the efforts to relabel some of the EU's activities also ran into trouble (Sieberson 2008: 49–55). Early ideas floated by Giscard d'Estaing and others in support of a dramatic new name for the EU, "United Europe," or the even more symbolically fraught "United States of Europe," never made it to the final stage because of the affront to sovereignty they implied (Sieberson 2008: 51). A proposal to similarly reframe all language about "community" activities to "federal" activities likewise fell by the wayside. As discussed in Chapter 7, the text of the constitution laid out the responsibilities of the "Union Minister for Foreign Affairs," a job that was fully retained in the Lisbon Treaty. The challenge to national sovereignty implied by the foreign minister name was viewed as a step too far, however. The title of the job was thus changed to "High Representative of the Union for Foreign Affairs and Security Policy" in Lisbon. More prosaically, the EU has long referred to its rules as "regulations," "directives," and "decisions." The constitution for the first time referred to "European laws," but even this was viewed as usurping sovereign power and was dropped out of the text of the Lisbon Treaty.

I do not mean to suggest that the failure of the constitution was driven only by the reaction to the inclusion of these blatantly national symbols. However, the relabeling of the constitution itself back to a "treaty," and the removal of all of these contentious elements described above while keeping most of the important substantive changes, indicates both the depth of the political union being formed, but also its cultural limits. While the failure of the constitution has often been interpreted as clear evidence of the rejection of "more Europe," we should recognize the complexity and nuance of the politics surrounding this hugely ambitious project. The French "no" in 2005 occurred at a moment of economic prosperity and expansion of opportunity. Ironically, it was a moment of peak overall support for European integration (Bruter 2012: 24). At that time, in fact, the comparative levels of trust in national governments versus the European Commission were tilted very strongly across almost all countries of the EU toward the commission (Bruter 2012: 25). Careful empirical work on the debate in France over the European Constitution has found that the opposition forces were successful in part because they were able to change the meaning of the referendum from a simple "do you approve the bill ratifying the treaty establishing a Constitution for Europe" to the broader question, "which Europe do we want?" (Sternberg 2013: 154). In France, much of the debate centered on whether to pursue a more market or more socially oriented EU, with various interpretations of what each meant. This explains why, despite 88 percent of post-referendum French citizens surveyed feeling that French membership in the EU was a "good" thing, so many were drawn into the "no" camp for the vote. Some of those voting against the constitution did so because of their desire for a discussion about specific shortcomings of the EU—sometimes including a preference for deeper, not less, integration.

If nothing else, the rise and fall of the European Constitution effort demonstrates the difficulties the EU has in directly and openly appropriating the symbolic trappings of the nation states, even under welcoming circumstances. The constitution's demise can be understood as an episode that brought the banal authority of symbols and practices out into the open, but to publics and politicians not ready for it.

But Can "Banality by Design" Solve Europe's Challenges?

So what does Europe's particular type of banal authority mean for the future of the EU and its policies going forward from the Eurozone crisis and beyond? Will it provide enough of a cultural infrastructure and social foundation for dealing with the challenges ahead—be they economic malaise, insufficient democratic representation, xenophobia, or exclusion? My account makes sense of the EU's seeming deadlock on many contentious issues by illuminating the basic nature of the EU as a new form of governance, one that must carefully navigate the prerogatives of the ever enduring nation states, even as it takes over many national functions. The particularly banal legitimation that arises from the symbols and practices of the EU's imagined community has been constructed to support European political development, but is not necessarily well equipped to deal with the serious challenges facing the EU as it evolves as an evermore significant source of governance. Deracinated and localized understandings of Europe, and citizens' places within it, are a weak foundation for the type of solidarity and sacrifices demanded in the face of Europe's economic, social, and geopolitical challenges.

Most obviously, the stresses and strains of the Eurozone crisis present a stark challenge to the European project and the trajectory of political development that I have traced in this book. Those groups that are suffering disproportionately from the crisis are confronting the meaning of the EU in new ways. Its "under-the-radar", taken-for-granted status has been swept aside by a new politicization of Europe—what the EU means, who it is for, and how it should be governed. The effects of the sovereign debt crisis that started with Greece in late 2009 continue to plague much of Southern Europe, while Northern EU states, most notably Germany, have seen their economic prospects only get rosier. The differing prescriptions for what to do to solve the crisis—with Germany in the person of Chancellor Angela Merkel successfully demanding austerity and the cutting of public budgets and services—have made what was a sore point into a painful fault line across the EU states and their publics.

Arguably, the euro crisis would not have occurred without the bursting of the bubble of the US subprime mortgage market in 2007 and the shock waves it sent through the vast panoply of questionable financial instruments built up during two decades of financial sector deregulation and expansion (Matthijs 2014a). And ultimately, the real problems of the so-called PIIGS countries (Portugal, Ireland, Italy, Greece, and Spain) were rooted not in the euro or the EU, but in national-level issues. The overexpansion of private debt and bad banking practices were to blame across the afflicted countries, in addition to, in the case of Greece, dodgy public finance. But the lack of adequate EU-level political institutions to support the euro, such as joint fiscal policy and a European-wide debt instrument, likely had made some sort of euro crisis inevitable in the long run, whatever the broader financial situation (McNamara 2015).

The key political challenge for the EU lies in the fact that the euro crisis has had such uneven effects across Europe's political community, with seemingly intractable youth unemployment soaring in the Mediterranean states while robust economic opportunities open up for new generations of Germans and other Northern Europeans (Matthijs 2014b). Does the EU have the overall social solidarity and sense of political community to support the pooling and transfer of resources from the haves to the have nots that the crisis seems to require? The public debate has suggested there is little sense of collective belonging, even in circumstances where the richer states arguably gain the most from the continuation of the Eurozone and the EU's larger economic integration. But despite this, the EU states together have pledged in the neighborhood of €1 trillion to keep the Eurozone afloat and the member states financially stable. European summits too numerous to count have been held, and a new layer of institutions, most prominently the European Stability Mechanism for back-up funding in times of crisis along with a European Banking Union, are being built at the EU level, further moving political authority to the center of the EU polity. These moves have been acquiesced to by the European public, if not embraced or even fully understood. They could not have been possible without the decades of slow accumulation of everyday symbols and practices detailed in this book, that created a permissive consensus for such political developments. Indeed, the most effective and active actor in the Eurozone crisis has been the European Central Bank, a relatively opaque and political independent body that has more in common with the EU legacy of deracinated, technocratic governance than with any new emergent sense of impassioned European political identity and solidarity. Yet as austerity policies continue to be the price paid by the laggard states for their debt issues, the close identification of those policies with "Europe" is an association that is piercing the banal authority the EU has been built on, and creating new challenges for legitimation.

A second major area of challenge for the EU goes far beyond any particular economic crisis. How can the EU improve overall democratic representation and citizens' participation in European-level politics? The topic of whether there is a democratic deficit in Europe has been discussed and debated by many academics, policymakers, and pundits over the years (Weiler, Haltern, and Mayer 1995; Majone 1998; Moravcsik 2002). I have offered in this book a different perspective by framing the EU as a new, emergent polity best understood using social and cultural theories of comparative political development and state formation. If we situate the EU as a case of political development, we notice that most comparative cases of the shift in power upward involve violent struggle, strife, and contestation that far outstrip anything that has occurred in the EU to date, despite the squabbling and inaction on the part of European leaders.

My argument suggests that one way forward is to enhance democracy in the EU through less banality and more political contestation—but contestation of a healthy and inclusive kind. Because of the veneer of banality that the EU's symbols and practices create, the salience of EU issues for everyday citizens is low, and it is difficult for the "mobilization of bias" to occur and drive debate and effective democratic participation (Schattschneider 1960). Although it seems counterintuitive, I argue that the EU needs more overt contestation and direct discussion of its policies, and debate over its leaders. The EU is profoundly shifting governance to the European level, even those areas that formally were considered core state powers (Genschel and Jachtenfuchs 2014). Conflict and contestation are the growing pains of any new polity, but they need to be directed into effective, legitimate, and appropriate channels of representation and partisanship (Follesdal and Hix 2006). Hix has outlined a series of institutional and other practical reforms to move the EU toward a more healthy politicization, or what he calls "limited democratic politics" (Hix 2008). These include increasing attention to already transparent political contests, such as in majority voting in the European Council and the work of the European Parliament. But, Hix argues, we need more publicity and accountability in the contest for president of the European Commission, and more attention to the relative balance of parties in the European Parliament and the job done there, rather than having European elections reflect national issues as they largely do now. Finally, the council should emphasize more open deliberations and clearer position taking across the national representatives so as to normalize its politics in a democratic way, away from the intergovernmental secrecy that still seems to be the norm.

As of this writing, there are some indications that we are moving in this direction, albeit with some important caveats. The 2014 European Parliament elections were much more publicly contested than any before in EU history, with wide coverage in national newspapers, and various trans-European interest groups—from students to environmental activists to high-priced consultants—setting up websites and generating information relevant to their EU-wide constituencies. Some small steps were made toward a true electoral contest for the European president to replace Herman Van Rompuy as the second president since the Lisbon Treaty. A heavily promoted television debate, social networking, and advertisements on various media all created an awareness of the European-level decision making completely unprecedented in EU history. But it was not to be the end of the EU's traditions of banality or deracination by any means. The voting result for the European president was not definitive, but only to be taken under advisement. The ultimate choice of Jean-Claude Juncker, a Luxembourg prime minister and confirmed technocrat, did not move the EU very far beyond its business as usual, even in a time of extraordinary tension over the euro crisis and the EU's future.

The argument made in this book suggests that any institutional fixes to improve EU democracy will need to work hand in hand with changes in the cultural infrastructure for European governance. The meaning currently infused into the symbols and practices of life in Europe, as both directly and indirectly shaped by EU policies, is one that does not easily support increasing democratic contestation. A shift will have to occur at every level of cultural experience in order to make this happen. In settled times, as Swindler points out, culture can directly influence political action by providing a "tool kit" or repertoire of social resources to construct strategies of action (Swindler 1986). The symbols and practices of banal authority have done so in the EU, creating a foundation for an extraordinary expansion of governance since World War II. Now, the unsettled times ahead will provide different opportunities for culture to shape outcomes. New cultural repertoires will need to arise to shape the meaning attached to the EU and increase the role of citizens and active political participation. Most importantly, the cultural strategies of deracination that support the EU need to be replaced with a more honest and open assessment of partisanship, and the winners and losers from various policies. Localization, or the careful symbolic balancing of local- and state-level attachments and powers, will continue to be necessary. Thinking about the EU as a federal system in formation, or a "coming together federalism" (Stepan 1999; Kelemen 2014), a voluntary grouping of previously independent states, offers a template for the foundation of political culture that can live with the tension in levels of political authority implied by the EU.

My emphasis on the need for increased politicization and a more impassioned, less technocratic sense of European identity might make some readers very nervous. After all, nationalism was the cause of much injustice and bloodshed over the past century. Should we be worried about a new more strident version of political identity being constructed at the European level? Efforts to create a European identity might well end up exclusionary and could support policies of social exclusion, military aggression, and xenophobia. In the same way that Ernst Gellner (1983) viewed nationalism as a malign force historically, so writers such as Delanty (1995) and Shore (2000) see the policies and dynamics I describe in this book as deeply pernicious. Delanty sees the "European idea" as a "totalising re-appropriation of forces that lie deep in European history" (Delanty 1995: viii). He writes about the "myth of Europe as a unifying and universalising project" linking it to the "enforced and violent homogenisation" that occurred historically (Delanty 1995: vii).

Although these are real and important concerns, the arguments and evidence presented throughout this book do not support these fears. The EU has some powerful symbolic and practical tools at its disposal; however, the process of authority construction is incomplete, lumpy, and highly attenuated, varying across different EU national settings and social and economic groups, and can often be contradictory in its effects. There have been clear examples of xenophobia in Europe, with anti-Muslim and anti-Semitic activities on the rise, but evidence also of an alternative type of political space, more peacefully overlapping and coexisting with national identity (Soysal 2002). The idea of Europe as a post-national, liberal enlightenment project is an underlying narrative throughout the various empirical areas surveyed in earlier chapters. The EU is not a perfect liberal democracy and never will be. But the accomplishments of the EU over the postwar era indicate that it has been, on balance, a force for the common good that need not necessarily repeat the excesses of nationalism.

The Often Unpleasant Path of Political Development

The consolidation of political power and the capacity to rule has historically involved deep cleavages, contestation, and often, bloodshed and war (Fukuyama 2011). US political development was initially sparked when the new colonies broke away from Britain in the War of Independence, but the true consolidation of power to Washington happened only with the ravages of the American Civil War. Germany only became a nation state when Bismarck fought a series of wars with the Duchies and wrestled control to Berlin. Switzerland, Belgium, and Italy are all relatively recent political inventions from the second half of the nineteenth century, and their development paths and political histories have been far from smooth. While the drama of war and modernization of markets were critical to state building, the slow, wavering, bloody process of centralizing political power also has included the hard-won accumulation of symbolic power as a key dynamic in all these cases and beyond (Bourdieu 1999: 40).

Seeing the EU in terms of the process of political development makes us better prepared for the inevitable ugliness, messiness, contestation, and seeming dysfunction that accompanies such politics. The virulent backlash against the EU evidenced by the success of far right and far left parties in the European elections of May 2014 should not surprise us, given the ongoing and deep penetration of the EU into citizens' lives across a range of everyday experiences. The severe economic crisis that began in late 2009, and the harsh impact of austerity policies that have kept growth slow and unemployment high, have rightly caused sometimes dramatic political contestation over the EU, far beyond any seen before. While the EU is unique among new political authorities in being constructed voluntarily, not at the point of a gun, it will not be immune from harsh criticism or social protests, nor should it be.

In the face of these developments and the deepening of the EU across multiple realms of policymaking, most pundits, politicians, academics, and casual observers struggle with how to think about the EU. On the one hand, the progress that it has made in institutionalizing governance at the European level across a wide range of areas—the euro, the European Central Bank, the single market, the European Defence and Security Policy—has lulled many journalists, academics, and policymakers into believing the EU will act as a coherent entity, decisively and cohesively responding to crises in the way a nation state might. The recent global financial crisis brought on a stream of articles and op-eds that chastised the EU for not coming up with a coordinated fiscal response along the lines of the US stimulus package and bank bailout packages. Early in the Eurozone crisis, an article in the *New York Times* expressed consternation at persistent national cleavages over who would pay for what, and expressed surprise that European "countries have worked to bail out their own banks and rescue national factories of global automobile companies" rather than working together at the EU level (Erlanger 2009). In the context of months of inaction on the part of the US Congress faced with cleaning up the mess at home, observers in the US and elsewhere pay an astonishing compliment to the EU in bashing it for not reacting in unified and harmonious ways, a compliment that would have been unthinkable a few decades ago. But the EU is a creature that will never fit neatly into the dominant nation state standard. The EU is a unique structure that overlays, and fits between, the member states as best it can, seeking to navigate the existing national politics and institutions while improving upon them.

Over a century ago, the killing of Austria's Archduke Franz Ferdinand by Bosnian military assassins set off a chain of events that would propel Europe toward decades of warfare and suffering. World War I, and its settlement, proved devastating to winners and losers alike, while the Great Depression that followed caused untold millions to go hungry and homeless across Europe. World War II brought Europe the worst loss of life and destruction of property known in history. Throughout, weak political parties, shaky governing institutions, unchecked geopolitical and military competition, and nationalism fanned by self-interested political leaders plagued Europe and its citizens. Yet by the end of the very same century, Europe would rebuild its economy and its national political systems and evolve into an exemplar of peace and prosperity. The innovative governance structure within which this remarkable feat happened is the European Union.

Yet the fact that the countries of Europe, locked in mortal combat mere decades ago, today are closely knit together across a variety of political, social, and economic policy realms is cold comfort to the new generation of Europeans who have grown up in this changed world. Delivering peace among the previously warring states of Europe is not enough, in this new age, to ensure political support for the EU. Today, the EU is riven by conflict and deeply shaken by financial crises. These challenges are by far the most serious that the EU has faced since the tumultuous years before its founding.

I have suggested in this book that we can only fully make sense of the bumpy trajectory of the EU if we step back—really far back—almost so far that we have to squint to see it. Rather than analyzing in detail the various ins and outs of Brussels bureaucracy and EU laws, reading the cultural infrastructure, the symbols and practices undergirding the EU, allows us to see what the EU represents in terms of innovations in governance more generally. Like a Chuck Close painting, the details of each particular aspect of the EU can obscure the overall picture of what it is. If we place the EU in a long list of historical political forms from medieval times onward, we get a better sense of what is new and innovative, what represents continuity from the past, and how we might be venturing into the future. The challenge is a big one, however, as our conceptual toolkit is woefully limited in its ability to depict the transformations in the form and content of rule evinced in changing forms of governance beyond the nation state. Fortunately, the lens of comparative political development can help. Situating Europe in terms of the long history of innovative forms allows us to unpack the various component parts of the EU's governance and better understand its accomplishments and shortcomings. The symbols and practices that create the cultural infrastructure of governance in the EU are a crucial part of the EU's political authority, just as with the nation state. In the long run, the better we understand what the EU is, the better we can understand what it does, and where it might be going.

References

Abdelal, Rawi, Yoshiko M. Herrera, Alastair Iain Johnston, and Rose McDermott, eds. 2009. *Measuring Identity*. Cambridge: Cambridge University Press.

Adler, Emmanuel and Vincent Pouliot, eds. 2011. *International Practices*. Cambridge: Cambridge University Press.

Adler-Nissen, Rebecca 2014. "Symbolic Power in European Diplomacy: The Struggle Between National Foreign Services and the EU's External Action Service." *Review of International Studies* 40: 657–81.

Afionis, Stavros 2009. "European Union Coherence in UNFCCC Negotiations under the New Treaty of Lisbon (Reform Treaty)." *Sustainable Development Law & Policy* 9 (2): 43–7, 73.

Alter, Karen and Sophie Meunier-Aitsahalia 1994. "Judicial Politics in the European Community: European Integration and the Pathbreaking Cassis De Dijon Decision." *Comparative Political Studies* 26 (4): 535–61.

Anderson, Benedict 1993. *Imagined Communities: Reflections on the Origins and Spread of Nationalism, Revised Edition*. London: Verso.

Anderson, Karen 2015. *Social Policy in the European Union*. Basingstoke: Palgrave Macmillan.

Anderson, Karen and Michael Kaeding 2013. "European Integration and Pension Policy Change: Variable Patterns of Europeanization in Italy, the Netherlands and Belgium." *British Journal of Industrial Relations*. doi: 10.1111/bjir.12030.

Ansell, Christopher and Giuseppe Di Palma, eds. 2004. *Restructuring Territoriality: Europe and North America*. Cambridge: Cambridge University Press.

Aron, Raymond 1974. "Is Multinational Citizenship Possible?" *Social Research* 41 (4): 638–56.

Aureli, Pier Vittorio, Veronique Patteeuw, Joachim Deklerck, and Martino Tattara, eds. 2007. *Brussels: A Manifesto Towards the Capital of Europe*. Brussels: Nai10 Publishers.

Austin, John L. 1962. *How to Do Things With Words*. Oxford: Clarendon Press.

Austin, John L., J. O. Urmson, and Geoffrey J. Warnock, eds. 1970. *Philosophical Papers*. Oxford: Oxford University Press.

Bach, David and Abraham Newman 2007. "The European Regulatory State and Global Public Policy: Micro-institutions, macro-influence." *Journal of European Public Policy* 16 (6): 827–46.

Bache, Ian and Matthew Flinders 2004. *Multi-level Governance*. New York: Oxford University Press.

References

Baker, Susan 2006. "Environmental Values and Climate Change Policy: Contrasting the European Union and the United States," in Sonia Lucarelli and Ian Manners (eds.), *Values and Principles in European Union Foreign Policy*. London: Routledge, pp. 77–96.

Balibar, Etienne 2004. *We, The People of Europe? Reflections on Transnational Citizenship*. Translated by James Swenson. Princeton, NJ: Princeton University Press.

Barker-Aguilar, Alicia 2003. "Iconography and Identity Constructing the Political Symbolism of the Euro." Unpublished undergraduate thesis, Princeton University.

Barnett, Michael and Martha Finnemore 1999. "The Politics, Power and Pathologies of International Organizations." *International Organization* 53 (4), Autumn: 699–732.

Barry, Andrew and Don Slater 2002. "Technology, Politics and the Market: An Interview with Michel Callon." *Economy and Society* 31 (2): 285–306.

Barth, Fredrik, ed. 1969. *Ethnic Groups and Boundaries: The Social Organization of Culture Difference*. Boston: Little, Brown.

Barth, Fredrik 2000. "Boundaries and Connections," in A. P. Cohen (ed.), *Signifying Identities*. London: Routledge, pp. 17–36.

Bartolini, Stefano 2005. *Restructuring Europe: Centre Formation, System Building and Political Structuring Between the Nation-state and the European Union*. Oxford: Oxford University Press.

Bátora, Jozef 2013. "The 'Mitrailleuse Effect': The EEAS as an Interstitial Organization and the Dynamics of Innovation in Diplomacy." *Journal of Common Market Studies* 51 (4): 598–613.

Bauböck, Rainer 1994. *Transnational Citizenship*. Aldershot: Edward Elgar.

Bauböck, Rainer and Virginie Guiraudon 2009. "Introduction: Realignments of Citizenship: Reassessing Rights in the Age of Plural Members and Multi-Level Governance." *Citizenship Studies* 13 (5): 439–50.

Bednar, Michael 2006. *L'Enfant's Legacy: Public Open Spaces in Washington, DC*. Baltimore: The Johns Hopkins University Press.

Bellier, Irène and Thomas M. Wilson 2000. "Building, Imagining, and Experiencing Europe: Institutions and Identities in the European Union," in Irène Bellier and Thomas Wilson (eds.), *An Anthropology of the European Union: Building, Imagining, and Experiencing the New Europe*. Oxford: Berg, pp. 1–30.

Bensel, Richard 1990. *Yankee Leviathan: The Origins of Central State Authority in America, 1859–1877*. New York: Cambridge University Press.

Berezin, Mabel 2006. "Great Expectations: Reflections on Identity and European Monetary Union," in Robert Fishman and Anthony Messina (eds.), *The Year of the Euro: The Cultural, Social and Political Import of Europe's Common Currency*. South Bend, IN: University of Notre Dame Press, pp. 97–110.

Berger, Peter L. and Thomas Luckman 1966. *The Social Construction of Reality: A Treatise on the Sociology of Knowledge*. Garden City, NY: Anchor Books.

Berman, Sheri 1998. *The Social Democratic Moment: Ideas and Politics in the Making of Interwar Europe*. New York: Cambridge University Press.

Berman, Sheri 2006. *The Primacy of Politics: Social Democracy and the Making of Europe's Twentieth Century*. Cambridge: Cambridge University Press.

Berman, Sheri and Kathleen R. McNamara 1999. "Bank on Democracy: Why Central Banks Need Public Oversight." *Foreign Affairs* 78, March/April: 2–8.

Bickerton, Chris, Bastien Irondelle, and Anand Menon 2011. "Security Co-operation Beyond the Nation-State: The EU's Common Security and Defence Policy." *Journal of Common Market Studies* 49 (1): 1–21.

Billig, Michael 1995. *Banal Nationalism*. London: Sage Publications.

Biscop, Sven 2001. "In Search of a Strategic Concept for the ESDP." *European Foreign Affairs Review* 7: 473–90.

Blyth, Mark 2002. *Great Transformations: Economic Ideas and Institutional Change in the Twentieth Century*. Cambridge: Cambridge University Press.

Borneman, John and Nick Fowler 1997. "Europeanization." *Annual Review of Anthropology* 26 (1): 487–514.

Börner, Stefanie and Monika Eigmüller, eds. 2015. *European Integration, Processes of Change and the National Experience*. Basingstoke: Palgrave Macmillan.

Börzel, Tanja and Madeleine O. Hosli 2003. "Brussels Between Bern and Berlin: Comparative Federalism Meets the European Union." *Governance* 16 (2): 179–202.

Bottoni, Piero 1938. *Urbanistica*. Milan: Hoepli.

Bouchard, Gerard 2013. "The Small Nation with a Big Dream: Quebec National Myths (Eighteenth–Twentieth Centuries)," in Gerard Bouchard (ed.), *National Myths: Constructed Pasts, Contested Presents*. New York: Routledge, pp. 1–23.

Bourdieu, Pierre 1977. *Outline of a Theory of Practice*. Cambridge: Cambridge University Press.

Bourdieu, Pierre 1980. *The Logic of Practice*. Trans. Richard Nice. Stanford, CA: Stanford University Press.

Bourdieu, Pierre 1984. *Distinction: A Social Critique of the Judgment of Taste*. Cambridge, MA: Harvard University Press.

Bourdieu, Pierre 1984. "Rethinking the State: Genesis and Structure of the Bureaucratic Field." Trans. Loic J. D. Wacquant and Samar Farage. *Sociological Theory* 12 (1): 1–18.

Bourdieu, Pierre 1991. *Language and Symbolic Power*. Cambridge, MA: Harvard University Press.

Bourdieu, Pierre 1998. *Practical Reason: On the Theory of Action*. Palo Alto, CA: Stanford University Press.

Brain, David 1994. "Cultural Production as 'Society in the Making': Architecture as an Exemplar of the Social Construction of Cultural Artifacts," in Diana Crane (ed.), *The Sociology of Culture: Emerging Theoretical Perspectives*. Oxford: Blackwell, pp. 191–220.

Braun, Emily, ed. 1989. *Italian Art in the 20th Century*. Munich: Prestel.

Brooks, Sarah, Raphael Cunha, and Layna Mosley 2014. "Categories, Creditworthiness and Contagion: How Investors' Shortcuts Affect Sovereign Debt Markets." *International Studies Quarterly*. doi: 10.1111/isqu.12173.

Brubaker, Rogers 1989. *Immigration and the Politics of Citizenship in Europe and North America*. Lanham, MD: University Press of America.

Brubaker, Rogers 1992. *Citizenship and Nationhood in France and Germany*. Cambridge, MA: Harvard University Press.

References

Brubaker, Rogers and Frederick Cooper 2000. "Beyond Identity." *Theory and Society* 29: 1–47.

Bruter, Michael 1999. "Diplomacy without a State: The External Delegations of the European Commission." *Journal of European Public Policy* 6 (2): 183–205.

Bruter, Michael 2003. "Winning Hearts and Minds for Europe: The Impact of News and Symbols on Civic and Cultural European Identity." *Comparative Political Studies* 36: 1148–79.

Bruter, Michael 2005. *Citizens of Europe? The Emergence of a Mass European Identity.* Basingstoke: Palgrave Macmillan.

Bruter, Michael 2012. "The Difficult Emergence of a European People," in Jack Hayward and Rüdiger Wurzel (eds.), *European Disunion: Between Sovereignty and Solidarity.* Basingstoke: Palgrave Macmillan, pp. 17–31.

Bukovansky, Mlada 2002. *Legitimacy and Power Politics: The American and French Revolutions in International Political Culture.* Princeton, NJ: Princeton Univeristy Press.

Burley, Anne-Marie and Walter Mattli 1993. "Europe Before the Court: A Political Theory of Legal Integration." *International Organization* 47: 41–76.

Butler, Judith 1993. *Bodies That Matter: On the Discursive Limits of "Sex".* London and New York: Routledge.

Buzan, Barry and Ole Waever 2003. *Regions and Powers: The Structure of International Security.* Cambridge: Cambridge University Press.

Callon, Michel 1998. "Introduction: The Embeddedness of Economic Markets in Economics," in Michel Callon (ed.), *The Laws of the Market.* Oxford: Blackwell, pp. 1–57.

Caporaso, James A. 1996. "The European Union and Forms of State: Westphalian, Regulatory or Post-Modern?" *Journal of Common Market Studies* 34 (1): 29–52.

Caporaso, James A. and Sidney Tarrow 2009. "Polanyi in Brussels: Supranational Institutions and the Transnational Embedding of Markets." *International Organization* 63 (4), October: 593–620.

Carlsnaes, Walter 2006. "European Foreign Policy," in Karl Jørgensen, Mark Pollack, and Ben Rosamond (eds.), *Handbook of European Union Politics.* London: Sage, pp. 545–61.

Castano, Emanuele 2002. "European Identity: A Social-Psychological Perspective," in Richard K. Herrmann, Thomas Risse-Kappen, and Marilynn B. Brewer (eds.), *Transnational Identities: Becoming European in the EU.* Lanham, MD: Rowman & Littlefield, pp. 40–58.

Channel 4 News, October 1, 2012, "Ryder Cup 'Hijacked by the EU'," 2012, accessed February 11, 2013, <http://channel4.com/news/ryder-cup-hijacked-by-eu>.

Checkel, Jeffrey, ed. 2007. *International Institutions and Socialization in Europe.* Cambridge: Cambridge University Press.

Checkel, Jeffrey and Peter Katzenstein, eds. 2009. *European Identity.* New York: Cambridge University Press.

Christiansen, Thomas 2005. "Towards Statehood? The EU's Move Towards Constitutionalisation and Territorialisation," *ARENA Working Paper* 21, Oslo.

Christiansen, Thomas, Knud Erik Jørgensen, and Antje Wiener, eds. 2001. *The Social Construction of Europe.* London: Sage.

Clark, Caryl 1997. "Forging Identity: Beethoven's 'Ode' as European Anthem." *Critical Inquiry* 23: 789–807.

Conant, Lisa 2006. "Individuals, Courts, and the Development of European Social Rights." *Comparative Political Studies* 39 (1), February: 76–100.

Conant, Lisa 2010. "Rights and the Limits of Transnational Solidarity in Europe," in Donald W. Jackson, Michael C. Tolley, and Mary L. Volcansek (eds.), *Globalizing Justice: Critical Perspectives on Transnational Law and the Cross-border Migration of Legal Norms.* New York: SUNY, pp. 141–60.

Cooper, Robert 2003. *The Breaking of Nations: Order and Chaos in the Twenty-First Century.* New York: Grove Press.

Council of European Communities 1984. "Conclusions of the European Council at Its Meeting in Fontainebleau, 26 June 1984." *Bulletin of the European Communities* No. 6 (1).

Cram, Laura 2001. "Imagining the Union: A Case of Banal Europeanism?" in Helen Wallace (ed.), *Interlocking Dimensions of European Integration.* London: Palgrave, pp. 343–62.

Cram, Laura 2006. "Inventing the People: Civil Society Participation and the Enhabitation of the EU," in Stijn Smismans (ed.), *Civil Society & Legitimate European Governance.* London: Edward Elgar, pp. 241–59.

Cram, Laura 2009. "Introduction. Banal Europeanism: European Union Identity and National Identities in Synergy." *Nations and Nationalism* 15 (1): 101–8.

Cram, Laura 2012. "Does the EU Need a Navel? Implicit and Explicit Identification with the European Union." *Journal of Common Market Studies* 50 (1): 71–86.

Crane, Diana, ed. 1994. *The Sociology of Culture: Emerging Theoretical Perspectives.* Oxford: Blackwell.

Cross, Maia K. Davis 2007. *The European Diplomatic Corps: Diplomats and International Cooperation from Westphalia to Maastricht.* New York: Palgrave.

Cross, Maia K. Davis 2011. *Security Integration in Europe: How Knowledge-Based Networks are Transforming the European Union.* Ann Arbor: University of Michigan Press.

Damro, Chad 2012. "Market Power Europe." *Journal of European Public Policy* 19 (5): 682–99.

Dannreuther, Roland and John Peterson 2006. "Introduction: Security Strategy as Doctrine," in Roland Dannreuther and John Peterson (eds.), *Security Strategy and Transatlantic Relations.* New York: Routledge, pp. 1–15.

David, Spence 2012. "The Early Days of the European External Action Service: A Practitioner's View." *The Hague Journal of Diplomacy* 7 (1): 115–34.

Delanty, Gerard 1995. *Inventing Europe: Ideas, Identity, Reality.* New York: St. Martin's Press.

Delanty, Gerard and Paul R. Jones 2002. "European Identity and Architecture." *European Journal of Social Theory* 5 (4): 453–66.

Della Salla, Vincent 2010. "Political Myth, Mythology and the European Union." *Journal of Common Market Studies* 48 (1): 1–19.

Delreux, Tom 2011. *The EU as International Environmental Negotiator.* Farnham: Ashgate.

Demey, Thierry 2007. *Brussels; Capital of Europe.* Brussels: Badeaux.

Deutsch, Karl W. 1953. *Nationalism and Social Communication.* Cambridge: MIT Press.

Deutsch, Karl, Sidney Burrel, Robert Kann et al. 1968/1957. *Political Community and the North Atlantic Area*. Princeton, NJ: Princeton University Press.

Dickinson, Edward 1902. *Music in the History of the Western Church*. New York: Haskell House.

Díez Medrano, Juan 2003. *Framing Europe: Attitudes to European Integration in Germany, Spain, and the United Kingdom*. Princeton, NJ: Princeton University Press.

Dinan, Desmond 1994. *Ever Closer Union?* London: Macmillan.

Dobbin, Frank 1994. "Cultural Models of Organization: The Social Construction of Rational Organizing Principles," in Diana Crane (ed.), *The Sociology of Culture: Emerging Theoretical Perspectives*. Oxford: Blackwell, pp. 117–53.

Douglas, Mary and David Hull, eds. 1992. *How Classification Works*. Edinburgh: Edinburgh University Press.

Douglas, Mary and Baron Isherwood 1996. *The World of Goods: Towards an Anthropology of Consumption*. 2nd Edition. London: Routledge.

Downing, Brian 1992. *The Military Revolution and Political Change: Origins of Democracy and Autocracy in Early Modern Europe*. Princeton, NJ: Princeton University Press.

Duchêne, François 1972. "Europe's Role in World Peace," in Richard Mayne (ed.), *Europe Tomorrow: Sixteen Europeans Look Ahead*. London: Fontana, pp. 32–47.

Duchêne, François 1973. "The European Community and the Uncertainties of Interdependence," in Max Kohnstamm and Wolfgang Hager (eds.), *A Nation Writ Large? Foreign Policy Problems before the European Community*. Basingstoke: Macmillan, pp. 1–21.

Duchesne, Sophie 2011. "National Identification, Social Belonging and Questions on European Identity," in Markus Thiel and Rebecca Friedman (eds.), *European Identity and Culture: Narratives of Transnational Belonging*. Surrey, England: Ashgate, pp. 53–74.

Duchesne, Sophie, Elizabeth Frazer, Florence Haegel, and Virginie Van Ingelgom, eds. 2013. *Citizens' Reactions to European Integration Compared: Overlooking Europe*. Basingstoke: Palgrave Macmillan.

Durkheim, Émile 1939. *The Rules of Sociological Method*. New York: Free Press.

Durkheim, Émile 1973. *Moral Education: A Study in the Theory and Application of the Sociology of Education*. New York: Free Press.

Durkheim, Emile and Marcel Mauss 1963. *Primitive Classification*. Chicago: University of Chicago Press.

Dyson, Kenneth and Kevin Featherstone 1999. *The Road to Maastricht: Negotiating Economic and Monetary Union*. Oxford: Oxford University Press.

The Economist 2009. "Behold, Two Mediocre Mice." *The Economist*, November 26. Accessed online December 20, 2014 at <http://www.economist.com/node/14966247>.

Edelman, Murray 1964. *The Symbolic Uses of Politics*. Urbana: University of Illinois Press.

Edelman, Murray 1971. *Politics as Symbolic Action: Mass Arousal and Quiescence*. New York: Academic Press.

Edelman, Murray 1988. *Constructing the Political Spectacle*. Chicago: University of Chicago Press.

Egan, Michelle 2001. *Constructing a European Market: Standards, Regulation, and Governance.* Oxford: Oxford University Press.

Egan, Michelle. Forthcoming. *Single Markets: Economic Integration in Europe and the United States.* New York: Oxford University Press.

Emerson, Michael, Daniel Gros, and Alexander Italianer 1992. *One Market, One Money: An Evaluation of the Potential Benefits and Costs of Forming an Economic and Monetary Union.* New York: Oxford University Press.

Erlanger, Steven 2009. "Economy Shows Cracks in European Union." *New York Times.* June 8.

Erlanger, Steven 2013. "Mediating as French Culture and Economics Collide." *New York Times.* July 30, p. A10.

EurActiv 2011. "UK to Abstain from 'European Heritage Label' Scheme." Published online on May 23. Accessed May 6, 2014 at <http://www.euractiv.com/culture/uk-abstain-eu-heritage-label-scheme-news-505011>.

European Commission 1998a. "Commission Communication on the Information Strategy for the Euro." *Euro Papers 16*, Brussels.

European Commission 1998b. "Summary of Experts Reports Compiled for the Euro Working Group/European Commission DG XXIV on Psycho-Sociological Aspects of the Changeover to the Euro." *Euro Papers 29*, Brussels.

European Commission 2003. *It's your Europe: Living, Learning and Working Anywhere in the EU.* Luxembourg: Office for Official Publications of the European Communities.

European Commission 2009. *Eurobarometer 71: Public Opinion in the European Union. Full Report.* Luxembourg: Office for Official Publications of the European Communities.

European Commission 2013a. "On the way to ERASMUS+: A Statistical Overview of the ERASMUS Programme in 2011-12." November. Unit C1 'Higher Education; Erasmus', Directorate-General for Education and Culture, European Commission, Brussels, Belgium.

European Commission, 2013b. "European Heritage Label: Frequently Asked Questions." MEMO/13/1068 November 28. Accessed May 6, 2014 at <http://europa.eu/rapid/press-release_MEMO-13-1068_en.htm>.

European Commission 2014a. "Preserving European Cultural Heritage." Accessed May 6, 2014 at <http://ec.europa.eu/news/culture/110610_en.htm>.

European Commission 2014b. "The European Company: Your Business Opportunity?" Europa Website. Accessed December 20, 2014 at <http://ec.europa.eu/internal_market/company/societas-europaea/index_en.htm>.

European Communities 1987. *Treaties Establishing the European Communities (ECSC, EEC, EAEC), Single European Act, Other Basic Instruments.* Brussels: Office for Official Publications of the European Communities.

European Council 1973. *Declaration on European Identity (Copehagen Declaration). European Council Meeting in Copenhagen 14–15 December 1973.* Accessed December 20, 2014 at <http://aei.pitt.edu/4545/1/epc_identity_doc.pdf>.

European Council 2001. *Presidency Conclusions, European Council Meeting in Laeken 14 and 15 December 2001.* Accessed December 20, 2014 at <https://www.consilium.europa.eu/uedocs/cms_data/docs/pressdata/en/ec/68827.pdf>.

References

European Council 2003. *European Security Strategy: A Secure Europe in a Better World.* Accessed December 20, 2014 at <http://www.eeas.europa.eu/csdp/about-csdp/european-security-strategy/>.

European Union, Europa 50th Anniversary of the Treaty of Rome, Brussels, viewed May 22, 2013, <http://europa.eu/50/index_en.htm>.

European Union 1992. *Treaty on European Union (Consolidated Version), Treaty of Maastricht.* O.J. C 325/5.

European Union 1997. *Treaty of Amsterdam Amending the Treaty on European Union, the Treaties Establishing the European Communities and Certain Related Acts.* Oct. 2. 1997 O.J. C 340.

European Union 2004. *Draft Treaty Establishing a Constitution for Europe.* O.J. C 310/1.

European Union 2006. *Decision of the European Parliament and of the Council Establishing the Culture Programme: Annex,* O.J. C 313E/96.

European Union 2008. *Consolidated Version of the Treaty on European Union Declaration on the symbols of the European Union,* O.J. C 115/355, at 355.

Evans, Peter B., Dietrich Rueschemeyer, and Theda Skocpol, eds. 1985. *Bringing the State Back In.* Cambridge: Cambridge University Press.

Express Tribune, with the International *New York Times* 2014. "Philharmonic flashmobs pay tribute to Ukraine's fallen protesters." Published: March 31, 2014, accessed August 26, 2014 at <http://tribune.com.pk/story/689494/philharmonic-flashmobs-pay-tribute-to-ukraines-fallen-protesters/>.

Fabbrini, Sergio, ed. 2005. *Democracy and Federalism in the EU and US: Exploring Post-National Governance.* London: Routledge.

Favell, Adrian 2003. "Eurostars and Eurocities: Towards a Sociology of Free Moving Professionals in Western Europe." *The Center for Comparative Immigration Studies Working Paper* 71, San Diego.

Favell, Adrian 2008. *Eurostars and Eurocities: Free Movement and Mobility in an Integrating Europe.* Malden, MA: Blackwell.

Favell, Adrian and Virginie Guiraudon, eds. 2011. *Sociology of the European Union.* Basingstoke: Palgrave Macmillan.

Favell, Adrian and Ettore Recchi, eds. 2009. *Pioneers of European Integration: Citizenship and Mobility in the EU.* Cheltenham: Elgar.

Favell, Adrian, Ettore Recchi, Theresa Kuhn, Janne Solgaard Jensen, and Juliane Klein 2011. "The Europeanisation of Everyday Life: Cross Border Practices and Transnational Identification among EU and Third-Country Citizens." *State of the Art Report for FP7 EUCROSS Project, Working Paper* #1, October.

De Federico de la Rúa, Ainhoa 2005. "Redes de amistad e identificación eurpea. Las redes transnacionales y las identidades de los estudiantes Erasmus," in Oscar Santacreu, (ed.), *European Union Social Changes: Migrations, Participation and Democracy.* OBETS, Universidad de Alicante, pp. 191–226.

Fioretos, Orfeo 2007. "The European Company Statute and the Governance Dilemma," in Sophie Meunier and Kathleen R. McNamara (eds.), *Making History: European Integration and Institutional Change at Fifty.* New York: Oxford University Press, pp. 157–73.

Fishman, Robert and Anthony Messina, eds. 2006. *The Year of the Euro: The Cultural, Social and Political Import of Europe's Common Currency*. South Bend, IN: University of Notre Dame Press.

Fligstein, Neil 1990. *The Transformation of Corporate Control*. Cambridge, MA: Harvard University Press.

Fligstein, Neil 1996. "Markets as Politics; A Political Cultural Approach to Market Institutions." *American Sociological Review* 61: 656–73.

Fligstein, Neil 2002. *The Architecture of Markets: An Economic Sociology of Twenty-First Century Capitalist Societies*. Princeton, NJ: Princeton University Press.

Fligstein, Neil 2008. *Euro-clash: The EU, European Identity, and the Future of Europe*. Oxford: Oxford University Press.

Fligstein, Neil and Luke Dauter 2007. "The Sociology of Markets." *Annual Review of Sociology* 33: 105–28.

Fligstein, Neil and Iona Mara-Drita 1996. "How to Make a Market: Reflections on the Attempt to Create a Single Market in the European Union." *American Journal of Sociology* 102 (1): 1–33.

Fligstein, Neil and Alec Stone Sweet 2001. "Institutionalizing the Treaty of Rome," in Alec Stone Sweet, Wayne Sandholtz, and Neil Fligstein (eds.), *The Institutionalization of Europe*. Oxford: Oxford University Press, pp. 29–55.

Fligstein, Neil and Alec Stone Sweet 2002. "Constructing Markets and Polities: An Institutionalist Account of European Integration." *American Journal of Sociology* 107 (5): 1206–43.

Follesdal, Andreas and Simon Hix 2006. "Why There is a Democratic Deficit in the EU: A Response to Moravcsik." *Journal of Common Market Studies* 44 (3): 533–62.

Foucault, Michel 1977. *Discipline and Punish: The Birth of the Prison*. New York: Vintage Books.

Foucault, Michel 1983. "Afterword: The Subject and Power" in Hubert Dreyfus and Paul Rabinow (eds.), *Michel Foucault: Beyond Structuralism and Hermeneutics*, 2nd edition. Chicago: University of Chicago Press, pp. 208–26.

Foucault, Michel 1991. "Governmentality," in Graham Burchell et al. (eds.), *The Foucault Effect: Studies in Governmentality*. Chicago: University of Chicago Press, pp. 87–104.

Fourcade, Marion 2009. *Economists and Societies: Discipline and Profession in the United States, Britain and France, 1890s–1990s*. Princeton, NJ: Princeton University Press.

Frank, David John, Suk-Ying Wong, John W. Meyer, and Francisco O. Ramirez 2000. "What Counts as History: A Cross-National and Longitudinal Study of University Curricula." *Comparative Education Review* 44 (1): 29–53.

Fukuyama, Francis 2011. *The Origins of Political Order: From Prehuman Times to the French Revolution*. New York: Farrar, Straus and Giroux.

Gaventa, John 1982. *Power and Powerlessness: Quiescence and Rebellion in an Appalachian Valley*. Champaign, IL: University of Illinois Press.

Gearan, Anna 2014. "Kerry Tells Iran that Existing Sanctions Will Remain in Place as Negotiations Continue." *The Washington Post* February 2. Accessed December 20, 2014 at <http://www.washingtonpost.com/world/national-security/kerry-tells-i

ran-that-existing-sanctions-will-stay-in-place-as-negotiations-continue/2014/02/02/54a225e0-8c32-11e3-9ed8-259977a48789_story.html>.

Geertz, Clifford 1973. *The Interpretation of Cultures: Selected Essays*. New York: Basic Books.

Gellner, Ernest 1983. *Nations and Nationalism*. Ithaca: Cornell University Press.

Genschel, Philipp and Markus Jachtenfuchs, eds. 2014. *Beyond the Regulatory Polity? The European Integration of Core State Powers*. Oxford: Oxford University Press.

Gieryn, Thomas F. 2002. "What Buildings Do." *Theory and Society* 31: 35–74.

Gilbert, Mark 2008. "Narrating the Process: Questioning the Progressive Story of European Integration." *Journal of Common Market Studies* 46 (3): 641–62.

Glancey, Jonathan 2008, "Let There Be Light," *The Guardian*, accessed March 5, 2013, <http://www.guardian.co.uk/artanddesign/2008/dec/02/eu-court-of-justice-architecture>.

Glazer, Nathan and Mark Lilla, eds. 1987. *The Public Face of Architecture*. New York: The Free Press.

Goddard, Stacy E. 2009. *Uncommon Ground: Indivisible Territory and the Politics of Legitimacy*. Cambridge: Cambridge University Press.

Goldberg, David Theo 1997. *Racial Subjects: Writing on Race in America*. New York: Routledge.

Goldstein, Leslie 2001. *Constituting Federal Sovereignty: The European Union in Comparative Context*. Baltimore: The Johns Hopkins University Press.

Gordon, David, ed. 2006. *Planning Twentieth Century Capital Cities*. New York: Routledge.

Gorski, Philip S. 1993. "The Protestant Ethic Revisited: Disciplinary Revolution and State Formation in Holland and Prussia." *American Journal of Sociology* 99 (2): 265–316.

Gorski, Philip S. 2003. *The Disciplinary Revolution*. Chicago: University of Chicago Press.

Gourevitch, Peter and James Shinn 2005. *Political Power and Corporate Control: The New Global Politics of Corporate Governance*. Princeton, NJ: Princeton University Press.

Gramsci, Antonio 1971. *Selections from the Prison Notebooks*. New York: International Publishers.

Gray, Julia 2013. *The Company States Keep: International Economic Organization and Sovereign Risk in Emerging Markets*. Cambridge: Cambridge University Press.

Green Cowles, Maria 2012. "The Single European Act," in Erik Jones, Anand Menon, and Stephen Weatherill (eds.), *The Oxford Handbook of the European Union*. Oxford: Oxford University Press.

Greenwood, Justin 2011. *Interest Representation in the European Union*. 3rd Edition. Basingstoke: Palgrave Macmillan.

Greenwood, Justin and Mark Aspinwall 1998. *Collective Action in the European Union: Interests and the New Politics of Associability*. London: Routledge.

Gros, Daniel and Niels Thygesen 1999. *European Monetary Integration*. London: Longman.

Gutmann, Amy and Dennis Thompson 2004. *Why Deliberative Democracy*. Princeton, NJ: Princeton University Press.

Guzzini, Stefano and Anna Leander, eds. 2006. *Constructivism and International Relations: Alexander Wendt and his Critiques*. New York: Routledge.

Haas, Ernst B. 1964. *Beyond the Nation State: Functionalism and International Organization*. Palo Alto, CA: Stanford University Press.

Habermas, Jürgen 2000. *The Postnational Constellation*. Cambridge: Polity Press.

Habermas, Jürgen 2001. "Why Europe Needs a Constitution." *New Left Review* 11, Sept–Oct: 5–26.

Hacking, Ian 1986. "Making Up People," in T. C. Heller et al. (eds.), *Reconstructing Individualism*. Stanford, CA: Stanford University Press, pp. 222–36.

Harvey, David 2003. *Paris, Capital of Modernity*. New York; Routledge.

Haus, Leah 2009. "Europeanization, Education, and School Curricula: The Role of Historical Legacies in Explaining Policy Variation Between England and France." *Comparative Political Studies* 42 (7), July: 916–44.

Hein, Carola 2004. *The Capital of Europe. Architecture and Urban Planning for the European Union*. Westport, CT: Greenwood/Praeger.

Hein, Carola 2006a. "Brussels—Capital of Belgium and 'Capital of Europe'," in David Gordon (ed.), *Planning Twentieth Century Capital Cities*. New York: Routledge, pp. 237–52.

Hein, Carola, ed. 2006b. "Bruxelles l'Européene: Capitale de qui? Ville de qui?/ European Brussels. Whose capital? Whose city?" *Cahiers de la Cambre – Architecture* n 5, Brussels: La Lettre Volée.

Hein, Carola and Willa Seldon 2000. *Censoring History: Citizenship and Memory in Japan, Germany and the United States*. Armonk, NY: ME Sharpe.

Heisenberg, Dorothee 1999. *The Mark of the Bundesbank: Germany's Role in European Monetary Cooperation*. Boulder, CO: Lynne Rienner Publishers.

Helleiner, Eric 1998. "National Currencies and National Identities." *American Behavioral Scientist* 41(10): 1409–36.

Helleiner, Eric 2002. *The Making of National Money: Territorial Currencies in Historical Perspective*. Ithaca, NY: Cornell University Press.

Herrmann, Richard K., Thomas Risse-Kappen, and Marilynn B. Brewer, eds. 2004. *Transnational Identities: Becoming European in the EU*. Lanham, MD: Rowman & Littlefield.

Hewett, Alexander 2009. "Constructing the Capitals of the European Union: Contributing to the Creation and Expression of a Supranational European Identity," Government 314 Imaging Europe, Unpublished paper, Georgetown University, Washington, DC.

Hicks, Dan and Mary C. Beaudry 2010. *The Oxford Handbook of Material Culture Studies*. Oxford: Oxford University Press.

Hill, Christopher 1993. "The Capabilities–Expectations Gap, or Conceptualizing Europe's International Role." *Journal of European Common Market Studies* 31 (3): 305–28.

Hill, Christopher and Michael Smith, eds. 2011. *International Relations and the European Union*. Oxford: Oxford University Press.

Hintze, Otto 1975. *The Historical Essays of Otto Hintze*. Oxford: Oxford University Press.

Hix, Simon 2008. *What's Wrong with the EU and How to Fix It*. Cambridge: Polity Press.

Hix, Simon and Bjorn Hoyland 2011. *The Political System of the European Union*. London: Palgrave Macmillan.

Hobsbawm, Erik J. 1990. *Nations and Nationalism since 1780: Programme, Myth, Reality*. Cambridge: Canto.

Hobsbawm, Eric J. and Terence Ranger, eds. 1983. *The Invention of Tradition*. Cambridge: Cambridge University Press.

References

Hobson, John and Leonard Seabrooke, eds. 2007. *Everyday Politics of the World Economy.* Cambridge: Cambridge University Press.

Hoffmann, Leif 2008. "Ever Closer Markets: Public Procurement and Services in the EU and the USA." *Political Perspectives* 2, No. 2. Available at <http://www.politicalperspectives.org.uk/wp-content/uploads/2010/08/Vol2-2-2008-2.pdf>.

Hoffmann, Leif 2011. "Land of the Free, Home of the (Un)Regulated: A Look at Market-Building and Liberalization in the EU and the US." Ph.D. Dissertation, Department of Political Science, University of Oregon at Eugene.

Hoffmann, Stanley 1995. *The European Sisyphus; Essays on Europe, 1964-1994.* Boulder, CO: Westview Press.

Hoffmann, Stanley and Robert O. Keohane 1991. *The New European Community: Decisionmaking and Institutional Change.* Boulder, CO: Westview.

Hooghe, Liesbet and Gary Marks 2001. *Multilevel Governance and European Integration.* Lanham, MD: Rowman and Littlefield.

Hooghe, Liesbet and Gary Marks 2004. "Contrasting Visions of Multi-Level Governance?" in Ian Bache and Matthew Flinders (eds.), *Multi-Level Governance.* Oxford: Oxford University Press, pp. 15–30.

Hubbard, William 1987. "A Meaning for Monuments," in Nathan Glazer and Mark Lilla, (eds.), *The Public Face of Architecture.* New York: The Free Press, pp. 124–41.

Huntington, Samuel 1993. "The Clash of Civilizations." *Foreign Affairs* 72 (3) Summer: 22–49.

Hurd, Ian 1999. "Legitimacy and Authority in International Politics." *International Organization* 53 (2): 379–408.

Hymans, Jacques 2004. "The Changing Color of Money." *European Journal of International Relations* 10 (1): 5–31.

Hymans, Jacques 2006. "Money for Mars: The Euro Banknotes and European Identity," in Robert Fishman and Anthony Messina (eds.), *The Year of the Euro: The Cultural, Social and Political Import of Europe's Common Currency.* South Bend, IN: University of Notre Dame Press, pp. 15–36.

Ikenberry, G. John 2001. *After Victory.* Princeton, NJ: Princeton University Press.

Ikenberry, G. John and Charles Kupchan 1990. "Socialization and Hegemonic Power." *International Organization* 44 (3): 283–315.

Imig, Doug and Sidney Tarrow 2001. *Contentious Europeans.* New York: Rowman & Littlefield.

Jabko, Nicolas 2006. *Playing the Market: A Political Strategy for Uniting Europe, 1985–2005.* Ithaca, NY: Cornell University Press.

Jacoby, Wade 2004. *The Enlargement of the European Union and NATO.* Cambridge: Cambridge University Press.

Jenson, Jane 1995. "Mapping, Naming and Remembering: Globalization at the End of the Twentieth Century." *Review of International Political Economy* 2 (1): 96–116.

Johnston, Alistair Iain 1995. *Cultural Realism: Strategic Culture and Grand Strategy in Chinese History.* Princeton, NJ: Princeton University Press.

Jones, Dan, ed. 2014. *Deloitte Football Money League.* Deloitte Consulting, Sports Business Group. Accessed December 20, 2014 at <http://www2.deloitte.com/content/dam/

Deloitte/uk/Documents/sports-business-group/deloitte-uk-deloitte-football-mo
ney-league-2014.pdf>.

Jørgensen, Knud Erik Sebastian Oberthur, and Jamal Shahin 2011. "Introduction:
Assessing the EU's Performance in International Institutions: Conceptual
Framework and Core Findings." *Journal of European Integration* 33 (6): 599–620.

Kaelberer, Matthias 2004. "The Euro and European Identity: Symbols, Power and the
Politics of European Monetary Union." *Review of International Studies* 3 (2): 161–78.

Kagan, Robert 2002. "Power and Weakness." *Policy Review* 113 (June/July): 3–28.

Katzenstein, Peter, ed. 1996. *The Culture of National Security: Norms and Identity in World
Politics*. New York: Columbia University Press.

Kelemen, R. Daniel 2004. *The Rules of Federalism: Institutions and Regulatory Politics in
the EU and Beyond*. Cambridge, MA: Harvard University Press.

Kelemen, R. Daniel 2005. "The Politics of Eurocracy: Building a New European State?,"
in Nicolas Jabko and Craig Parsons (eds.), *The State of the European Union, Volume
7: With US or Against US? European Trends in American Perspective*. Oxford: Oxford
University Press, pp. 173–89.

Kelemen, R. Daniel 2007. "Built to Last? The Durability of EU Federalism," in Sophie
Meunier and Kathleen R. McNamara (eds.), *Making History: European Integration and
Institutional Change at Fifty*. Oxford: Oxford University Press, pp. 51–66.

Kelemen, R. Daniel 2010. *Eurolegalism: The Transformation of Law and Regulation in the
European Union*. Cambridge, MA: Harvard University Press.

Kelemen, R. Daniel 2014. "Constructing the European Judiciary." Paper prepared for
LAPA Seminar, March 24, 2014, Princeton University, Princeton, New Jersey.

King, Russell and Enric Ruiz-Gelices 2003. "International Student Migration and the
European 'Year Abroad': Effects on European Identity and Subsequent Migration
Behaviour." *Population, Space and Place* 9 (3) May/June: 229–52.

Kirk, Terry 2005. *The Architecture of Modern Italy: The Challenge of Tradition, 1750–1900*.
New York: Princeton Architectural Press.

Kirschbaum, Erik 2005. "New Wave of Euro Pix Avoids Europudding Curse." *Variety*
October 30. Accessed June 1, 2013 at <http://variety.com/2005/film/news/new-
wave-of-euro-pix-avoids-europudding-curse-1117931911/>

Krasner, Stephen 1999. *Sovereignty: Organized Hypocrisy*. Princeton, NJ: Princeton
University Press.

Krebs, Ronald 2004. "A School for the Nation? How Military Service Does Not Build
Nations, and How it Might." *International Security* 28 (4): 85–124.

Krebs, Ronald and Jennifer K. Lobasz 2007. "Fixing the Meaning of 9/11: Hegemony,
Coercion, and the Road to War in Iraq." *Security Studies* 16 (3) (July–September): 409–51.

Krotz, Ulrich 2010. "Regularized Intergovernmentalism: France-Germany and Beyond
(1963–2009)." *Foreign Policy Analysis* 6 (2): 147–85.

Krotz, Ulrich 2011. *Flying Tiger: International Relations Theory and the Politics of Advanced
Weapons*. Oxford: Oxford University Press.

Kuhn, Theresa 2012. "Why Educational Exchange Programmes Miss Their
Mark: Cross-Border Mobility, Education and European Identity." *Journal of Common
Market Studies* 50 (6): 994–1010.

References

Kuhn, Theresa 2015. *Experiencing European Integration: Transnational Lives and European Identity*. Oxford: Oxford University Press.

Ladd, Brian 1997. *The Ghosts of Berlin: Confronting German History in the Urban Landscape*. Chicago: University of Chicago.

Lakoff, George 1987. *Women, Fire, and Dangerous Things: What Categories Reveal about the Mind*. Chicago: University of Chicago Press.

Lamont, Michele and Virág Molnár 2002. "The Study of Boundaries Across the Social Sciences." *Annual Review of Sociology* 28: 167–95.

Lasansky, D. Medina 2005. *The Renaissance Perfected: Architecture, Spectacle, and Tourism in Fascist Italy*. University Park, PA: Penn State University Press.

Lavenex, Sandra and John Peterson 2012. "The EU as a Security Actor," in Elizabeth Bomberg, John Peterson, and Richard Corbett (eds.), *The European Union: How Does it Work?* Oxford: Oxford University Press, pp. 185–202.

Limerick, Patricia 1988. *The Legacy of Conquest: The Unbroken Past of the American West*. New York: W. W. Norton & Company.

Loveman, Mara 2005. "The Modern State and the Primitive Accumulation of Symbolic Power." *American Journal of Sociology* 110 (6): 1651–83.

Lucarelli, Sonia 2006. "Introduction," in Sonia Lucarelli and Ian Manners (eds.), *Values and Principles in European Union Foreign Policy*. London: Routledge, pp. 1–18.

Lucarelli, Sonia and Ian Manners, eds. 2006. *Values and Principles in European Union Foreign Policy*. London: Routledge.

Lukes, Steven 1974. *Power: A Radical View*. London: Macmillan.

Luzón, Antonio 2005. "Europe in Spanish Textbooks: A Vague Image in the Space of Memory," in Hanna Schissler and Yasmin Soysal (eds.), *The Nation, Europe, and the World: Textbooks and Curricula in Transition*. New York: Berghahn Books, pp. 163–90.

Maas, Willem 2007. "The Evolution of EU Citizenship," in Sophie Meunier and Kathleen R. McNamara (eds.), *Making History: European Integration and Institutional Change at Fifty*. New York: Oxford University Press, pp. 231–45.

MacKenzie, Donald 2006. *An Engine Not a Camera: How Financial Models Shape Markets*. Cambridge, MA: The MIT Press.

Majone, Giandomenico 1994. "The Rise of the Regulatory State in Europe." *West European Politics* 17 (3): 77–101.

Majone, Giandomenico 1998. "Europe's Democratic Deficit." *European Law Journal* 4: 1.

Malkki, Liisa H. 1995. *Purity and Exile: Violence, Memory, and National Cosmology among Hutu Refugees in Tanzania*. Chicago: University of Chicago Press.

Malkki, Liisa H. 1996. "National Geographic: The Rooting of Peoples and the Territorialization of National Identity among Scholars and Refugees," in Geoff Eley and Ronald Grigor Suny (eds.), *Becoming National: A Reader*. Oxford: Oxford University Press, pp. 434–55.

Manners, Ian 2002. "Normative Power Europe: A Contradiction in Terms?" *Journal of Common Market Studies* 40 (2): 235–58.

Manners, Ian 2006. "The Constituent Nature of Values, Images and Principles in the European Union," in Sonia Lucarelli and Ian Manners (eds.), *Values and Principles in European Union Foreign Policy*. London: Routledge, pp. 19–41.

Manners, Ian 2011. "Symbolism in European Integration." *Comparative European Politics* 9: 243–68.

Marks, Gary 1997. "A Third Lens: Comparing European Integration and State Building," in Jutta Klausen and Louise Tilly (eds.), *European Integration in Social and Historical Perspective: 1850 to the Present*. Lanham: Rowman & Littlefield, pp. 23–43.

Marks, Gary 2012. "Europe and its Empires: From Rome to the European Union." *Journal of Common Market Studies* 50 (1): 1–20.

Marshall, T. H. 1950. *Citizenship and Social Class*. Cambridge: University Press.

Matthijs, Matthias 2014a. "The Eurozone Crisis: Growing Pains or Doomed from the Start?," in Manuela Moschella and Catherine Weaver (eds.), *Handbook of Global Economic Governance: Players, Power, and Paradigms*. Abingdon: Routledge, pp. 201–17.

Matthijs, Matthias 2014b. "Mediterranean Blues: The Crisis in Southern Europe." *Journal of Democracy* 25 (1): 101–15.

Matthijs, Matthias and Mark Blyth 2015. "Introduction," in Matthias Matthijs and Mark Blyth (eds.), *The Future of the Euro*. New York: Oxford University Press.

Mattli, Walter 1999. *The Logic of Regional Integration: Europe and Beyond*. New York: Cambridge University Press.

McCrea, Ronan 2010/2009. "Religion as a Basis of Law in the European Union." *Columbia Journal of European Law* 16 (1), Winter: 81–119.

McNamara, Kathleen R. 1998. *The Currency of Ideas: Monetary Politics in the European Union*. Ithaca: Cornell University Press.

McNamara, Kathleen R. 2001. "Where Do Rules Come From? The Creation of the European Central Bank," in Alec Stone Sweet, Wayne Sandholtz, and Neil Fligstein (eds.), *The Institutionalization of Europe*. Oxford: Oxford University Press, pp. 155–70.

McNamara, Kathleen R. 2002. "Rational Fictions: Central Bank Independence and the Social Logic of Delegation." *West European Politics* 25 (1): 47–76.

McNamara, Kathleen R. 2006. "Managing the Euro: The European Central Bank" in John Peterson and Michael Shackleton (eds.), *The Institutions of the European Union*. Oxford: Oxford University Press, pp. 164–85.

McNamara, Kathleen R. 2008. "A Rivalry in the Making? The Euro and International Monetary Power." *Review of International Political Economy* 15 (3), August: 439–59.

McNamara, Kathleen R. 2010. "Constructing Europe: Insights from Historical Sociology." *Comparative European Politics* 8: 127–42.

McNamara, Kathleen R. 2011. "Historicizing the Unique: Why EMU Has No Fiscal Authority and Why It Matters." *Mortara Center for International Studies Working Paper* (2011–11–15). Available at <https://repository.library.georgetown.edu/handle/10822/551531>.

McNamara, Kathleen R. 2013. "Imaginary Europe: The Euro as Symbol and Practice," in Giovanni Moro (ed.), *The Single Currency and European Citizenship*. London: Bloomsbury, pp. 22–35.

McNamara, Kathleen R. 2015. "Forgotten Embeddedness: History Lessons for the Euro," in Matthias Matthijs and Mark Blyth (eds.), *The Future of the Euro*. New York: Oxford University Press.

References

Menon, Anand 2014. "Defence Policy and the European State: Insights from American Experience," in Desmond King and Patrick Le Gales (eds.), *The Reconfiguration of the State in Europe*. In preparation.

Mérand, Frédéric 2006. "Social Representations in the European Security and Defence Policy." *Cooperation and Conflict* 41 (2): 131–52.

Mérand, Frédéric 2008. *European Defence Policy: Beyond the Nation State*. Oxford: Oxford University Press.

Mérand, Frédéric, Martial Foucault, and Bastien Irondelle 2011. "Theorizing Change in the European Security Environment," in Frédéric Mérand, Martial Foucault, and Bastien Irondelle (eds.), *European Security Since the Fall of the Berlin Wall*. Toronto: University of Toronto Press, pp. 3–24.

Merriman, John 2006. "Some Observations on the Transition to the Euro in France," in Robert Fishman and Anthony Messina (eds.), *The Year of the Euro: The Cultural, Social and Political Import of Europe's Common Currency*. South Bend, IN: University of Notre Dame Press, pp. 37–64.

Messina, Anthony 2006. "Why Doesn't the Dog Bite? Extreme Right Parties and the 'Euro' Skepticism within the EU," in Robert Fishman and Anthony Messina (eds.), *The Year of the Euro: The Cultural, Social and Political Import of Europe's Common Currency*. South Bend, IN: University of Notre Dame Press, pp. 131–60.

Meunier, Sophie 2000. "What Single Voice? European Institutions and the EU–US Trade Negotiations." *International Organization* 54 (1), Winter: 103–35.

Meunier, Sophie 2005. *Trading Voices: The European Union in International Commercial Negotiations*. Princeton, NJ: Princeton University Press.

Meunier, Sophie 2014. "Integration by Stealth: How the European Union Gained Competence over Foreign Direct Investment." Paper prepared for the 7th Annual Conference of the Political Economy of International Organizations, January 16–18, Princeton University.

Meunier, Sophie and Kalypso Nicolaïdes 1999. "Who Speaks for Europe? The Delegation of Trade Authority in the European Union." *Journal of Common Market Studies* 37 (3): 477–501.

Meunier, Sophie and Kalypso Nicolaidis 2006. "The European Union as a Conflicted Trade Power." *Journal of European Public Policy* 13 (6): 908–27.

Meyer, John W, John Boli, and George M Thomas 1987. "Ontology and Rationalization in the Western Cultural Account," in George M Thomas, John W. Meyer, Francisco O. Ramirez, and John Boli (eds.), *Institutional Structure: Constituting State, Society, and the Individual*. London: Sage, pp. 2–37.

Meyer, John W., John Boli, George M. Thomas, and Francisco O. Ramirez 1997. "World Society and the Nation-State." *American Journal of Sociology* 103 (1) July: 144–81.

Meyer, John W. and Ronald L Jepperson 2000. "The 'Actors' of Modern Society: The Cultural Construction of Social Agency." *Sociological Theory* 18 (1): 100–20.

Mitchell, Kristine 2012. "Student Mobility and European Identity: Erasmus Study as a Civic Experience?" *Journal of Contemporary European Research* 8 (4): 490–518.

Mitchell, Kristine 2014. "Rethinking the 'Erasmus Effect' on European Identity." *Journal of Common Market Studies*: 1–19. Article first published online: April 11, 2014. DOI: 10.1111/jcms.12152.

Mitzen, Jennifer 2006. "Anchoring Europe's Civilizing Identity: Habits, Capabilities and Ontological Security." *Journal of European Public Policy* 13 (2): 270–85.

Moravcsik, Andrew 1998. *The Choice for Europe: Social Purpose and State Power from Messina to Maastricht.* Ithaca, NY: Cornell University Press.

Moravcsik, Andrew 2002. "In Defence of the Democratic Deficit: Reassessing Legitimacy in the European Union." *Journal of Common Market Studies* 40 (4): 603–24.

Moravcsik, Andrew 2010. "Europe: Rising Superpower in a Bipolar World," in Alan Alexandroff and Andrew Cooper (eds.), *Rising States, Rising Institutions: Challenges for Global Governance.* Washington, DC: Brookings Institution Press, pp. 151–74.

Moro, Giovanni 2012. *Citizens in Europe: Civic Activism and the Community Democratic Experiment.* New York: Springer.

Moskos, Charles C., John Allen Williams, and David R. Segal 2000. *The Postmodern Military: Armed Forces After the Cold War.* Oxford: Oxford University Press.

Neumann, Iver B. 2002. "Returning Practice to the Linguistic Turn: The Case of Diplomacy." *Millennium: Journal of International Studies* 31 (3): 627–51.

Newman, Abraham 2008. *Protectors of Privacy: Regulating Personal Data in the Global Economy.* Ithaca: Cornell University Press.

Nexon, Daniel 2009. *The Struggle for Power in Early Modern Europe.* Princeton, NJ: Princeton University Press.

Nicolaides, Kalypso and Robert Howse, eds. 2001. *The Federal Vision.* Oxford: Oxford University Press.

Niemann, Arne 2012. "The Common Commercial Policy: From Nice to Lisbon," in Finn Laursen (ed.), *The EU's Lisbon Treaty: Institutional Choices and Implementation.* Surrey: Ashgate, pp. 205–28.

Norheim-Martinsen, Per 2013. *The European Union and Military Force Governance and Strategy.* Cambridge: Cambridge University Press.

Nye, Joseph 2004. *Soft Power: The Means to Success in World Politics.* New York: Public Affairs.

Olsen, Espen D. H. 2008. "The Origins of European Citizenship in the First Two Decades of European Integration." *Journal of European Public Policy* 15 (1): 40–57.

Olsen, Espen D. H. 2012. *Transnational Citizenship in the European Union: Past, Present, and Future.* New York: Continuum.

Olsen, Espen D. H. 2013. "European Citizenship: Mixing Nation State and Federal Features with a Cosmopolitan Twist." *Perspectives on European Politics and Society* 14 (4): 505–19.

Padgen, Anthony, ed. 2002. *The Idea of Europe: From Antiquity to the European Union.* Cambridge: Cambridge University Press.

Pahl, Ray 1991. "The Search for Social Cohesion: From Durkheim to the European Commission." *European Journal of Sociology* 32 (2): 345–60.

Palmer-Rae Associates 2004. *European Cities and Capitals of Culture.* Study Prepared for the European Commission. Accessed September 13, 2014 at <http://ec.europa.eu/culture/tools/actions/documents/ecoc/cap-part1_en.pdf>.

Papademos, Lukas 2005. "Introductory statement on the winning design chosen in the international urban planning and architectural design competition for the new ECB premises." Brussels, accessed May 1, 2009 at <http://www.ecb.int/press/pressconf/2005/html/is050120_1.en.html>.

Papadopoulos, Alex G 1996. *Urban Regimes and Strategies: Building Europe's Central Executive District in Brussels*. Chicago: University of Chicago Press.

Paris, Roland 2001. "Human Security: Paradigm Shift or Hot Air?" *International Security* 26 (2): 87–102.

Parsons, Craig 2003. *A Certain Idea of Europe*. Ithaca, NY: Cornell University Press.

Petersen, William 1987. "Politics and the Measurement of Ethnicity," in William Alonso and Paul Starr (eds.), *The Politics of Numbers*. New York: Russell Sage, pp. 187–233.

Peterson, John 2012. "The EU as a Global Actor" in Elizabeth Bomberg, John Peterson, and Richard Corbett (eds.), *The European Union: How Does it Work?* Oxford: Oxford University Press, pp. 203–23.

Peterson, John and Michael Shackleton, eds. 2006. *The Institutions of the European Union*. Oxford: Oxford University Press.

Poggi, Gianfranco 1978. *The Development of the Modern State*. Palo Alto: Stanford University Press.

Polanyi, Karl 1944. *The Great Transformation*. Second edition 2001, New York: Beacon Press.

Pollack, Mark 2003. *The Engines of European Integration: Delegation, Agency and Agenda Setting in the European Union*. New York: Oxford University Press.

Porter, Bruce 1994. *War and the Rise of the State*. New York: Free Press.

Pouliot, Vincent 2007. " 'Sobjectivism:' Toward a Constructivist Methodology." *International Studies Quarterly* 51: 359–84.

Pouliot, Vincent 2008. "The Logic of Practicality: A Theory." *International Organization* 62: 257–88.

Pouliot, Vincent 2010. *International Security in Practice: The Politics of NATO–Russia Diplomacy*. Cambridge: Cambridge University Press.

Raento, Pauliina, Anna Hämäläinen, Hanna Ikonen, and Nella Mikkonen 2004. "Striking Stories: A Political Geography of Euro Coinage." *Political Geography* 23 (8): 929–56.

Raykoff, Ivan 2007. "Camping on the Borders of Europe," in Ivan Raykoff and Robert Tobin (eds.), *A Song for Europe: Popular Music and Politics in the Eurovision Song Contest*. Farnham: Ashgate, pp. 1–12.

Raykoff, Ivan and Robert Tobin, eds. 2007. *A Song for Europe: Popular Music and Politics in the Eurovision Song Contest*. Hampshire: Ashgate.

Recchi, Ettore and Adrian Favell, eds. 2009. *Pioneers of European Integration: Citizenship and Mobility in the EU*. Cheltenham: Edward Elgar.

Risse, Thomas 2003. "The Euro between National and European Identity." *Journal of European Public Policy* 10 (4): 487–503.

Risse, Thomas 2010. *A Community of Europeans? Transnational Identities and Public Spheres*. Ithaca, NY: Cornell University Press.

Romanczyk, Katarzyna M. 2012. "Transforming Brussels into an International City: Reflections on 'Brusselsization'." *Cities* 29 (2): 126–32.

Rosato, Sebastian 2011. *Europe United: Power Politics and the Making of the European Community.* Ithaca, NY: Cornell University Press.

Roy, William G. 1997. *Socializing Capital: The Rise of Large Industrial Corporation in America.* Princeton, NJ: Princeton University Press.

Ruggie, John Gerard 1982. "International Regimes, Transactions, and Change: Embedded Liberalism in the Postwar Economic Order." *International Organization* 36, Summer: 379–415.

Ruggie, John Gerard 1993. "Territoriality and Beyond: Problematizing Modernity in International Relations." *International Organization* 47 (1): 139–74.

Sandholtz, Wayne 1993. "Choosing Union: Monetary Politics and Maastricht." *International Organization* 47 (1): 1–39.

Sandholtz, Wayne and John Zysman 1989. "1992: Recasting the European Bargain." *World Politics* 42 (1): 95–128.

Sandholtz, Wayne and Alec Stone Sweet, eds. 1998. *European Integration and Supranational Governance.* Oxford: Oxford University Press.

Salamonska, Justyna, Lorenzo G. Baglioni, and Ettore Ricchi 2013. "Navigating the European Space: Physical and Virtual Forms of Cross-Border Mobility among EU Citizens." *EUCROSS Working Paper* 5, Università di Chieti-Pescara, Chieti.

Santacreu, Oscar, Emiliana Baldoni and María Carmen Albert 2009. "Deciding to Move: Migration Projects in an Integrating Europe" in Ettore Recchi and Adriane Favell (eds.), *Pioneers of European Integration: Citizenship and Mobility in the EU.* Cheltenham and Northhampton: Edward Elgar.

Sassatelli, Monica 2002. "Imagined Europe: The Shaping of a European Cultural Identity through EU Cultural Policy." *European Journal of Social Theory* 5 (4): 435–51.

Saurugger, Sabine and Frédéric Mérand 2010. "Does European Integration Theory Need Sociology?" *Comparative European Politics* 8: 1–18.

Sbragia, Alberta 1992. "Thinking about the European Future: The Uses of Comparison," in Alberta Sbragia (ed.), *Euro-Politics: Politics and Policymaking in the "New" European Community.* Washington, DC: Brookings, 257–92.

Sbragia, Alberta 2004. "Territory, Representation, and Policy Outcome: The United States and the European Union Compared," in Christopher K. Ansell and Guiseppe Di Palma (eds.), *Restructuring Territoriality: Europe and North America.* Cambridge: Cambridge University Press, 205–24.

Sbragia, Alberta 2005. "Territory, Electorates, and Markets in the United States: The Construction of Democratic Federalism and its Implications for the European Union," in Sergio Fabbrini (ed.), *Democracy and Federalism in the EU and US: Exploring Post-National Governance.* London: Routledge, pp. 93–103.

Schattschneider, E. E. 1960. *The Semi-Sovereign People: A Realist's View of Democracy in America.* New York: Holt, Rinehart and Winston.

Schimmelfennig, Frank 2003. *The EU, NATO, and the Integration of Europe: Rules and Rhetoric.* Cambridge: Cambridge University Press.

Schissler, Hanna and Soysal, Yasemin Nuhoğlu, eds. 2005. *The Nation, Europe, and the World: Textbooks and Curricula in Transition.* New York: Berghahn Books.

Schmidt, Vivien 2006. *Democracy in Europe: The EU and National Polities.* Oxford: Oxford University Press.

References

Schmidt, Vivien 2008. "Discursive Institutionalism: The Explanatory Power of Ideas and Discourse," *Annual Review of Political Science* 11: 303–26.

Schmidt, Suzanne K. and R. Daniel Kelemen, eds. 2013. *The Power of the European Court of Justice*. London: Routledge.

Scott, James 1985. *Weapons of the Weak: Everyday Forms of Peasant Resistance*. New Haven: Yale University Press.

Scott, James 1998. *Seeing Like a State: How Certain Schemes to Improve the Human Condition Have Failed*. New Haven: Yale University Press.

Searle, John R. 1969. *Speech Acts: An Essay in the Philosophy of Language*. Cambridge: Cambridge University Press.

Searle, John R. 1992. *The Construction of Social Reality*. New York: The Free Press.

Sewell, William H. 1995. "A Theory of Structure: Duality, Agency and Transformation." *American Journal of Sociology* 98 (1): 1–29.

Shaw, Jo 2008. *The Transformation of Citizenship in the European Union*. Cambridge: Cambridge University Press.

Shore, Bradd 1996. *Culture in Mind: Cognition, Culture, and the Problem of Meaning*. New York: Oxford University Press.

Shore, Cris 2000. *Building Europe: The Cultural Politics of European Integration*. London: Routledge.

Shore, Cris 2006. "'In Uno Plures' (?) EU Cultural Policy and the Governance of Europe." *Cultural Analysis* 5: 7–26.

Sieberson, Stephen C. 2008. "Did Symbolism Sink the Constitution? Reflections on the European Union's State-Like Attributes." *U.C. Davis Journal of International Law & Policy* 14: 1–57.

Sieg, Katrin 2013. "Cosmopolitan Empire: Central and Eastern Europeans at the Eurovision Song Contest." *European Journal of Cultural Studies* 16 (2): 244–63.

Sigalas, Emmanuel 2010. "Cross-Border Mobility and European identity: The Effectiveness of Intergroup Contact during the ERASMUS Year Abroad." *European Union Politics* 11 (2): 241–65.

Silver, Larry 2008. *Marketing Maximillian: The Visual Ideology of a Holy Roman Emperor*. Princeton, NJ: Princeton University Press.

Singh, J. P. 2011. *Globalized Arts: The Entertainment Economy and Cultural Identity*. New York: Columbia University Press.

Skowronek, Stephen 1982. *Building a New American State: The Expansion of National Administrative Capacities, 1977–1920*. Cambridge: Cambridge University Press.

Smith, Karen Elizabeth 2008. *European Union Foreign Policy in a Changing World*. Cambridge, UK: Polity Press.

Smith, Michael E. 2004. *Europe's Foreign and Security Policy: The Institutionalization of Cooperation*. Cambridge: Cambridge University Press.

Smith, Michael E. and Roy Ginsberg 2007. "Understanding the European Union as a Global Political Actor: Theory, Practice, and Impact," in Sophie Meunier and Kathleen R. McNamara (eds.), *Making History: European Integration and Institutional Change at Fifty*. Oxford: Oxford University Press, pp. 267–82.

Soysal, Yasemin 1994. *Limits of Citizenship: Migrants and Postnational Membership in Europe*. Chicago: University of Chicago Press.

Soysal, Yasemin 2002. "Locating Europe." *European Societies* 4 (3) September: 265–84.

Soysal, Yasemin 2002. "Locating European Identity in Education," in António Nóvoa and Martin Lawn (eds.), *Fabricating Europe: The Formation of an Education Space*. New York. NY: Kluwer Academic Publishers, pp. 55–66.

Spruyt, Hendrik 1994. *The Sovereign State and its Competitors*. Princeton, NJ: Princeton University Press.

Starr, Paul 1987. "The Sociology of Official Statistics," in William Alonso and Paul Starr (eds.), *The Politics of Numbers*. New York: Russell Sage, pp. 7–57.

Starr, Paul 1992. "Social Categories and Claims in the Liberal State," in Mary Douglas and David Hull (eds.), *How Classification Works*. Edinburgh: Edinburgh University Press, pp. 154–79.

Steinmetz, George, ed. 1999. *State Culture: State Formation after the Cultural Turn*. Ithaca, NY: Cornell University Press.

Stepan, Alfred 1999. "Federalism and Democracy: Beyond the US Model." *Journal of Democracy* 10 (4): 19–34.

Sternberg, Claudia Schrag 2013. *The Struggle for EU Legitimacy: Public Contestation 1950–2005*. Basingstoke, Hampshire: Palgrave Macmillan.

Stoeckel, Florian 2014. "Contact and Community: The Role of Social Interactions for a Political Identity," unpublished paper, University of North Carolina at Chapel Hill. Available at SSRN: <http://dx.doi.org/10.2139/ssrn.2416971>.

Stone Sweet, Alec 2004. *The Judicial Construction of Europe*. Oxford: Oxford University Press.

Stone Sweet, Alec 2010. "The European Court of Justice and the Judicialization of EU Governance." *Living Reviews in European Governance* 5 (2): 1–50.

Stone Sweet, Alec and James A. Caporaso 1998. "From Free Trade to Supranational Polity: The European Court and Integration," in Wayne Sandholtz and Alec Stone Sweet (eds.), *European Integration and Supranational Governance*. Oxford: Oxford University Press, pp. 92–134.

Stone Sweet, Alec, Wayne Sandholtz, and Neil Fligstein, eds. 2001. *The Institutionalization of Europe*. Oxford: Oxford University Press.

Strasbourg Seat Study Group n.d. *Brussels-Starsbourg Study*. European Parliament. Accessed April 2013 at <http://www.brusselsstrasbourgstudy.eu/4.html>.

Swedberg, Richard 1994. "The Idea of 'Europe' and the Origin of the European Union: A Sociological Approach." *Zeitschrift für Soziologie* 23: 378–87.

Swindler, Ann 1986. "Culture in Action: Symbols and Strategies." *American Sociological Review* 51 (2): 273–86.

Swindler, Ann 2002. "Cultural Power and Social Movements," in Lyn Spillman (ed.), *Cultural Sociology*. Malden, MA: Blackwell, pp. 311–23.

Taylor, Charles 2004. *Social Imaginaries*. Durham: Duke University Press/ Public Planet Books.

Terry, Laurel S. 2008. "The Bologna Process and its Impact in Europe: It's So Much More than Degree Changes." *Vanderbilt Journal of Transnational Law* 41: 107–228.

Thomas, George M., John W. Meyer, Francisco O. Ramirez, and John Boli 1987. *Institutional Structure: Constituting State, Society and the Individual*. London: Sage.

Thrift, Nigel 2007. *Non-Representational Theory: Space, Politics, Affect*. London: Routledge.

References

Tilly, Charles, ed. 1975. *The Formation of National States in Western Europe*. Princeton, NJ: Princeton University Press.

Tilly, Charles 1990. *Coercion, Capital, and European States, AD 990–1992*. Cambridge, MA: Blackwell Press.

Tilly, Charles 1998. *Durable Inequality*. Berkeley: University of California Press.

Tobin, Robert Deam 2007. "Eurovision at 50: Post-Wall and Post-Stonewall," in Ivan Raykoff and Robert Deam Tobin (eds.), *A Song for Europe: Popular Music and Politics in the Eurovision Song Contest*. Hampshire: Ashgate, pp. 25–36.

Toje A. 2005. "The 2003 European Union Security Strategy: A Critical Appraisal." *European Foreign Affairs Review* 10 (1): 117–33.

Torpey, John C. 2000. *The Invention of the Passport*. Cambridge: Cambridge University Press.

Trachtenberg, Mark 1999. *A Constructed Peace: The Making of the European Settlement 1945-1963*. Princeton; Princeton University Press.

Treitler, Leo 1984. "Reading and Singing: On the Genesis of Occidental Musicwriting." *Early Music History* 4: 135–208.

Tretter, Eliot 2011. "The 'Value' of Europe: The Political Economy of Culture in the European Community." *Geopolitics* 16 (4), 926–48.

Trevor-Roper, Hugh 1983. "The Invention of Tradition: The Highland Tradition of Scotland," in Eric J. Hobsbawm and Terence O. Ranger (eds.), *The Invention of Tradition*. Cambridge: Cambridge University Press, pp. 15–42.

Tsoukalis, Loukas 1977. *The Politics and Economics of Monetary Integration*. London: Allen & Unwin.

Tuan, Yi-Fu 1977. *Space and Place: The Perspective of Experience*. University of Minneapolis: University of Minnesota Press.

Turner, William Jackson 1994. *Rereading Frederick Jackson Turner: The Significance of the Frontier in American History and Other Essays*. With commentary by John Mack Faragher. New York: Henry Holt.

USA Today 2013. "Missouri Halts US Execution by Propofol." October 11 (no author). Accessed December 10, 2014 at <http://www.usatoday.com/story/news/nation/2013/10/11/missouri-halts-propofol-execution/2967607/>.

Vachudova, Milada. 2005. *Europe Undivided: Democracy, Leverage and Integration After Communism*. Oxford: Oxford University Press.

Vale, Lawrence 1992. *Architecture, Power, and National Identity*. West Hanover: Yale University Press.

De Valk, Helga A. G. and Juan Díez Medrano 2014. "Special Issue: Meeting and Mating Across Borders: Union Formation in the European Union Single Market." *Population, Space and Place* 20 (2): i–ii, 103–99.

Van Der Wusten, Herman 2000. "Dictators and Their Capital Cities: Moscow and Berlin in the 1930s." *GeoJournal* 52: 339–44.

Van Der Wusten, Herman 2004. "Public Authority in European Capitals: A Map of Governance, An Album with Symbols." *European Review* 12: 143–58.

Van Mol, Christof 2011. "The Influence of European Student Mobility on European Identity and Subsequent Migration Behaviour," in Fred Dervin (ed.), *Analysing the Consequences of Academic Mobility and Migration*. Newcastle: Cambridge Scholars, pp. 29–50.

Van Mol, Christof 2013. "Intra-European Student Mobility and European Identity: A Successful Marriage?" *Population, Space and Place* 19 (2): 209–22.

Velicogna, Marco 2014. "The Making of Pan-European Infrastructure: From the Schengen Information System to the European Arrest Warrant," in Francesco Contini and Giovan Francesco Lanzara (eds.), *The Circulation of Agency in E-Justice: Interoperability and Infrastructures for European Transborder Judicial Proceedings*. Utrecht: Springer Netherlands, pp. 185–215.

Verdun, Amy 1999. "The Role of the Delors Committee in Creating EMU: An Epistemic Community?" *Journal of European Public Policy* 6 (2): 308–28.

Wall Street Journal 2009. "Europe's Grey Mice." *Wall Street Journal*, Opinion Europe. November 23. Accessed December 10, 2014 at <http://www.wsj.com/articles/SB100 01424052748704779704574551633245643074>.

Walzer, Michael 1967. "On the Role of Symbolism in Political Thought." *Political Science Quarterly* 82 (2): 191–204.

Watt, Nicolas 2009. "Lady Ashton: Principled, Charming... or Just Plain Lucky?" *The Guardian*, November 20. Accessed December 20, 2014 <http://www.theguardian. com/politics/2009/nov/20/cathy-ashton-eu-foreign-job>.

Weber, Eugen 1976. *Peasants into Frenchmen*. Palo Alto, CA: Stanford University Press.

Weber, Max 1918 [1991]. "Politics as a Vocation," in H. H. Gerth and C. Wright Mills (eds.), *From Max Weber: Essays in Sociology*. London: Routledge, pp. 77–128.

Weber, Max 1922 [1978]. *Economy and Society*. Berkeley: University of California Press.

Weber, Max 1946. *From Max Weber: Essays in Sociology*. New York: Oxford University Press.

Weber, Max 1947. *The Theory of Social and Economic Organization*. New York: Oxford University Press.

Wedeen, Lisa 1999. *Ambiguities of Domination: Politics, Rhetoric, and Symbols in Contemporary Syria*. Chicago: University of Chicago Press.

Wedeen, Lisa 2002. "Conceptualizing Culture: Possibilities for Political Science." *American Political Science Review* 96 (4): 713–28.

Wedeen, Lisa 2008. *Peripheral Visions: Publics, Power, and Performance in Yemen*. Chicago: University of Chicago Press.

Weiler, Joseph H. H. 1991. "The Transformation of Europe." *The Yale Law Journal* 100 (8) *Symposium: International Law*: 2403–83.

Weiler, Joseph H. H., Ulrich R. Haltern, and Franz Mayer 1995. "European Democracy and its Critique." *West European Politics* 18 (3): 4–39.

Welsh, Ian 2006. "Values, Science and the European Union," in Sonia Lucarelli and Ian Manners (eds.), *Values and Principles in European Union Foreign Policy*. London: Routledge, pp. 59–76.

Wendt, Alexander 1999. *Social Theory of International Politics*. Cambridge: Cambridge University Press.

Wessels, Ramses A. 2011. "The Legal Framework for Participation of the European Union in International Institutions." *Journal of European Integration* 33 (6): 621–35.

Wiener, Antje 1998. *"European" Citizenship Practice: Building Institutions of a Non-State*. Boulder, CO: Westview Press.

References

Williams, Michael C. and Iver B. Neumann 2000. "From Alliance to Security Community: NATO, Russia, and the Power of Identity." *Millennium—Journal of International Studies* 29: 357–87.

Wilson, Iain 2011. "What Should We Expect of 'Erasmus Generations'?" *Journal of Common Market Studies* 49 (5): 1113–40.

Wintle, Michael 1996. "Europe's Image: Visual Representations of Europe from the Earliest Times to the Twentieth Century," in Michael Wintle (ed.), *Culture and Identity in Europe*. Avebury/ Ashgate: Aldershot, UK, pp. 52–97.

Woll, Cornelia 2008. *Firm Interests: How Governments Shape Firm Lobbying on Global Trade*. Ithaca, NY: Cornell University Press.

Young, Alasdair and John Peterson 2014. *Parochial Global Europe: 21st Century Trade Politics*. Oxford: Oxford University Press.

Zaiotti, Ruben 2011. *Cultures of Border Control: Schengen and the Evolution of European Frontiers*. Chicago: University of Chicago Press.

Zelizer, Viviana 1994. *The Social Meaning of Money: Pin Money, Paychecks, Poor Relief and other Currencies*. Princeton, NJ: Princeton University Press.

Zelizer, Viviana 1998. "The Proliferation of Social Currencies," in Michel Callon (ed.), *The Laws of the Market*. Oxford: Blackwell, pp. 58–68.

Zerubavel, Eviatar 1997. *Social Mindscapes: An Invitation to Cognitive Sociology*. Cambridge, MA: Harvard University Press.

Zerubavel, Yael 1995. *Recovered Roots: Collective Memory and the Making of Israeli National Tradition*. Chicago: University of Chicago Press.

Index